SO-ARK-780

**NILES
PUBLIC
LIBRARY
DISTRICT**

6960 Oakton Street
Niles, Illinois 60714
(847) 663-1234

DATE DUE	DATE DUE
FEB 2 0 2000	
MAR 2 6 2000	

CRIMEBUSTING
Breakthroughs in Forensic
Science

CRIMEBUSTING
Breakthroughs in Forensic Science

JENNY WARD

BLANDFORD

Blandford Press
An Imprint of the Cassell Group
Wellington House, 125 Strand, London WC2R 0BB

Distributed in the USA by Sterling Publishing Co. Inc.,
387 Park Avenue South, New York, NY 10016-8810.

© Dr Jenny Ward, 1998
All rights reserved. No part of this book may be reproduced or
transmitted in any form or by any means electronic or mechanical
including photocopying recording or any information storage and
retrieval system without permission in writing
from the Publisher.

British Library Cataloguing-in-Publication Data:
a catalogue record for this book is available from the British Library

ISBN 0-7137-2639-3

Designed and edited by DAG Publications Ltd.
Designed by David Gibbons; edited by John Gilbert;
printed and bound in Great Britain.

CONTENTS

INTRODUCTION

Our fascination for all things criminous dates back at least to 1811 when the very first sensational murder case hit the national press. During the dark winter nights of December that year, in the vicinity of Ratcliffe Highway, in the East End of London, seven people in two separate households were brutally clubbed to death over a period of twelve days. The murders gripped the public imagination with a horror that had never been known before. *The Times* gave the crimes pride of place over almost every other news for three weeks. Public frenzy lasted well beyond the arrest and suicide in prison of the suspect, John Williams, who was probably innocent.

Fuelled by the press, the populace felt that Williams had cheated the gallows and they wanted revenge. To appease the mob, his body was brought from Newgate in procession through the crowded streets of London in a cart guarded by a large body of constables. The route led past the scenes of the crimes, and Williams was buried, with a stake through his body, at the crossroads near the church of St George's in the East.

Public outrage at the murders was countrywide, reaching as far, at least, as the Lake District, 300 miles away, where Thomas De Quincey was living, having taken over Dove Cottage from Wordsworth. The essayist was enthralled by the story. 'The panic was indescribable,' he wrote, in *On Murder Considered as One of the Fine Arts*. The press, of course, were responsible. They spread the panic, afflicting the whole population with a sense of insecurity out of all proportion to the events themselves, then called for a better system of policing to cope with the increasing depravity of the metropolis.

The US newspapers practised, at first, a more restrained approach. Crime reporting didn't really get under way until 1835 when James Gordon Bennett, of the *New York Herald*, started to add a little 'salt' to his news stories by covering vice. Police and crime reporting soon spread, and one particular story, the murder of Mary Cecilia Rogers, in New York in 1836, was picked up by Edgar Allan Poe to form the basis of his story, *The Mystery of Marie Roget*, in 1842. It was the second story to feature Auguste Dupin, the first being *The Murders in the Rue Morgue*. Dupin himself was inspired by the memoirs of Sûreté chief Eugène François Vidocq, which caught the public imagination in the USA and England when they appeared in 1828. Dorothy L. Sayers was to say later that the five Dupin stories laid down the rules for detective fiction. Without them we wouldn't have had the *Adventures of Sherlock Holmes*, written to the Poe formula: the wise detective and his admiring satellite, the personal eccentricities, the locked room mystery, and so on.

Conan Doyle's stories were immensely popular in France at the turn of the century and inspired scientific methods of detection in real life. Dr Edmond Locard, who founded the French police laboratory in Lyons in 1910, acknowledged Holmes' inspiration in the British *Police Journal*. It was Locard, incidentally, who is said to have coined the phrase, 'Every contact leaves a trace', the watchword of British forensic science.

Oddly enough, the effect of the Holmes stories on criminalistic development in the United Kingdom was minimal, if not negative. We might think, reading Conan Doyle now, that there was no professional medico-legal work going on at the end of the Victorian era, but this is far from the truth. The popularity of Holmes and Watson has obliterated from folk memory their true-life counterparts. There were a number of private detectives in London in Holmes' day, many of them ex-coppers, but Scotland Yard didn't call any of them in on tricky cases. The under-secretary of state summoned the Home Office analyst, Dr Thomas Stevenson. Furthermore, Dr Watson wouldn't have bumbled about the corpses. The Yard would have called in the divisional police surgeon, a man of some experience in medico-legal cases, especially in central London.

These late Victorian experts and their forebears practised 'forensic medicine', 'legal medicine' or 'medical jurisprudence' – different names for more or less the same thing. Forensic medicine is a translation of the Latin *medicina forensis*, medicine of the courtroom, from the open-air *forum*, where justice was dispensed. Legal medicine is a translation from the French *médecine légale*, or German *gerichtliche Medizin*. There was also a more general term, *criminalistique* in French, or *Kriminalistik* in German. The English equivalent – 'criminalistics' – is in fact more commonly used in the USA than in Britain.

Criminology – the study of crime and criminals in the criminal justice system – has a different background. Its best remembered pioneer is Cesare Lombroso (1835–1909), who developed the notion of the born criminal. The subject was originally taught in law faculties at the end of the nineteenth century.

The two disciplines – criminology and criminalistics – merged to be taught side by side from 1912 by Enrico Ferri, a former pupil of Lombroso's, at La Scuola d'Applicazione Giuridico-Criminale in Rome. One of Ferri's pupils in 1928 was Leon Radzinowicz, renowned for his multi-volume work *The History of the English Criminal Law* (Oxford 1948–86). Sir Leon, born in 1906 and still with us, introduced the study of criminology to England in 1938 and founded the Institute of Criminology at Cambridge in 1959, where it is part of the law faculty. It is studied at postgraduate level by social scientists, police officers, lawyers and others, and as part of the undergraduate law degree.

Although Radzinowicz was the first president of the British Academy of Forensic Sciences at its foundation in 1960, the teaching of criminalistics didn't come over from Italy to be part of English criminology. Somehow it got left behind. The subject of scientific crime investigation is taught in only a few places in the UK. The best-known courses are postgraduate courses at King's College, London, and the University of Strathclyde in Glasgow.

Forensic medical training is done as part of a doctor's general medical education; and pathologists and forensic medical examiners (formerly known as police surgeons) can take the two-part Diploma in Medical Jurisprudence of the Society of Apothecaries of London to supplement their other qualifications. The Department of Forensic Pathology at Sheffield runs training courses for would-be pathologists in the UK and abroad, and also provides a professional service to local coroners. The University of Glasgow offers more general postgraduate courses in forensic medicine and forensic toxicology for students involved in the criminal justice system and court work, such as lawyers, scientists, social scientists and doctors.

Because I have a doctorate, people often ask me if I am a forensic scientist, but in fact my academic background is criminological, not criminalistic. I took my master's degree in criminology at Radzinowicz's Institute before moving into history for my PhD.

The Institute is set in a quiet, leafy Cambridge street, in a large Victorian house set back from the road. The jewel in its crown is the Radzinowicz Library, glowered over by a portrait of the master himself. Anyone who reads crime books, true crime or fiction, would welcome being snowed up in this library. I have actually begged to be locked in at lunchtimes in the long vac, when the library is shut for an hour, rather than go for a meal. Most of the Notable British Trials series of books are here, arranged in their red covers side by side from Eugene Aram to Oscar Wilde. There are books on piracy and smuggling, the CIA and the FBI, insanity and fingerprinting. Some books are so rare that they are kept under the eye of the librarian, Helen Krarup, in her office. Helen and her assistants, Jean Arnold, Betty Taylor and Caroline Dethridge, have been such a help to me in writing both my thesis and this book that a simple acknowledgement is inadequate. Many of the books and papers listed in the selected sources are in the Radzinowicz Library. Others are found in the main Cambridge University Library across the road. My thanks to the library staff there over the years as well.

It was reading Crippen's trial in the Radzinowicz Library that inspired my interest in the history of the forensic side of criminology. I tried

9

to find a written history of the subject when I was researching Crippen for a radio documentary a few years ago. I found that reminiscences of pathologists were, with the odd exception, unreliable. The only useful source was Jurgen Thorwald's series of books *The Century of the Detective*, and his companion volume, *Crime and Science*, all published in the 1960s. Thorwald has been stripped bare by forensic historians ever since, though new cases have been added to the canon. The most comprehensive recent book, aside from the encyclopedias, is Colin Wilson's wide-ranging *Written in Blood*. The cases I have chosen are not necessarily all the great sensational cases using medical evidence, but the ones which had some influence on the course of scientific crime investigation on the Continent, in the UK and in the USA. The list is narrower than Thorwald's and Wilson's but the research is deeper, and provides a more unified whole.

Much of the new information presented here is the result of original historical research, and represents hours of ploughing through medical journals, ancient and modern. I've tried to acknowledge the most important of my sources, but I apologise if anyone feels aggrieved.

Apart from the staff of the Cambridge Library, I am also indebted to the following for help, advice and moral support: Jim Bamberg, Jeffrey Bloomfield, Jennifer Brown, Brian Caddy, Michael Clark, Cathy Crawford, Rachel Dormor, Roderick Dymott, John Forsyth, Michael Green, Roy Ingleton, John Jennings, Valerie Johnson, Jessie Keating, Sue King, Bernard Knight, Anthony Rae, Neill Spencer and Margaret Wright.

Jenny Ward, Cambridge, November 1997

CHAPTER ONE

BURKE AND HARE
Immigrant enterprise

The centre of Edinburgh in the 1820s was what we now call the Old Town: a high granite hill, dominated by the Castle, with steep narrow streets and stepped alleys, punctuated here and here by wide thoroughfares like Grassmarket, then the main trading area. The old Royal Infirmary and the University Medical School were within easy walking distance from here – unless you had a heavy load to carry.

William Burke and his lady, Nelly MacDougal, met William and Margaret Hare for the first time over a drink in November 1827. Burke, an Irishman, was a cobbler of sorts. He bought second-hand shoes, which he soled and heeled for Nelly to sell on the streets. Hare, also Irish, worked as a boatman from time to time on the canal that he had helped to build. Margaret, between drinks, ran a squalid lodging house in Tanners Close, West Port. This was a continuation of Grassmarket, a poor, overcrowded area of stark, high tenement buildings.

William and Nelly moved in with the Hares as their tenants soon after they met. It must have been quite crowded. There were two main rooms with beds in them, apparently on the ground floor, as passers-by could see in through the window overlooking the close. Beyond these largish rooms was a small closet which looked out on a pigsty and a dead wall.

While Nelly and William Hare were out at work all day, Burke and Margaret were thrown on each other's company, and that of the lodgers, who came and went casually. On 29 November of that year an aged tenant called Donald died of the dropsy, and owing rent. Donald was an old soldier in receipt of a small pension, and the Hares had been content to let him live with them on credit until his next instalment came through, probably at Christmas, the next quarter-day. With his untimely departure, the Hares were £4 out of pocket and Donald would have to be buried on the parish.

It wasn't until the coffin was almost at the door that Hare hit upon the notion of selling Donald's body to aid medical science. This wasn't a new idea. In 1506, James IV of Scotland had granted the Edinburgh Guild of Surgeons and Barbers the bodies of executed criminals for dissection. Carried out in public, the desecration of dissection was meant to be an additional ignominy, quite literally a fate worse than death.

From the medical point of view, however, dissection helped to increase the understanding of human anatomy, and by the mid-eighteenth century it was widely used by medical schools for anatomy demonstrations. Even so, the old stigma remained as the general public still regarded it as a post-mortem punishment. The growing shortage of bodies for medical use led to a swift trade in fresh corpses, often with coffin shavings attached. In fact, grave-robbing became so prevalent that guards were set by those who could afford them to watch over the dearly departed in churchyards most at risk. It's said in police circles that this is the origin of the phrase 'the graveyard shift'.

But why go to the trouble of digging up a body when there was one to hand? Burke and Hare let the parish representatives nail Donald down in his coffin, and when they were gone Hare forced open the lid and the two men lifted out their erstwhile room-mate and hid him in the bed. Tanners Close was aptly named. There were four tanneries in the immediate neighbourhood, one at the end of the close. The conspirators fetched in some tanners' bark that was lying nearby to use as a make-weight, covered it decently with a sheet, and replaced the lid.

Once the parish representatives had taken the bark-filled coffin away for solemn burial, the two entrepreneurs tried to work out their next move. Burke confessed before his execution that Hare was 'at a loss how to get the body disposed of'. It was Burke's idea to ask at the university, just a few streets away. There they enquired of a student, who directed them to Dr Knox, at 10 Surgeons Square. They were seen by three of his assistants, who asked no questions but told them to come back after dark. They returned with the late lodger in a sack and were invited to lay him out on the dissecting table for inspection.

Dr Robert Knox now enters the story. He was an odd-looking man, in his mid-thirties, with a face disfigured by smallpox, thanks to which he had lost the sight of one eye. He was a popular lecturer in anatomy, catering to more than 400 students. It wasn't a question of having a leg apiece on individual tables, as in Paris. In Edinburgh the lecturer would dissect to an audience. But he still needed a steady supply of corpses.

Knox offered Burke and Hare £7 10s and asked Thomas Wharton Jones, one of his assistants, to settle with them. Jones handed over the money and bade them farewell, adding that the pair would be welcome whenever they had another body for disposal. Burke gave Hare £4 5s and himself kept £3 5s, a good deal more than they were making at their day jobs, and certainly way beyond the fee they were expecting. No doubt they walked home thoughtfully.

During the first few weeks of 1828, a lodger known as Joseph the miller caught a fever and was expected to die. It would be difficult to find tenants if it became known that someone had died there from a fever. Burke and Hare precipitated the inevitable and despatched the miller to his maker early. Burke smothered him with a pillow while Hare sat on his legs to keep him still. This time they got £10, apparently the going rate. With Donald, Knox had taken advantage of their inexperience.

Soon afterwards, another lodger developed jaundice and was easily put out of his misery. Abandoning the pillow, Burke slipped his thumb under the sick man's chin to close his mouth, and stopped up his nose by squeezing it between two fingers. Hare's job, as before, was to hold him down. This method of murder later entered the dictionary as 'burking'.

From despatching the sick as a kindness, the two murderers progressed to luring in friendless strangers with an eye to profit. During a merry evening, the stranger's genial hosts would enquire as to family and friends of the nearly departed, and the stranger, giving a satisfactory reply, would be intoxicated, burked and folded into a tea-chest ready for delivery before rigor mortis had set in.

As 1828 warmed into spring, the two men became careless. Golden-haired Mary Paterson was well known in the Canongate where she had recently plied her trade. In fact, she was still clutching 2½d (the going rate?) in her hand on the dissecting table. William Fergusson, one of Knox's assistants, recognised her, as did several of the class, and he asked where Burke and Hare had got her. They answered that she had died of drink and they had bought the corpse off an old hag. Nevertheless, the buyers must have been suspicious, as they made Burke cut off her golden hair to disguise her looks.

As spring turned into a fruitful summer, and then autumn, the murderers lost count of their victims. It could have been as many as sixteen, or seventeen, counting old Donald, the natural death. Burke was having trouble with his conscience, which he dulled with alcohol, and he kept a bottle and a twopenny candle by the bed to ward off the nightmares.

In about September, Burke and Nelly moved out of the Hares' to a place of their own nearby, a 'sunk flat' below a shop. This may have been as the result of a row, as there is some evidence to show that Hare was conducting business on his own account, cutting out Burke. Alternatively, it may just have been that as business improved Nelly and Burke moved to a place of their own. Burke explained to Nelly that he was an entrepreneur in the 'resurrection' business (the polite term for grave-robbing), and she seems to have accepted the story of this lesser evil, for the time being. Despite living apart, the two men remained business partners, and one would invite the other over, as Owen Dudley Edwards' book puts it, 'for murder and light refreshments'.

In October, Burke was called over to the Hares, who were entertaining Daft Jamie Wilson, a sturdy 19-year-old with the mind of a simple child. Jamie had lived with his widowed mother and his sister until he ran away after a beating for pulling down a crockery cupboard. This was another careless choice of guest, as Daft Jamie, with his deformed, unshod feet, was a well-known street character, existing on handouts. Margaret Hare had met him in the Grassmarket that morning, when he told her he was looking for his mother. Margaret told him that she was at Tanners Close and took him home with her. He proved difficult to get drunk as he preferred snuff. He refused further drink and kept asking for his mother.

According to Burke's confession, they invited him into the little back room where he lay down, with Hare lying on the bed behind him, his head raised and resting on his hand. Burke remained standing, watching over the boy until he fell asleep. Privacy was assured them by Margaret, who went out, locked the outer door, and slipped the key back underneath. When it seemed safe, Hare threw himself down on Jamie, pressed one hand on his mouth and held his nose with the other. As their victim woke, they both fell off the bed and struggled while Burke held the boy's hands and feet until he was still.

They got £10 from Knox, but, as with Mary Paterson, Daft Jamie was recognised at Surgeons Square. Once it was known abroad that the boy was missing, it seemed prudent to dissect him out of turn. Fergusson began by cutting off his head and his distinctive feet.

Inevitably, the whole thing blew up in their faces. On Friday, 31 October 1828, Burke chanced upon a lonely Irishwoman, Mary Docherty, in Rymer's bar on the corner of Tanners Close and West Port. She was in Edinburgh looking for her adult son. Burke said his mother's maiden name was Docherty and claimed a tentative kinship with the woman which called for a drink, or two, or three. The difficulty with doing business on this particular night was that Burke and Nelly had guests staying with them, James and Ann Gray, a couple with a small child. Burke persuaded the Grays to sleep over with the Hares, but prospective business didn't stop the Hallowe'en celebrations from taking place, and there was a good deal of traffic in and out of the Burkes' lodgings that night, most of it drunken. The Hares and other Irish folk had been invited, Hallowe'en being an Irish celebration, but not a Scottish one. At one stage the party moved to the neighbours, the Connoways, where there was dancing and drinking. Mary Docherty, plied with whisky, did her share of the merry-making.

The business being done sometime during the night, it was all right for the Grays to come back next morning. Burke went over to the Hares' before breakfast with a dram of spirits for Gray and an invitation to breakfast. Ann Gray did the cooking and during the meal Ann Connoway came in, enquiring what had happened to Docherty. Nelly said that she had become over friendly with Burke and she had kicked her out of the house.

At some point, Ann Gray, pipe in mouth, started looking for her child's stockings, which she thought were under the bed, where Burke kept straw, potatoes and corpses. Burke shouted at her for taking a pipe so near to the straw, but her suspicions were aroused. Later that day she and her husband managed to find the room unoccupied and they discovered Docherty hidden in the straw, naked, with blood about her mouth and one side of her face.

As they ran horrified up the stairs to the street, they met Nelly MacDougal coming in and told her what they had found. Nelly begged them to be quiet about it, offering them £10 a week for their silence. As they went along the street, pursued by Nelly, they met Margaret Hare, who suggested they went into a public house to talk it over, instead of making such a commotion in the roadway.

The room was unoccupied just then because Burke and Hare had gone to arrange transport. They had bought their own horse and cart earlier in the year, but the horse refused to pull the cargo – an incident of super-stitious significance – and the pair reverted to the use of a porter. While the women were in the tavern with the Grays, the men returned to the flat and boxed up their last victim in a tea-chest, accompanying her and the porter to Surgeons Square.

When the party left the tavern, James Gray went to the police office where he told his story to Police Sergeant-Major John Fisher, a 'criminal officer' – the word 'detective' not yet being in common usage. Fisher and John Findlay, a member of the more humble uniformed 'patrol', returned with Gray to the Burkes' room. William and Nelly, now at home, were both taken to the police office and arrested, and a search party returned to the room, where they found Mrs Docherty's striped and bloodstained bed-gown under the bed. Early on Sunday morning the body was discovered in Knox's cellar below the lecture room, and William and Margaret Hare were arrested soon afterwards.

The body was taken to the police office and three medical men were called in. The most junior was Alexander Black, who had been surgeon to the Edinburgh police establishment for twenty of its twenty-three years of existence. He was obliged to tell the court that he had no medical degree but was 'merely a surgeon'. The other two were William Newbigging, a respected Edinburgh surgeon, and his friend and former colleague at the Royal Infir-mary, Robert Christison. Christison was professor of medical jurisprudence and medical police at the university.

Forensic medicine had been brought to Scotland from the Continent in 1795 by Andrew Duncan, professor of the Institutes of Medicine, along with the novel idea of public health, or 'medical police' as it was then called. Both subjects were referred to as 'state medicine' since the practitioners, in Edinburgh as in Berlin, Vienna and Paris, were paid out of the public purse. After lecturing on the subject for a few years, Duncan petitioned the author-ities for a regius professorship, as on the Continent, for the purpose of 'elucidating doubtful questions in courts of law'. This definition is still the basis of the entry for forensic medicine in the current edition of *Chambers Dictionary*, an Edinburgh publication.

The chair of medical jurisprudence and medical police was founded in 1806. It was the first chair of its kind either in the UK or the USA. It was followed in 1808 by the establishment of a chair at Columbia University, New York, by James Stringham. Stringham was a native of New York who had come over to Edinburgh to obtain his MD in 1799 before returning home to base his course on the one he had attended in Scotland.

Robert Christison became the Edinburgh professor in 1822 when he was only 23 years old, so by the time of the West Port murders he was in his early thirties. He often appeared as a medical witness in criminal and civil cases but, more significantly, he was prominent at the precognition stage. In Scots law the procurator fiscal – the public prosecutor – can take precognitions (statements) from witnesses to determine whether to prosecute. This had the effect, in these early days, of minimising the investigative role of the police. Christison would interrogate both sides at these hearings with the aim of getting at the truth, rather than speaking for one side or the other. In the matter of Burke and Hare, Christison stated in his autobiography that he was the 'chief party' in the professional investigations.

Christison's portrait shows a white-haired man, one time president of the British Medical Association; a tall, thin-lipped figure in black, looking like a dehydrated corpse. We must imagine him as a younger man, more loose-limbed and lively. His first task in the case of Mary Docherty was the post-mortem, performed at the police office, no doubt in primitive and unhygienic conditions. He and Newbigging found vague signs of death by asphyxia but no external marks to show how respiration had been obstructed. There was some bruising on the body, attended by swelling but no discoloration. This suggested that the bruising was recent, but as yet they were uncertain whether it had occurred before or after death. Other bruises to the neck and back could have been caused by forcing the victim into the tea-chest, pressing her head downwards to fit the box. This action could have been the cause of death.

Christison decided to experiment on another dead body, which he beat with a stick to see whether bruising could be produced after death. He found that whereas livid marks resulted, there was no swelling, nor were any small blood clots formed in the bruises. This cadaveric bruising was so shallow that the outer layer of skin could be peeled back to remove all the discoloration. He concluded that in Mary Docherty's case the bruises with swelling had been inflicted shortly before death – the swelling indicated a flow of blood to the site – but that the shallow bruising to neck and back was inflicted after death, showing that she was dead when she was forced into the chest. Unfortunately, this did not clear up the cause of death, which was consistent with smothering, but with no positive proof.

This was the first recorded instance in Britain of an experiment being conducted expressly for a criminal trial, although scientific experimental evidence had been given in a civil case in London a few years earlier. A fire in a sugar bakers in the City of London in November 1819 gave rise to a complex insurance case. The sugar bakers, Severn, King and Company, had installed new heating equipment without informing the insurers, who refused to pay up. The question was whether the new oil-fuelled process was more dangerous than its old-fashioned predecessor. Had it caused the fire? Each side of the dispute called on as many notable men of science as they could find to conduct experiments to prove their case. The experts included such chemical pioneers as William Thomas Brande, John Dalton and Michael Faraday. After half an hour's deliberation, the jury decided in favour of the sugar bakers. *The Times* blamed a lighted candle for the 'conflagration'. Faraday's experiments for the case, incidentally, are believed to have led to his discovery of benzene in 1825 and to the subsequent evolution of the oil industry.

The chemists were treated very churlishly by the legal profession when they tried to get paid for their expert witnessing, and the matter went up for a Judges' Ruling. Their lordships refused to allow the claim on the grounds that a chemist – a new word in 1819 – was not a professional man like a lawyer, a physician or a divine, but was a mechanic of some sort since he worked with his hands. The giving of medical evidence in court had been accepted without question since the Middle Ages, or even earlier, but non-medical scientists have had to fight every step of the way.

Christison considered himself a practical hands-on chemist as well as a physician, and was working on his *Treatise on Poisons* at the time of the West Port murders. He described his cadaveric experiments in the *Edinburgh Medical and Surgical Journal* in 1829 and these passed into the folklore of the medical school. The report was picked up some years later by student Arthur Conan Doyle who attributed the experiment to the young Sherlock Holmes in *Study in Scarlet*.

Another of Christison's tasks as official investigator was to interview Dr Knox. Surely Knox had noticed that the body of Mary Docherty had been delivered while still warm and flexible? Knox replied that his providers watched low lodging houses and purchased bodies from tenants before anyone could claim them for burial. Christison, though sceptical, considered Knox 'deficient in principle and heart', but nothing worse.

There were moves behind the scenes to protect Knox and the Edinburgh medical profession from damaging court appearances. Was Christison orchestrating these as well, to protect his colleagues? Originally the quartet of prisoners was to be charged with three sample cases, Mary Paterson, Daft Jamie and Mary Docherty. It would have been difficult for Knox and his team to wriggle out of complicity in the first two murders, yet in the third there was not enough evidence to show how the victim had died, despite Christison's expertise. Matters were arranged backstage that the

Hares would turn King's Evidence in return for immunity from prosecution, and that Burke and MacDougal would stand trial for the murder of Mary Docherty alone.

Hare, coached in a version of the truth which was terminologically inexact, gave his evidence with unblushing effrontery, and Burke was found guilty. The case against MacDougal was 'not proven', to Burke's relief. He turned to her in the dock and said, 'Nelly, you are out of the scrape.' Burke was hanged, and was dissected at the university, where his skeleton remains today. Margaret Hare, with the babe in arms which accompanied her into the witness box, took the sailing boat *Fingal* to Belfast and was never heard of again. William Hare was last reported, alone, on the road south from Carlisle.

The teaching of forensic medicine moved down from Edinburgh to London in the 1820s, in the person of Dr John Gordon Smith. He had a medical degree from the University of Edinburgh but couldn't practise as a physician in London because of the closed shop operated by the Royal College of Physicians, which required members to hold a degree from either Oxford or Cambridge. Smith scratched a living at first by writing a textbook on forensic medicine, *Principles of Medical Jurisprudence* (1821), one of the first in the English language. Then he set up a series of lectures for medical students. The first of these was at the Webb Street School, St Thomas's Hospital, in 1823. Later, in 1826–8, he gave some talks at the Royal Institution, alternating with Faraday's chemistry classes. The university didn't yet offer medical degrees of its own. In 1828 it offered tuition for the licentiate of the Society of Apothecaries of London (LSA), as did the many other medical schools in the capital.

Meanwhile, he made a successful application to become professor of medical jurisprudence at the new University of London, which opened its gates for the first time in October 1828. He was a useless lecturer, a waffler. The *Morning Chronicle* was at his inaugural lecture. 'Condensation,' the paper reported, 'is not a virtue of Dr Smith's'. Because of this and because medical jurisprudence was not a compulsory examination subject, no one came to the classes. Apart from £4 per annum, Smith's salary was paid from students' fees. Consequently, he petitioned the university, and then the Society of Apothecaries of London, to put forensic medicine on the compulsory curriculum.

Medicine was a three-tier profession in early nineteenth-century London. The physicians, an élite of some 200 Oxbridge men, would not demean themselves by touching the patient; they merely diagnosed and prescribed. Practical doctoring, such as lancing boils and sawing off legs, was done by the surgeons, who were members of the College of Surgeons.

At the bottom of the pile were the apothecaries, who ran shops and dispensed drugs. Each body had its own examinations. A surgeon could not dispense drugs without qualifying with the Society of Apothecaries, so surgeon-apothecaries, or 'general practitioners' as they were just beginning to be called, were becoming more usual; the student would first get his LSA, then take the membership of the College of Surgeons (MCS). Smith could have retrained in this way but he may have considered it beneath his professional dignity.

The Society of Apothecaries refused his petition and the situation looked impossible, but there was another card in the pack. Thomas Wakley, a medical man and editor of *The Lancet*, was trying to become elected as a London coroner, and in August 1830 he was approached by the family of a young Irishwoman, Catherine Cashin, to attend her inquest on their behalf. Catherine, a consumptive, had died after being treated by John St John Long, a Harley Street quack.

Long professed to cure consumption by two methods; one was inhalation through rubber tubes from a mechanical contraption, the other was by rubbing on the back or the chest of the patient a corrosive mixture which raised sores. This suppuration was alleged to relieve the inner problems of the lungs. Although this might seem obvious charlatanism today, Long had a large and fashionable clientele, many of whom supported him in court.

Thanks to Wakley's intervention, the inquest jury brought in a verdict of manslaughter and Long was arrested. He was later found guilty at the Central Criminal Court in Old Bailey and was fined £250, an immense sum, which he paid in cash before driving away in the Marquess of Sligo's curricle.

Wakley used the case in his electoral campaign to illustrate the benefits of medical coronerships and forensic medical training for medical students. Public meetings were held, and bills were posted all over London and in the newspapers promoting Wakley on the grounds that he was well qualified 'in the investigation of all subjects connected with medical jurisprudence'. The affair thus brought forensic medicine to the London public's attention for the first time, and within a month the Society of Apothecaries announced that a compulsory, i.e. examined, three-month second-year course in forensic medicine would commence for all their students on 1 January 1831.

Smith's scheme now backfired. Once the subject was compulsory, the university replaced him with someone who could actually do the job and he died a drunk in a debtors' prison in 1833, abandoned by everyone except his obituarist. The new professor was Dr Anthony Todd Thomson, already professor of materia medica at the university. He, too, was an Edinburgh physician, but had already taken his LSA and MCS in London.

Once the subject was approved for examination, every other medical school in London similarly appointed lecturers in medical jurisprudence; in fact there was more teaching of forensic medicine in London in 1831 than there is today. The standard of both teaching and practice, however, was very poor in comparison with the situation in Edinburgh. We know this from a parallel case in London to that of Burke and Hare in the autumn of 1831, when teaching in forensic medicine was just a few months old.

Whereas Burke and Hare were enthusiastic amateurs, John Bishop, Thomas Williams and James 'Blaze Eye Jack' May were professional resurrectionists and dealers in unburied stiffs. They, too, took to murdering only those who never would be missed. The story has a familiar ring. On Guy Fawkes Day, Saturday, 5 November 1831, the three men arrived at London's King's College, beside the Thames, accompanied by a market porter, Michael Shields, who was carrying the body of a 14-year-old boy in a hamper on his head. The men had been turned away from Guy's Hospital and Graingers, a private crammer, and they had already drunk the profit from the sale when they turned up at King's.

Shields tipped the body out for inspection by the dissecting room porter, William Hill, as was the custom. The teeth had already been removed for sale to a dentist: sound teeth fetched a good price for making up into false sets. This was not unusual, but the boy also had a cut head, a swollen face and bloodshot eyes. One arm was turned up towards his head and his fist was clenched. Hill, seeing the cut, asked how he had died. Bishop blamed May for handling the body carelessly. Hill then left the room to speak to the anatomy demonstrator, Richard Partridge. Partridge came in to examine the body for himself and evidently shared the porter's suspicions, leaving Hill with the four men while he quietly sent for the police. The four were arrested and taken to the police station of 'F' Division of the Metropolitan Police, by the side of St Paul's Church, in Covent Garden.

The Edinburgh autopsy, in the case of Burke and Hare, had been conducted by the professor of medical jurisprudence. King's College had a lecturer in forensic medicine in 1831, a Mr Watson, but he wasn't called upon, nor was Professor Thomson at the University of London, at that time a rival establishment. It was an opportunity lost. The post-mortem was left to George Beaman, parish surgeon, who had been the first to examine the boy's body, Herbert Mayo, professor of anatomy at King's, and Partridge himself. Mayo had an MD from the University of Leyden and was a prominent London surgeon. Surprisingly, he was not called to give evidence either at the inquest or the trial. This was given by Beaman, and was confirmed by Frederick Tyrell, a surgeon from St Thomas's, who was not even present at the autopsy. It may indicate the lower esteem with which forensic medicine was regarded in London compared with Edinburgh.

The post of divisional police surgeon was created when the Metropolitan Police was founded in 1829. The surgeon for 'F' Division was Charles Snitch, a local general practitioner. He didn't attend the post-mortem himself but sent his apprentice, James Fernandez Clarke, whose unpleasant task it was to sew up the body afterwards. This was bad luck for Clarke, but a stroke of good fortune for history, as Clarke wrote his memoirs in the 1870s and gave a first-hand account of the autopsy:

> There were no external marks of violence on any part of the body. The internal organs were carefully examined: there was no trace of injury or poison. Mr Mayo, who had a peculiar way of standing very upright with his hands in his breeches pockets, said, with a kind of lisp he had – 'By Jove! the boy died a nathral death.' Mr Partridge and Mr Beaman, however, suggested that the spine had not been examined, and after a short consultation it was determined to examine the spinal column. Upon this being done, one or more of the upper cervical vertebrae were found fractured. 'By Jove!', said Mr Mayo, 'this boy was murthered.'

In fact, there was no fracture to the spine. The internal bruising and coagulated blood in the spinal column showed that the victim had been killed by blows to the back of the neck. The boy was first thought to be an Italian street entertainer called Carlo Ferrari, who begged by exhibiting a tortoise and white mice. There were several of these Italian boys around London. They paid 4d a night for lodgings and then paid the owners of the animals a sum ranging from 1s 6d for a box of white mice to 3s per day for a monkey in uniform, to assist in begging. They could earn an average of 6 or 7 shillings a day by this method. The Italian beggar-master who identified his exhumed body as Ferrari had been too upset to look at the boy's face. He turned out to be a Lincolnshire lad whom Bishop and Williams had spotted as he drove cattle to Smithfield Market.

Bishop and Williams, and their wives, lived in mean dwellings in Bethnal Green, in the East End. When police dug up their garden, they discovered clothing, and in the privy they found the hair and scalp of a woman. By now Shields, the porter, had been released, but Bishop, Williams and May were charged with further murders. Rumours suggested up to sixty victims, although it could have been as few as three or four. They were each found guilty. The confessions of Bishop and Williams exonerated May of any direct involvement and he was sentenced to transportation for life. The two explained how the murders had been committed. The victims had been made drunk with a mixture of rum and laudanum and then taken to a sunken water tank in the garden where they were pushed in and hung by their feet until they stopped breathing.

Bishop and Williams were publicly hanged outside Newgate on 5 December, exactly a month after the discovery of the crime. The trial and execution caused as much commotion in London as its counterpart in Edinburgh. About 30,000 people crammed into the streets that met at the Newgate crossroads, at the top of Old Bailey, just by the Central Criminal Court. Barriers had been erected at all approaches, but when figures appeared on the scaffold the crowd pressed forward and one of the barriers gave way, filling a ward at St Bartholomew's Hospital with casualties, including officers of the City of London Police.

There had recently been a growing campaign to stamp out body-snatching by a change in the law. A bill brought by Henry Warburton in 1829 after the Edinburgh murders narrowly failed, but now the Anatomy Act was passed only days after the London hanging, amid calls in both Houses of Parliament for measures to prevent further bloodshed. While it stamped out the practice of body-snatching from graveyards, it created another problem. By decreeing, effectively, that unclaimed bodies could be used for medical purposes, it condemned the poor to be dissected after their death. People who claimed a body from a workhouse or hospital were obliged to cart it away and be responsible for the burial. This involved expense, and so paupers tended to be left unclaimed. Poverty, like murder, would now be punished by dissection. The destitute and friendless feared such an end even more than the death which made it possible, and one evil was replaced by another.

Robert Christison had spent some time in Paris in 1822 as part of his medical education, and had attended lectures given by M. J. B. Orfila, the pioneering toxicologist. It was this Paris interlude which had inspired him to experimental methods in forensic medicine and toxicology, and to become for Scotland what Orfila had become for France. The *Affaire Lafarge* (1840) was Orfila's last case.

CHAPTER TWO

MARIE LAFARGE
The gateau from the chateau

Marie Cappelle was a spoilt child who quickly learned how to get her own way. It was not that she feigned sickness. She really did make herself ill, probably by not eating. There were some things, though, that making herself ill was powerless to change: the death of her beloved father after a shooting accident, and her mother's speedy remarriage.

In about 1829, her new stepfather took the family to live with him at the castle of Ittenwillers, in Alsace. Here, Marie, an impressionable 13-year-old, obsessed by grief for her father, retreated into a world of her own. She read the latest romances, imagining herself to be Diana Vernon, Walter Scott's heroine, riding her white horse across the Scottish heather, and wrote verses and long letters. Everything around her fed these daydreams – the superb Alsace scenery, the rocky passes, the feudal castles and the gothic ruins.

When she was about 18, her mother died, and Marie went to stay with her critical Aunt Garat, who lived in a sumptuously furnished apartment over the Banque de Paris, where her husband held a good position. Aunt Garat thought Marie impractical and affected. She was not as pretty as her Parisian cousins, although she had beautiful long black hair, and she was very thin and pasty faced. Moreover, she was poor. Her mother had left her a mere 100,000 francs, only a small fortune. It would be difficult to find a husband for her.

Aunt Garat felt it her duty to correct Marie's faults. One of her letters read: 'Again you have been telling untruths; but I have not been taken in... You flatter everyone, you coax everyone, in a way that is not at all frank. I wish your intelligence would teach you not to be false and clever, but good, friendly and simple... Remember that people who are double-faced make themselves loved to begin with, but are detested afterwards when one gets to know them. Instead of dreaming about a whole lot of useless things, concentrate on correcting yourself.'

It would have been an unhappy time for Marie without the friendship of a wealthier companion, Marie de Nicolai, who lived nearby. The two girls were allowed out to explore the shops and other delights of Paris chaperoned by Marie de Nicolai's former governess, Mlle Delvaux. Pretty, rich Marie de Nicolai, however, was soon married and, as the Vicomtesse de Léautaud, moved to her husband's country estate at Pontoise, outside Paris. She invited Marie Cappelle to visit her.

Marie found the household in a state of excitement due to the imminent wedding of a relative and neighbour. Marie de Léautaud, swept up in the romance of the occasion, tried to persuade Marie to marry her governess's brother Georges, a dull civil servant. Marie, the poor orphan, felt humiliated by this social snub. On the eve of the relative's wedding, Marie de Léautaud brought out her own wedding gift from the Vicomte to show around. It was a beautiful necklace of pearls and diamonds, a family heirloom. Careless and trusting, she left the jewel box lying around the drawing room, and to the horror of the whole household, the necklace went missing. Suspicion fell on the servants, as usual, but despite a search, the culprit was not found. In an age when the police were more deferential to 'quality', the guests' belongings remained untouched.

In Marie Cappelle's absence, her uncle had engaged the Parisian matrimonial agency of Monsieur Foy to find a suitable husband for his difficult niece. M. Foy suggested Charles Lafarge. He was a 28-year-old ironmaster from the Limousin region (not far from the Dordogne) and was presented to Marie on her return in the most glowing terms. His estate, Le Glandier, was built on the ruins of a gothic abbey with cloisters and an ancient church. He ran an ironworks nearby which provided a handsome income. He spent six months in Paris on business and six months at the chateau. Marie saw herself as chatelaine of a property that her friends would give their eye teeth for. She was disappointed on first meeting Lafarge to discover that he was a plain, provincial businessman with only trivial conversation.

Soon, though, testimonials arrived from his family lawyer, the curé and other local worthies from Le Glandier, who all praised the young ironmaster, and Marie began to think he had prospects after all. Lafarge told the Garats that he had an annual income of 30,000 to 35,000 francs, which would soon be augmented when a new smelting process that he was developing was patented, and when the planned railway came to the area. Marie was shown a delightful watercolour of the chateau depicting a terraced garden of flowers, with a fountain and classical statues. A well-kept lawn sloped down to a river bordered with weeping willows. A dark forest lay beyond, and, of course, there were the monastery ruins.

Marie was captivated, and allowed herself to be betrothed after a mere four days' acquaintance to a man only too keen to declare his love. It was not until just before the marriage that Marie discovered that Lafarge was a widower. His first wife had died suddenly, but Marie didn't find out until later that he had married her for the money to revive his ailing, mismanaged business. His marriage to Marie would achieve the same end.

The new marriage barely survived the coach journey to Le Glandier. Marie found Charles uncouth and over-eager to consummate their union at inns on the way. She used her maid and confidante, Clementine, to keep him at bay. Le Glandier was a bitter disappointment. When the carriage pulled up at the door in the pouring rain, Marie could see only poplar trees blackened by smoke from the all too close ironworks, and a dilapidated old house set in a wasteland of neglected ground. Greeted with enthusiasm by two women that Marie took to be servants, she realised, to her dainty horror, that these were Lafarge's mother and her new sister-in-law, Amena Buffière. Mère Lafarge was a drab woman in her sixties, while Amena, in Marie's opinion, was a common little woman.

She was dismayed. She sat in her room with Clementine and wrote a letter of abject despair to her husband which contained the most outrageous lies. She pleaded to be released from the marriage. She said that she was unworthy to be his bride. She had a lover who had followed her to Uzerche, a nearby town. She begged for two horses to start her on a journey to Smyrna where she would live by working or giving lessons. She threatened to kill herself and said she had taken poison at Orléans on the journey down. She became quite carried away by her own eloquence. Clementine pushed the note under Lafarge's door and ran back to her mistress. They stood in the locked room waiting for the inevitable scene.

Lafarge banged on the door, threatening to force the lock. Marie went to the window, as if intending to jump, and let Clementine unlock the door. Charles, seeing Marie at the window, didn't storm the chamber, but went for his mother and sister. In a scene of total pandemonium they all promised Marie the earth if she would only remain. Now they were talking her language. Marie hesitantly gave in and agreed to stay for a few days, to Lafarge's promises that he would treat her 'as a sister' and that she would be queen of the house. 'Tomorrow the masons and carpenters will arrive and everything shall be as you wish.'

Marie settled down to make the best of things, consoled by the fact that she was getting her own way. She imported Alfred, one of her aunt's servants, and Mme Mion, an excellent cook, from Paris. She installed a bath, a convenience unknown to Mère Lafarge, who (Marie said) slept in her clothes in a little room off the kitchen and never changed her bedding. She had the roof mended, and doors and windows knocked through – ignorant of the fact that Charles was heavily in debt.

Marie's enemies at Le Glandier soon increased with the arrival of Jean Denis Barbier and his wife. Marie detested Denis, Lafarge's right-hand man, calling him a low type, uneducated and pretentious. Lafarge had picked him up in Paris, where he was working, Marie said, behind the counter at a cheap café. But her word was notoriously unreliable.

In November, Charles left for Paris to try to patent his new smelting process and to raise a bank loan. While he was away, the household was further augmented by Emma Pontier, his young niece, and Anna Le Brun, an impoverished portrait painter. Emma, who was not yet 20, came as a companion to Marie, and Anna was invited to paint a miniature of Marie to send to Charles in Paris. Marie and Emma became devoted friends, while 24-year-old Anna – described by Marie as an 'old maid' – became a great crony of Mme Lafarge senior. And so the household split into twin camps under its two mistresses.

When the portrait was ready, Marie decided to send it together with a few cakes and some other necessities in a large parcel. Mère Lafarge made the cakes, with the household looking on, and Marie packed some of them in a box. Each cake was about the size of a small orange, and wrapped in paper. When the parcel arrived in Paris, on 17 December 1839, Charles fetched it himself from the post office and took it in a cab to his rooms in the rue Ste Anne.

The box, when opened, didn't contain the four or five small cakes that had been packed, but one flat, round 7-inch cake. A visitor later described it as looking rather dry, with a burnt edge. Lafarge ate a piece of the cake and left the rest on the mantelpiece. By next morning he was very ill with vomiting and diarrhoea. He stayed in bed.

Apparently on the mend, Charles returned home a couple of weeks later, on 3 January 1840, in cheerful mood. He had obtained the patent for his smelting process and had on him, he said, 25,000 francs in cash which he had raised on some property of Marie's. That evening he shared his wife's supper of game and truffles, but vomited immediately and was so ill during the night that the family physician, Dr Bardon, was sent for. Bardon didn't think the illness was serious and wrote out a prescription. Marie asked him to add 4 grams of arsenic to it as they were being troubled by rats at the chateau. She explained that she had ordered some rat poison a few weeks earlier, in December. A servant had made it up into a paste but the rats had refused to touch it. On 5 January, she sent Alfred into Uzerche for the prescription and a few ounces of gum arabic.

Charles grew steadily worse, attended by doctors Bardon, Massenat and Lespinasse, from the nearby town of Brive. In addition, there was a constant toing and froing of rival female attention, most notably from the patient's mother and wife. The rats were running about above the ceiling of the sick room and Marie, realising that 4 grams of arsenic would be inadequate, asked Denis to fetch her a larger amount from Tulle. He brought her 64 grams, which she gave to Alfred. This contained enough arsenic to poison over a hundred people.

As Charles weakened, the rivalry between the two chatelaines and their opposing camps broke into open hostility with accusations that Marie was poisoning her husband. On 10 January Charles' sister Amena said that she had seen Marie stirring a powder into a glass of egg beaten in milk. Marie replied that it was orange blossom sugar (a white powder). Charles drank only a sip, and it was placed on the mantelpiece while Dr Bardon paid a visit. During one of the constant passages in and out of the sick room by the women of the household, Anna Le Brun pointed out to Amena that small white flakes had floated to the surface of this drink. The women drew the doctor's attention to it. He thought perhaps it was ash from the fire, or that a speck of plaster had fallen from the ceiling. After his departure, Amena threw the eggnog into the fire and noticed that a sediment settled at the bottom of the glass, which she kept.

Later the same day, the suspicious (or malicious) Anna watched Marie take a drink of wine and water to a cupboard and, although Marie had her back to the portrait painter, Anna heard her stirring the mixture with a spoon. Charles complained that the drink burnt his throat. Marie said she wasn't surprised and that he shouldn't take wine when his throat was inflamed. Anna later found an opportunity to look in the cupboard. She found traces of a white powder on one of the shelves. She also saw specks of white in a glass of water that Marie brought her husband. Marie said it was gum arabic, refilled the glass from the same jug and drank it herself. She kept her gum arabic in a small malachite box which she always carried about with her.

Lafarge worsened and Dr Lespinasse was called in, having been warned beforehand that the family thought Marie was dosing the patient with arsenic. By now, Lafarge was drifting in and out of consciousness; his heartbeat was irregular and his hands and feet were cold. These were all symptoms, among other things, of arsenic poisoning. The nineteenth-century popularity of arsenic as a domestic poison, aside from its availability, stemmed mainly from the fact that its symptoms resembled those of cholera. When Marie was out of the room, Anna went to the cupboard and showed the doctor the traces of white powder on the shelf. Lespinasse scraped it up and threw it on the fire. It gave out the smell of garlic characteristically associated with arsenic.

Charles died at 6 o'clock the following morning, 14 January. As soon as he was dead, Madame Lafarge senior took possession of the house, including the two bags of money brought back from Paris. She declared this sum to amount to only 3900 francs, and not the 25,000 which Charles had said they contained. This mystery, like the cake substitution, was never cleared up. Mère Lafarge also declared that Charles had left her everything in his will, including Marie's dowry, and she took over Marie's rooms, engaging a locksmith to break into her desk. She removed all Marie's private papers.

The police were called in, and Moran, the examining magistrate in Brive, arrived at the chateau. He took possession of various items that Anna Le Brun had set aside: the eggnog glass, the remains of the soup and a glass of 'sugar water' that also contained a white sediment. These things, together with Charles Lafarge's vomit, were placed carelessly in a basket. Moran asked doctors Bardon, Massenat and Lespinasse to analyse these substances, and to perform an autopsy on the victim, with examination of the stomach contents. This was the usual procedure at the time.

The provincial doctors added hydrogen sulphide to the eggnog, soup and sugar water. This primitive method yielded a heavy yellow precipitate – or sediment – which dissolved in ammonia. The doctors decided that this indicated considerable quantities of arsenic to be present in the substances. The vomit yielded only a slight yellowish tinge, an inconclusive result. The doctors obtained the same yellow sediment from treating the stomach contents and pieces of stomach wall with nitric acid, to which they added a solution of hydrogen sulphide. This mixture was put in a test tube with some charcoal and heated: unfortunately the test tube exploded. Examination of the stomach revealed inflamed patches and ecchymoses (post-mortem stains), plus a gangrenous patch in the duodenum. Despite what appears to have been an inconclusive post-mortem and analysis, the doctors announced that stomach and contents showed the presence of arse-nious acid (arsenic in its white powdered form). The malachite box had also found its way into police hands and Lespinasse heated part of the contents on glowing coals. A strong smell of garlic was given off.

Alfred, in a panic, had buried the remains of the rat poison in the garden when the police were called. This was dug up and analysed, together with the remains of the rat paste, still strewn about the attics. They were nothing but bicarbonate of soda. It seemed obvious to Moran that Marie had substituted bicarbonate of soda for the rat poison and given Charles the arsenic. She was arrested. Among her possessions was found the Vicomtesse de Léautaud's stolen necklace. Marie was first of all tried for theft in the spring of 1840. She was found guilty, but her lawyer appealed and a re-trial was set for a date after the murder trial. Newspaper coverage was intense.

It was the early autumn by the time the murder trial started, in Tulle. The situation for Marie looked grave. The prosecutor, Maître Decous, was the advocate general of France. In an emotional and vituperative address, he presented her to the court as a monster, coolly poisoning her husband under the noses of his loving family. To damn her even further in the eyes of the fourteen-strong jury, he brought up the matter of the necklace – a step that would not have been allowed in an English court, even in those early days.

The trial was poorly conducted and the circumstantial evidence was very muddled, confused even further by the gossip and hearsay which were allowed to be introduced – evidence again that would not have been permitted in England. It was hardly a fair trial in any system of justice, with the jury already convinced that the defendant was a liar and a thief.

The affair attracted nationwide publicity. Marie was well connected and seemed a sophisticated Parisienne in such a provincial setting. The whole of France was split into Lafargists and anti-Lafargists. Was she victim or villain? Marie had bought the arsenic. Having failed to get her husband to eat the entire cake in Paris, she had ample opportunity to poison him at home. Or had Charles died from a gastric complaint? Had some member or members of the household been sprinkling arsenic around and been playing games with cakes and bicarbonate of soda to implicate Marie.

Maître Paillet, Marie's lawyer, looked to the scientific evidence to clear his client's name. If he could successfully challenge the analyses and show that Charles had died a natural death, then he stood a chance of saving her. Before the trial, Paillet had visited Professor M. J. B. Orfila, dean of the Medical Faculty at the University of Paris. Mateo José Bonaventura Orfila was born a Spanish subject on Minorca in 1787 and studied medicine in Valencia. Finding the teaching pitiable, he set up a laboratory in his room, obtained the textbooks and taught himself. He arrived in Paris to take his medical degree in 1811 and stayed.

In 1813, a lecture he was delivering on the properties of arsenic went wrong when he experienced an unexpected colour reaction. Further experiments showed him that when arsenic was mixed with different substances, different colour reactions were obtained. He discovered that most of the poisons known at the time could not be detected for certain when mixed with animal or vegetable liquids. Orfila's experiments resulted in the first treatise on toxicology, *Traité des poisons ... et de la médecine légale*, published in 1814, and a lifelong study of poisons. He was credited with being the first person to set toxicology on a properly based scientific footing. What this meant practically was animal experiments. He poisoned dogs with a measured amount of poison, then hanged them. After their death he noted any changes in the tissues and organs, and attempted to recover the known doses of poison by various chemical methods.

In 1836 he started to experiment with a new method of analysis developed by an Englishman, James Marsh. Marsh was a chemist at Woolwich Arsenal, on the Thames estuary, who had set aside his military work in 1832 to assist the prosecution in a local poisoning case. He used the same reagents that the Brive doctors used in 1840 in the Lafarge case. Despite finding arsenic to his own satisfaction, Marsh was disappointed when the defendant was acquitted; to the ill-educated jury, the scientific evidence seemed so much mumbo jumbo. He decided to experiment with a method of analysing substances for arsenic that was more easily demonstrable to a jury, and came across the idea of the arsenic 'mirror', discovered in 1787 by Johann Daniel Metzger. This he adapted to his own use.

His apparatus was quite simple: a U-shaped test tube fixed to a stand by rubber bands, one arm being shorter than the other. (See illustration section). Marsh dropped an inch-long length of glass rod in the short arm, followed by a small piece of zinc, bent double. This came to rest on the glass rod. Then he fixed a stopcock in a hollow cork to the short arm. He mixed an extract of the suspect substance with a small amount of dilute sulphuric acid and poured it into the long arm of the test tube until it reached a quarter of an inch below the cork. The zinc reacted with any arsenic in the suspect substance to give off gas bubbles of arsenuretted hydrogen. This collected in the space under the cork. When the tap was opened, the escaping gas was lit with a taper and a piece of glass – the arsenic mirror – was held over the flame. Any arsenic would be deposited in a metallic state on the cold glass. If the mirror was coated first with ammonio-nitrate of silver, the arsenic would form yellow arsenite of silver. Unfortunately, other substances, such as antimony, could also cause a yellow deposit. Even so, it was an improvement on the earlier methods, especially if further tests, using, for example, silver oxide, were made to identify the arsenic with more certainty.

By the time of the Lafarge case, improvements had been made at the mirror end of the apparatus by the Swedish chemist Johan Jakob Berzelius. The glass mirror was likely to break if held over a naked flame, so instead of using a flat piece of glass, a horizontal length of test tubing was attached to the short arm of the apparatus, supported by stands, and the gas was heated gently. This had the advantage of allowing a roughly measurable amount of arsenic to be deposited on the inside of the horizontal tube. The deposit, again, had to be verified as arsenic by further testing. Orfila had made himself an expert on this method, and was able to send in a report to the court which cast doubt on the Brive analysis. This, he said, was not sufficiently thorough, it did not eliminate the possibility of other substances producing a yellow precipitate, and the test tube had exploded. The results were unreliable.

Maître Paillet, for Marie, read out Orfila's report in court and forced the medical witnesses to admit that they had never heard of James Marsh or his test. Paillet demanded that Orfila be brought to Tulle. Instead, the judge nominated two apothecaries from Limoges, Dubois, father and son, and the chemist, Dupuytren, to retest the remains according to methods recommended in Orfila's books. To the jubilation of the defence, they found no arsenic.

If the ecstatic Marie expected acquittal, disappointment was soon to follow. Since Maître Paillet had brought out Orfila's name in such triumph in court, Maître Decous had studied all his works. In a paper published in 1839, Orfila had described a breakthrough in toxicology which seems obvious to us now, but which was arrived at only through painstaking experimentation, again using dogs. He discovered that before death the arsenic travelled from the stomach via the bloodstream to the other organs, notably the liver and kidneys, and to a lesser extent the muscles and brain, to do its deadly work. In fact, any arsenic found in the stomach was not the poison which had caused death, but the residue which had failed to be absorbed into the system. Decous now wanted the body of Charles Lafarge exhumed, some eight months after his death, and all the organs subjected to experiments by the experts from both Brive and Limoges.

The Spectator described the exhumation for English readers:

> The coffin was little more than three feet below the surface, and when opened, the body presented a hideous spectacle, and so much decomposed, that instead of the usual instruments, it was necessary, in order to take from it what was wanted, [to use] a spoon, which was sent for from the village. This species of paste rather than flesh was put into earthen pots to be brought to Tulle. On their arrival, the chemists placed their alembics on the road which surrounds the Palais de Justice. Five or six furnaces were arranged in a circle, and supplied with charcoal from an enormous brazier, which was kept constantly at a red heat. The heights which commanded this extraordinary scene were crowded with spectators, looking at the operations of this laboratory in the open air, but they were hindered by a dense and foetid vapour from seeing much of what was going on. The odour emitted was so powerful that at the afternoon sitting, it was thought it would be impossible to remain in court.

No trace of arsenic was found in any of the organs. However, when the same experts retested the eggnog and the other substances, they found arsenic everywhere. The eggnog contained enough arsenic to kill ten people. Now, at last, Orfila was summoned by the prosecution to throw light on these contradictory and confusing results.

The great man swept down to Tulle on the express stage from Paris and went to work in a locked room. He was assisted by the previous experts, and used their test materials and reagents to dispel any suspicions that he might have brought reagents contaminated with arsenic from Paris. Zinc and sulphuric acid can both contain traces of arsenic, which is a very common metal in nature. Each reagent, therefore, had to be tested for purity before each experiment. Because the very sensitive Marsh test could easily detect arsenic even though it was merely a contamination from the materials, rigorous experimental conditions were essential.

Orfila informed the court, in a dramatic scene, that he had found small quantities of arsenic in an extract made from the stomach and stomach contents, and small but unmistakable amounts of arsenic in other organs, such as the liver and brain. He explained that the first tests, in Brive, had been done using outmoded methods. The Limoges chemists had used the latest method, but in their inexperience had probably heated the test tube too violently and driven off the arsenic. Further experiments with the soil around the grave did not yield arsenic. The arsenic had not, therefore, entered the body from the soil. The soil experiment also showed that Orfila's reagents were not contaminated, or positive results would have been obtained. Maître Paillet was dismayed, having himself demanded Orfila's presence as the leading authority.

The jury found Marie guilty within an hour and she was sentenced to life imprisonment. She spent the time in prison tolerably well, writing her memoirs and playing the celebrity with a large and fashionable correspondence. She died of tuberculosis shortly after her release in 1852, aged 36.

But was she guilty? Did Charles Lafarge die of arsenic poisoning? Did Denis murder his master for the bags of money? Did he, or Marie's enemies, scatter arsenic around to rid themselves of her when it looked as though her husband might die of gastro-enteritis? Or was Charles a chronic arsenic eater who died from the effects of its long-term use?

Keith Simpson, former professor of forensic medicine at London University, gave a summary of the symptoms of arsenic poisoning in his 1964 textbook *Forensic Medicine*:

> If there is sufficient oxide of arsenic in food, there may be some burning in the mouth. A short interval follows, then symptoms of intense gastro-enteritis develop quite suddenly, with nausea, pain in the abdomen, burning regurgitation into the throat, and vomiting. There is great prostration with the latter, and this is made worse by the diarrhoea which follows, the stool quickly becoming watery, often with blood.

We know that Charles complained that his wine and water burnt his throat and that he suffered severe gastric symptoms, but we don't have enough information regarding his general health to know if he took arsenic in the longer term as a medicament. It was an ingredient in the commonly used Fowler's solution, a general tonic and cure-all for every complaint from the ague (influenza) to eczema, cancer and syphilis. It was also frequently given to cure the gastric symptoms which it had probably caused in the first place. The small amounts of arsenic discovered by Orfila could have been taken innocently by Lafarge in a patent, or prescribed, medication.

Simpson also describes the autopsy findings of a typical case of arsenic poisoning:

> In acute forms the stomach and upper parts of the small intestine are highly inflamed, the mucus membrane having a typical velvety appearance, coloured bright red and puffed up by

inflammatory oedema. Stray particles of white oxide may still remain adherent to the wall, sometimes in erosions caused by their presence, and bleeding from these erosions often tinges the vomit.

From the amount of arsenic which was found in the analysed food items and in Marie's box, some traces of the powder, as a gritty deposit, might have been expected to be discovered in the stomach, but there were no overt signs of the poison. The stomach was certainly inflamed. The vomit yielded ambiguous results, but the poison might have left the stomach by the time of death, leading to these inconclusive findings.

One of the better known effects of arsenic poisoning is that the arsenic acts as a preservative and that on exhumation the body appears in remarkably good condition. A case in point is that of Mrs Armstrong, who died in 1921 in Hay-on-Wye, in England. Even after ten months' burial, Bernard Spilsbury, the Home Office pathologist, found her body unusually well preserved. His opinion was that she had taken arsenic shortly before death. Glaister's 1921 textbook also records this phenomenon.

This occurrence, however, may not have been noted and recorded by the medical profession as early as 1840. *The Spectator*'s description indicates that Lafarge's body was badly decomposed, so this seems to let him out as an arsenic eater. In order for arsenic to preserve a body, it would need to have pervaded all the tissues over some time during life. Spilsbury has been accused of over-confidence, at the very least, in giving the opinion that hanged Herbert Armstrong. It depends on where 'shortly before death' shades into 'chronic'.

It seems doubtful that Lafarge was poisoned at all. The French authorities may themselves have held this view. Orfila was about 53 years of age at the time of the case, and France's leading toxicologist, yet he never again appeared in court as an expert witness. According to his arch enemy, François-Vincent Raspail, the scientist and reformer, this was because after Marie's trial the Ministry of Justice requested the Academy of Medicine not to use him again as a toxicological expert. His breakthrough, that poison migrated through the system to other organs to do its deadly work, was his last legacy to the scientific world.

Even though he never testified in court again, Orfila continued to write, and to edit new editions of his great toxicology treatise; but he did not give an inch to Jean Servais Stas, the Belgian chemist who upstaged him in the Bocarmé case.

CHAPTER THREE

COUNT AND COUNTESS BOCARMÉ
Deadly nicotine

In the dock at Hainaut, Belgium, were Alfred Julien Gabriel Gerard Hippolyte Visart, Comte de Bocarmé, a landowner, and his wife, Lydie Victoire Josephe Fougnies, both aged 32. They were accused of poisoning Gustave Fougnies (30), brother of the countess, with nicotine in November 1850. Bocarmé had made a mistake in marrying Lydie Fougnies. She and her brother were the heirs of a retired grocer and Bocarmé thought she was wealthier than she actually was. Unfortunately, Lydie had made the same mistake about her new husband. Nevertheless, this didn't stop the happy couple from living in a style far beyond their means at the rural chateau of Bitremont, with a town house in Brussels.

Countess Bocarmé's father died in 1845, two years after the wedding, leaving the bulk of his estate to his son, Gustave, a bachelor, who was in poor health since the amputation of a leg. The Bocarmés soon ran through Lydie's much smaller inheritance and a year later the count had to borrow 43,000 francs off his solicitor. In fact, they were obliged to raise 95,000 francs on some property to repay him and to settle other debts. As time went on, the debts grew ever larger and more numerous, and they resorted to borrowing small sums from the servants, even as little as ten or fifteen francs.

By 1849 they were facing imminent financial ruin and were relying on Gustave to die young, unmarried, and soon, so that Lydie would inherit the rest of her father's estate. Indeed, the cautious count had actually consulted a physician on his future brother-in-law's life expectancy before marrying Lydie. Gustave, however, not only showed no signs of dying but suddenly announced that his marriage would take place in November 1850 to a widow, Madame Dudzeele, whose fertility was demonstrated in that she already had a daughter. Lydie tried sending her brother anonymous letters slandering Madame Dudzeele, but they failed to achieve their desired result. More certain methods were needed.

In 1823, Dr Edmé Castaing had been found guilty of the murder of a friend and patient, Auguste Ballet, by poisoning him with morphine. Although Castaing was found guilty and executed, the presence of morphine in the body had not been detected by any of the twelve experts who were brought to the witness stand. Morphine had first been extracted from opium in 1805. It was still a new drug, so new that the experts were unable to say what the fatal dose was, or whether administration of it widened, or narrowed, the pupils. This failure to detect the poison was given wide publicity throughout Europe and potential murderers were thus alerted to new possibilities in these modern vegetable poisons, or alkaloids, so called because of their organic base. Metallic poisons were easier to detect because they were not destroyed by the gross extraction methods such as Orfila employed. Boiling up whole corpses or charring the flesh and organs, in the manner of a cannibals' barbecue, served to concentrate metallic poisons like arsenic, but of course, would consume any vegetable matter.

Much interest was taken by the educated public in the new alkaloids, and in February 1850 a man calling himself Bérant presented himself at the laboratory of Professor Loppens, in Ghent. He asked the professor for information on extracting essential oils from vegetable matter. He had heard, he said, that the savages of North America poisoned their arrows with the sap from certain plants and he was doing some research on this for relatives in the United States. In particular, he consulted Loppens on how to distil the essential oil of tobacco, or nicotine. At the same time, he ordered a copper vessel and apparatus from Ghent on Loppens' recommendation.

Returning to Ghent in May, he showed Loppens a sample of impure nicotine which he had extracted from tobacco. He then worked for two days at the laboratory under the professor's guidance. The diligent student returned again to Ghent in October for further instruction and bought equipment for a grander scale of operation than his experiments had so far warranted. Bocarmé/Bérant installed this equipment in the outbuildings of the chateau and, after working solidly for ten days and nights, succeeded in obtaining two vials of pure nicotine by 10 November.

Lydie subsequently told the court that she had seen a retort heating something in the boiler in the back laundry and that Hippolyte had said he was making eau de Cologne. After pressing him on this, he had eventually confessed to his wife that it was nicotine for Gustave, and on 20 November he told her he was ready to 'do the business'.

The unsuspecting Gustave arrived for dinner at 10 o'clock in the morning. From the account of the case written by Orfila, it appears that the main meal was eaten in the late afternoon or early evening. The countess spent the whole day with her brother without warning him of the danger that he faced. She sent away those members of the household whose presence might hinder the execution of the crime. For instance, she arranged for the children to eat in their rooms with their governess and nurse, instead of downstairs in the kitchen. She despatched the coachman, Gilles Van den Berghe, on an unnecessary errand to Grandmetz, the home of the Dudzeeles, even though he had Gustave's horse to take care of. Instead of using Van den Berghe to serve at table, as was usual, the countess asked her maid, Emerance Bricourt, taking care to allow her to retire after the second course. When she came into the dining room unexpectedly with an offer to bring in some light, both the count and the countess replied at the same time: 'No, no, later.'

Emerance returned to the kitchen where Van den Berghe was eating his supper after returning from his errand. The countess went upstairs to say goodnight to the children and the two nurses, Justine Thibaut and Virginie Chevalier. Gustave now showed signs of leaving and the count sent François de Blicquy, the gardener, to get his coach ready. Unfortunately the stable was locked and Van den Berghe had the key. The count found Van den Berghe in the kitchen, sent him to the stable with a lantern and returned to the dining room.

Justine Thibaut came down the kitchen stairs just then from the nursery. She was on the last two steps when she heard a thud in the dining room and Gustave calling out: 'Oh, oh, pardon, Hippolyte!' She ran across the kitchen, heading for the small office and the hall that led to the dining room; but from the kitchen door she saw the Countess rush from the dining room and enter the office, shutting both doors behind her, to deaden the noise. Much alarmed, Justine went down a passage into the courtyard to skirt the house. As she passed the dining room windows she could still hear Gustave's cries. She returned to the children's rooms by another staircase. Emerance, meanwhile, came down the kitchen stairs. The countess, seeing her at the foot of the stairs, sent her back up.

The countess eventually called Van den Berghe into the dining room to tell him that Gustave had had a stroke and was dead. During the ensuing commotion, the servants all crowded into the dining room. The coachman was told to undress the dead man, and was sent to the cellar for vinegar. The count ordered him to pour vinegar into Gustave's mouth and to wash his body with it. Meanwhile the countess took his clothes to the laundry and made the cook wash them until well into the night. Then the countess herself spent some considerable time scrubbing the dining room floor. Later, she washed Gustave's crutches, although she burnt them the following day, together with his cravat and gilet. Afterwards she claimed that she had acted to save her husband, the father of her children. The count, for his part, blamed his wife for everything.

The servants, much troubled by the events at the chateau, went into the village of Bury to ask the advice of the priest. The matter was soon put in the hands of the law, and the examining magistrate, Heughebaut, visited the chateau on 22 November, accompanied by three surgeons and the town clerk. The floor of the dining room was littered with wood shavings and in the fireplace were remains of burnt books and papers. The count only reluctantly showed them to where Gustave was lying, in a servant's bedroom. His face was a ghastly sight, with cut cheeks and a blackened, burnt appearance to his mouth.

The doctors had the body carried to the coach-house for examination. There were scratches and corrosion around the mouth, and his tongue was swollen and bitten. They concluded that he had ingested some corrosive fluid and that the liquid, when spat out, had caused burning to the mouth and neck. Death was due to the corrosive liquid and the violence used by the attackers trying to stifle the cries of the victim. The liquid had also gone up the victim's nose and caused contusions which were a contributory factor to the cause of death.

The magistrate examined the count's hands and discovered a cut on the middle finger of his left hand which was obviously the result of a bite, the teeth marks still being visible. There was a pinkish tinge under his fingernails. The count's explanation was far from satisfactory. The magistrate ordered the doctors to remove the victim's tongue, digestive tract, stomach, intestines, liver and lungs for examination, and put the count and countess under arrest. Bocarmé's distilling equipment was nowhere to be found at the chateau and didn't come to light for six weeks, when it was discovered behind some panelling.

The organs were sent to Brussels to the laboratory of Jean Servais Stas, professor of chemistry at the Ecole Militaire. Stas was born in Louvain in 1813 and after qualifying in medicine went to work as a chemist in Paris where he made his name on the composition of carbonic acid. He returned to Belgium to take up his chair in 1841. Despite his status, he was obliged to set up a laboratory at his own expense in the garden of his home, and it was probably here that he conducted the experiments on the Bocarmé case.

Tobacco wasn't grown in Europe until the middle of the sixteenth century when the seeds were first brought to Lisbon by Jean Nicot, the French ambassador. It was taken to France in 1561 as a valuable medicinal plant, used originally to treat dropsy and palsy and in doses of from 3 to 10 grains as an emetic. The chief alkaloid of tobacco, called nicotine after the ambassador, was first extracted in 1828. It is a deadly poison and 30 grains can kill within the hour. The symptoms include faintness, nausea, vomiting, giddiness, delirium, trembling, loss of power and strength in the muscular system, purging and violent pain in the abdomen, coldness of the skin with clammy perspiration, convulsions, paralysis and death. No one knows which of these Gustave suffered, but the dose was large enough, mercifully, to kill him within five minutes.

Nicotine itself is a thin, volatile, oily liquid of a pale amber colour which gives off an acrid odour affecting the nose and eyes and resembling stale tobacco smoke. Its significance for the experimental toxicologist of the nineteenth century was that it is easily soluble both in water and in ether. Other vegetable alkaloids, though all are slightly soluble in water, tend to dissolve better in ether.

The organs in this case were sent in jars to Stas, preserved in alcohol, from which ether is derived. So some of the alkaloid was already beginning to dissolve. Stas's method – working in a vacuum as much as possible – was at first a matter of trial and error. He took a sample of the stomach contents, mixed it with water and filtered it. Then he added sulphuric acid, among other things, to dissolve the animal material. He was left with blobs of insoluble grey matter which he boiled down to a quarter of the volume and evaporated the liquid. He tested the residue to see if there were any poisonous mineral or other substances to account for death.

Then he took a portion of the filtered extract, which he had set aside, and evaporated it on a watch glass to a syrupy consistency. It was brownish, very acid and smelt of wine vinegar. When he treated this with concentrated alcohol, it partially dissolved. He evaporated the spirit and treated the residue with a selection of chemicals to hand, including caustic potash. When he added the latter, the substance browned and gave off a noxious animal odour. The ammonia smell that was emitted seemed to Stas reminiscent of mouse's urine, indicating an alkaloid. He agitated this mixture with ether and evaporated it on a watch glass. It left an oily ring with a disagreeable odour of tobacco. When he tasted it, it produced a burning sensation on the tongue which spread through the mouth, throat and oesophagus. He refined his procedure as he worked through all the organs, adding cold water when necessary to solidify any remaining blobs of animal fat, which would be left on the filter paper.

The advantage of this extraction method was that it was valid for all the alkaloids, not just nicotine. Several had been discovered by that time, including conia, aniline, morphine, codeine, strychnine, brucine, aconitine, atropine and hyoscyamine. Once the extract had been made, established tests could then be applied to the pure alkaloid to identify it more certainly. It is doubtful, however, whether these tests were specific enough by today's standards to pass muster.

As time passed, other items were brought to Stas from the chateau for examination, such as Bocarmé's clothes, the floorboards from the dining room and the gardener's trousers. The gardener, de Blicquy, had helped Bocarmé make his 'eau de Cologne' and his trousers showed that he had handled nicotine. The authorities had meantime found the remains of cats and ducks buried in the grounds. Presumably Bocarmé had tried out his poison on them first to get the dosage right. They were sent to Brussels, but were too badly decomposed for Stas to say for certain whether they had been given nicotine. On the other hand, the floorboards were positive for both nicotine and blood.

As well as testing a pauper's corpse for nicotine as a control, Stas poisoned two dogs by pouring nicotine into their mouths. He introduced vinegar, or acetic acid, into the mouth of the second dog. This resulted in

38

the same blackish burns that had been found round Gustave's mouth. He had probably struggled and spilt some of the nicotine and the murderous couple had tried to wash it away with the vinegar, with disastrous results.

Bocarmé had fixed on nicotine after having read, in the 1843 edition of Orfila's *Toxicologie*, that this alkaloid could not be detected in the body. By the time of the crime, Orfila, who was approaching the end of his career, was preparing the fifth edition of his book. He wrote to Stas on 4 April 1850 to ask for details of his work on nicotine and suggested that he, Orfila, should make some animal experiments if Stas had not already done so, before they met. Stas replied that he had already conducted animal experiments on dogs and told Orfila that he was engaged to present his research to the Belgian Academy of Medicine. However, Orfila plagiarised his research, and read his own paper first to the Academy of Medicine in Paris. The modest Stas was indignant at this behaviour and thought that Orfila should have had the common decency to wait until after he, Stas, had announced his results. As it was, Orfila claimed a joint success for an innovation which belonged to Stas alone. The younger man, however, was vindicated by posterity as the process is still referred to as 'Stas's'.

Orfila's work had a slightly different emphasis from that of Stas. His main concern, according to his Academy of Medicine paper, was to show that vegetable poisons as well as metallic poisons migrated through the system to do their poisonous work. He succeeded in this, at the expense again of several dogs. It was unnecessary research, though, as Stas's work on Fougnies' remains demonstrated unequivocally that this was so.

The Old World didn't have a monopoly on medico-legal murders; the New World also had its share. The 1849 murder of Harvard University Medical College's benefactor, Dr Parkman, by the chemistry professor, John Webster, will immediately spring to the mind of the true crime enthusiast as being a first for forensic dentistry. But really this didn't become a forensic speciality until the twentieth century. The case is more significant, historically, because it was the first time in the States that the microscope had been used in a criminal case to identify human blood.

CHAPTER FOUR

PROFESSOR WEBSTER
Killing the golden goose

John White Webster, besides being a doctor of medicine, was professor of chemistry and mineralogy at Harvard University Medical College in 1849. His laboratory and offices were in a new building, erected in 1846, the gift of Dr George Parkman. The two men had known each other since student days at Harvard but were not in the same social league. Webster, a plump, middle-aged man with side whiskers, was the son of a well-to-do apothecary who had left him enough money to buy a substantial family home in Cambridge, Mass., where he entertained on a scale beyond his income. Parkman, very tall and thin with a jutting lower jaw, was a member of a prominent local family and was wealthy enough to be a prime benefactor of the Medical College. Indeed, he had endowed the Parkman chair of anatomy and physiology, whose present incumbent was Dr Oliver Wendell Holmes, the dean of the college and future author of the *Autocrat of the Breakfast Table*.

When Webster ran into financial difficulties, then, it was not surprising that he turned to Parkman to bail him out in the form of a mortgage on his house, worth about $2500, which included the professor's collection of cabinet minerals. When this proved insufficient to save Webster from the imminent danger of losing his home, he raised a further $1200 (his annual university salary) from Robert Shaw, Parkman's brother-in-law. As surety, he gave Shaw a bill of sale on the mineral collection which he had already mortgaged to Parkman. Parkman discovered this fraud and angrily pursued Webster for payment, threatening public exposure and ruin.

By 19 November 1849, things were coming to a head. Webster's income from the Medical College was separate from his university stipend and was by way of sale of tickets to his lectures. This was paid to him at the beginning of term. Knowing, then, that Webster should have the money, Parkman called on him that day at his laboratory. This was a basement room with two large windows overlooking the Charles River. In fact, the river ran only a couple of feet below the windows at high tide, and the water closet, set into a far corner of the room beside the window, opened into a vault below which was flushed by the river at high tide.

The college janitor, Ephraim Littlefield, recalled the meeting between the two men. The janitor was with Dr Webster, assisting him in an experiment, towards evening: 'Dr Webster had three candles burning. He was looking at a chemical book. I stood at the stove, stirring some water, in which something was to be dissolved. I heard no footstep, but saw Dr

40

Parkman enter the room from the lecture-room. Dr Webster looked round, surprised to see him enter without being heard. He said, "Dr Webster, are you ready for me tonight?", speaking loud and quick. Dr Webster answered, "No, I am not ready tonight, doctor."' After a short exchange of words, Parkman left, saying: 'Something must be done tomorrow.'

The two men made an appointment to meet at the Medical College at half-past one on Friday, 22 November. Dr Parkman did not return from that appointment and was never seen again.

Parkman's family were unaware that he had arranged to meet Webster, only that he had an appointment at 1.30 p.m. They set up a wide search, including the Medical College, circulated handbills offering a substantial reward, and had the river dredged.

On the Sunday, the 25th, Webster went to visit the Revd Francis Parkman, the missing man's brother, and explained that he had been the mysterious Friday appointment. During this interview, Webster claimed that he had given Parkman $483.60 and that Parkman had promised to cancel the mortgage. Webster, having had time to get his story straight since the Friday, then repeated it to all and sundry, and appeared to the outside world to be acting quite normally, though perhaps with little sympathy for the missing man.

However, some of Webster's actions at the college over the weekend had aroused the deep suspicions of the janitor, who lived on the premises. Having heard the earlier exchange between the two men, he had an inkling of the ill feeling between them. He had seen Parkman approach the college at around 1.45 on the Friday, after lectures were over for the day, but had not seen him leave. At 2.15 he saw Dr Holmes out of the building, and as Holmes was usually the last to leave, Littlefield pursued his usual Friday routine of clearing away the items the dean had used during his lecture, attended to the furnaces and went to clear up Webster's laboratory, which was near to his own quarters. On this particular day he was unable to do this because the professor's door was bolted from the inside and he could hear him moving about. Littlefield saw Webster leave at around 5.30, blowing out his candle as he left the building.

Making his nightly rounds, the janitor found the laboratory still locked at 10 p.m. Then, on the Saturday, he was surprised to see Webster arrive at the college at around 11 a.m., where he spent the larger portion of the day in his laboratory, alone. Littlefield could hear water running all day.

Webster came across the janitor on the Sunday evening, while he was chatting to a friend in the street, and, entering into the spirit of the search, asked him when he had last seen Parkman. Littlefield replied that it had been on the Friday afternoon as he approached the college. 'That is the very time I paid him 483 dollars and 60 cents.' Webster told the janitor that he had counted the money down to Dr Parkman in his lecture room, and that

Parkman had grabbed the money from the table without counting it, and had run off as fast as he could go, up two or three steps at a time. As Webster went into detail, Littlefield became suspicious of the man's pale cheeks and uneasy manner. Littlefield shared his suspicions with his wife, who cautioned him to say nothing for fear of losing his job. Nevertheless, he determined to watch the professor's every step.

The following week was Thanksgiving and therefore a holiday, but although the college was closed, Webster was in his laboratory. On the Monday, Charles Kingsley, Parkman's business agent, came to the college with a search party. Littlefield let them in, and they met Dr Holmes on the stairs. The dean scarcely resembled the tall, lean fictional character named after him by Conan Doyle. The erudite and witty doctor was only 5 feet 5 inches tall and was slightly built, a chronic asthma sufferer. He asked the party in grim jest if they wanted to haul all the dissection subjects out of their chests, never imagining for one minute that the truth would be far more gruesome, or that the search party would indeed brave the dark vault where the remains of the subjects were thrown after dissection. The air in this cellar was reportedly so foul that it put out the candle – mercifully – for the search party. Webster was planning to do some chemical experiments on the air in this vault, so he knew how dank and foetid it was. With a little more forethought and a little less panic, he might have sawed Parkman into smaller chunks and scattered them among the human debris. That way, one of them, at least, might have kept his head.

When the party finally managed to persuade Webster grudgingly to let them into his laboratory, the room looked as if it had just been swept, and there was a bright fire burning in the furnace. In one corner of the room was a tea-chest containing tanners' bark and some minerals in twists of paper. The officers picked up some of the minerals and looked at them. One officer asked where the other door led to and Littlefield said it was Webster's lavatory. The professor casually called the search team's attention to something on the other side of the room, and the party moved on.

Webster wouldn't let Littlefield in to clear up or light the fires that week but tended to them himself. By Wednesday the janitor was so curious that he took to peeping through the keyhole, trying to pick a hole in the partition wall and lying on the floor to look under the door. Later, the furnace against the passage wall was giving out such a great heat into the passage that Littlefield couldn't hold his hand against the wall for more than a few moments. On Thanksgiving Day itself, the janitor decided to break through the wall into the lavatory.

He went into the vaults below the laboratory and passageway and, with the permission of two professors, started to chip into the brickwork with a hatchet and a chisel. By Friday afternoon he had progressed to a cold chisel and hammer when he was interrupted by some police officers. He told them what he was doing and to come back in twenty minutes. He broke through to the lavatory barely five minutes later, and, holding a candle through the hole, could discern a man's pelvis and two pieces of leg.

This was the beginning of the end for Webster. The police called for him at his house in Cambridge and took him by cab to the Leverett Street prison, where he was arrested and his belongings removed from his pockets, including a key labelled 'lavatory'. He presented a sorry spectacle in the cells, where, to Officer Starkweather's discomfort, he went completely to pieces. Starkweather asked the prisoner not to keep asking him questions, as it was not proper for him to answer them. Webster babbled: 'You might tell me something about it. Where did they find him? Did they find the whole of the body? How came they to suspect me? Oh! My children! What will they do! What will they think of me! Where did you get the information?' Starkweather asked the doctor if anyone had access to his private rooms. He answered: 'Nobody has had access to my private apartments but the porter, who makes the fires.' Then he paused, and exclaimed: 'Oh, that villain! I am a ruined man!', and paced to and fro wringing his hands. Then he put a hand into his waistcoat pocket, took something out and put it in his mouth. Immediately, he went into a spasm. Starkweather guessed that he had swallowed poison and kept him walking until help came. Webster had taken strychnine, but the dose was not high enough to kill him.

The professor was taken back to the laboratory in a cab, although he could barely stand, and the police forced the lock of the lavatory – the key still being in a drawer at the gaol. Webster was trembling and his teeth were chattering so much that he bit through a glass of water given him. The portions of body were brought up from the lavatory, in which were also found a pair of slippers, some towels and a pair of trousers, described at the trial as 'pantaloons', which seems quaint, even for 1850. The laboratory was searched meticulously and in the furnace ashes were found fragments of bone and some fused false teeth. The tea-chest was tipped out on to the floor to disclose a left thigh, a thorax and a hunting knife. The thigh was bound to the thorax by means of some thick twine, or marline, thicker than a clothes-line. In a cupboard were found some large fish-hooks bound with the same marline so as to form a grapple.

Webster was still in a distressed and trembling state on the way back to the gaol in the coach, and wet himself. He had to be carried into his cell, where he was left lying on his back in his damp clothes. He had sufficiently recovered by the next morning to write a note to his family, who were convinced of his innocence, and to throw all the blame on the janitor: 'This is no more Dr Parkman's body than it is my body; and how in the world it came there, I don't know. I never liked the looks of that Littlefield, the janitor. I opposed his coming there, all I could.'

The trial took place in Boston in March 1850 before Chief Justice Lemuel Shaw. It was the first major trial in the United States to use medical and scientific experimental evidence, the first to identify the victim by his teeth, and the first to use the microscope to identify blood. The reason for all this ground-breaking activity was not only the importance of the victim in Boston society but also the fact that he was the benefactor of the Medical College where the murder actually occurred. It was inevitable that colleagues of both accused and victim were called upon as experts to identify the remains and to determine the cause of death. With only a thorax, pelvis, two thighs and a left leg, there wasn't a lot to go on.

The medical committee, Doctors Charles T. Jackson, George H. Gay, James W. Stone, Winslow Lewis Jnr, and Jeffries Wyman, made a thorough, if not exemplary, post-mortem examination of the remains. The parts which had been down the lavatory were white, from being soaked in water. The thorax and left thigh, from the tea-chest, were discoloured, apparently from the bark chips as well as from some caustic substance. There was a greenish area under one armpit where decomposition had set in, and some blueness where the arms had been sawn off. The head had been sawn off at the seventh vertebra and the breastbone had been removed by someone with anatomical skills. There was a ragged opening under the left nipple, about 1½ inches long, extending into the chest cavity. This perforation had signs of chemical activity about it. Under examination, the medical team wouldn't say that the perforation was done with a knife; it looked more like the mark of a cane or stick.

The committee estimated the height of the victim as 5 feet 10½ inches, Dr Parkman's height. Even so, the medical witnesses wouldn't swear that it was he, only that there were no signs to contradict the identification. It was not, at least, a body which had been prepared for dissection. Unlike the victim, all the dissection bodies were injected with antiseptic and wax into the arteries to prepare them for use. Besides, Webster taught chemistry, so had no need for human subjects.

The furnace yielded a quantity of small bones, some gold and some porcelain teeth. These were examined by Dr Jackson, as were parts of the discoloured thorax and thigh. He analysed portions of skin and found that they contained potash mixed with a very little sea salt. It was never explicitly stated in court why this should be, but Jackson found himself answering questions as to how long it would take to dissolve a body using potash and whether nitric acid would not be more efficient, especially if the remains were heated. Potash, it seemed, was best, and about 70 lbs would be required to dissolve Dr Parkman, who weighed 140 lbs. 'Potash softens and dissolves human flesh gradually,' he told the court, 'and when heat is applied, very rapidly. If attempting to dissolve a body in potash, one would dissolve the potash and boil it, precisely as in making soap.' One would also need a very large kettle, such as a boiler for washing clothes. There was no vessel large enough in Webster's laboratory to do this. Nitric acid, on the other hand, would take 140 lbs, the whole body weight, and would give off a disagreeable and unhealthy odour. So don't try this at home.

There were some green splashes on the white-painted laboratory wall, which Jackson lifted with filter paper. The splashes, when analysed, proved to be nitrate of copper. Nitrate of copper absorbs moisture from the air so the stains would remain fluid for a long time. The significance of this finding became apparent when Dr Jeffries Wyman, professor of anatomy, took the stand. He had performed some experiments on the effect of nitrate of copper on blood. He placed some blood under the microscope and applied a solution of nitrate of copper. After a few hours the blood discs disappeared. Webster, the chemist, had tried to dissolve the bloodstains to defy investigation. Wyman, however, found some further spots of blood, detected by the microscope, from the trousers and one of the slippers found in the lavatory.

This statement slipped through unchallenged at the time, but the next issue of the *Boston Medical and Surgical Journal* ran a letter from a Dr A. C. Castle, sceptical of the worth of any tests for blood. He helpfully listed previous cases in the United States which involved blood and none of them had used the microscope. He doubted the new technology. Boston Medical College, however, was at the forefront of microscopy since Dr Holmes had brought the college's very first instrument back with him from a trip to Europe in 1835. The microscope was undergoing a great revolution in the middle of the nineteenth century. Modifications and improvements since 1830 had eliminated the distortions and coloured fringes which were common in instruments until then, and the new achromatic lenses would now enable modern science to evolve. It was around this time, for example, that modern cell biology began to develop.

Holmes was both a keen microscopist and photographer and had put microscopy on the curriculum at Harvard. But could the microscopes of the time detect blood? The leading English forensic medical expert was Alfred Swaine Taylor, of Guy's Hospital Medical School, London. His *Manual of Medical Jurisprudence* considered the problem across several editions mid-century. At first Taylor was sceptical but by 1849 he noted that menstrual blood could be distinguished from wound blood on a microscope slide, as the former contained epithelial cells from the vagina.

The dental evidence was much more dramatic. Dr Nathan Cooley Keep had been Parkman's dentist for nearly twenty-five years and had made a set of false teeth for him in 1846. He remembered the date very well. Parkman had asked him when the teeth would be ready as the new Medical College building was shortly to be opened and he might have to speak at the ceremony. Keep first made a model of his client's distinctive jaw from a wax impression and moulded a lower plate to this, repeating the procedure with the upper jaw.

Once he knew the moulds would fit, he copied them in gold, then set the white porcelain teeth into them in three separate blocks. Spiral springs connected the upper and lower sets to let the patient open and shut his mouth without dislodging the plates. He finished the job with thirty minutes to spare before the ceremony. Afterwards, Parkman had returned to the dentist saying he felt he had no room for his tongue and Keep ground the plate carefully on the inside of the lower jaw. When he was shown the teeth from the furnace, he recognised his workmanship immediately and found the mould. The teeth fitted exactly and Keep passed them around the court to much effect.

The dentist considered that the teeth had been put into the furnace inside the head. Teeth, in use, absorbs tiny particles of water. If these were to be heated suddenly, the surface would become closed, the water inside would turn to steam and the teeth would explode. But if they had been heated inside the head, only a small portion at the front would be exposed to the fire and the temperature would be raised only gradually. This would explain why the teeth were intact, and cracked only at the front.

Webster was found guilty. Once he knew that his appeal had failed and he would hang, he confessed, to the dismay of his family, who until then had thought he was the victim of a ghastly mistake. Parkman had demanded the money from Webster, threatening to have him turned out of the Medical College. When he thrust his fists into Webster's face, the timid chemist saw red and seized the nearest implement, a stick of wood. He struck Parkman just one blow on the side of the head and his benefactor dropped to the floor, insensible. Instead of rushing out of the room to fetch help for someone who was perhaps not even dead, Webster panicked and thought to hide the body. He tried unsuccessfully to dissolve it with potash by boring a hole in the chest, and only then resorted to the saw. He cut the body up in the sink, washing the blood away with water from the running tap.

Littlefield, the curious janitor, scooped a reward of $3000 for finding the body, a huge sum bearing in mind that Webster's salary as a full professor was only $1200 per annum basic. Keep also benefited from the case. By a quirk of fate, the Harvard Medical College building became the Harvard Dental School in 1867, the first university dental school in the States, with Dr Nathan C. Keep, the first forensic dental hero, as dean.

Alfred Taylor had become lecturer in forensic medicine at Guy's in 1831, one of the first cohort of lecturers appointed when forensic medicine became an examined subject for the LSA. He rose to prominence following the publication of his *Manual of Medical Jurisprudence* in 1844, but despite his renown in the medico-legal world, his performance in both the laboratory and the courtroom was deeply flawed. The Rugeley poisoning in 1855–6, a first for strychnine, was his most notable case.

CHAPTER FIVE

DR WILLIAM PALMER
The Rugeley poisoner

John Parsons Cook, aged 28, a racehorse owner and bon viveur, died in absolute agony in room 10 of the Talbot Arms Inn, Rugeley, Staffordshire, on 21 November 1855. He had made the mistake of befriending serial killer William Palmer, a charming and easy-going surgeon who, having married money, had given up his practice to follow the turf.

Palmer's poisoning career, according to rumour, had started young. Even as a medical student he had laced his companions' drinks with a pinch of this or that from the poisons cupboard at the infirmary. One friend was foolish enough to enter into a drinking contest with the plump and benevolent looking Palmer for a bet. The friend lost the bet, and his life. He was found outside the public house next morning in a pile of straw. He could have choked on his own vomit, or perhaps he was poisoned.

Palmer qualified as a surgeon in 1846, after studying in Stafford and at St Bartholomew's Hospital in London. He returned to Staffordshire, leaving his debts behind him in the capital, to marry Ann Thornton. Before their marriage Ann had inherited a large sum from her father which enabled Palmer to give up his short-lived medical practice and live the life of a country gentleman and racehorse owner. They settled in Rugeley, in a handsome house opposite the Talbot Arms, and soon produced a son and heir, also called William.

Mrs Thornton, Palmer's mother-in-law, was the first of the family to die, in 1849. William had his eye on the £12,000 that she would undoubtedly leave to her only daughter. On a visit to William and Ann, Mrs Thornton became ill and retired to her bed complaining of headaches and sickness. William treated her most solicitously, taking up all her meals, but she died suddenly, the death being put down to apoplexy by elderly Dr Bamford. Unfortunately for Palmer, Mrs Thornton didn't leave her daughter a small fortune for her husband to spend. He had been mistaken.

In the next three years, between 1851 and 1854, Ann produced four more children, three boys and a girl, who all died soon after birth of convulsions. Rumour later had it that their father smeared his finger in poison and coated it with sugar for the babies to suck. He often complained that large families were ruinously expensive.

The life of a country gentleman cost more than Palmer expected, and by 1854 he was in serious financial difficulties. He decided to insure his wife's life to raise a loan on the policy, a common enough practice even then. He took out a policy with the Prince of Wales' insurance company for £13,000 and had paid only the first annual premium, £760, when Ann caught a chill. Palmer again called in Dr Bamford, a man nearing 80 years old. When Ann died, Dr Bamford attributed her death to English cholera. Palmer sobbed throughout the funeral and, as the coffin was lowered into the vault, cried: 'Take me, O God, take me with my darling treasure.' Then he claimed the £13,000.

The money failed to solve all Palmer's problems, and in December of the same year he insured his brother Walter's life, also with the Prince of Wales', this time for £14,000. Over the next few months he borrowed £12,500 on this policy at 60 per cent from one Thomas Pratt, a Mayfair moneylender.

Walter was a drunkard and a wastrel, and William had every expectation that he would soon drink himself to death; and, indeed, he gave instructions to Walter's manservant (whose salary he was paying) to let Walter have all the drink he wanted. This didn't do the trick quickly enough for Palmer, so by August 1855 he decided to give nature a hand. On 14 August, he bought an ounce of prussic acid in Wolverhampton, some miles away, and went to visit his brother. Walter died two days later, and William arranged to collect the money.

This time, the insurance company was suspicious and refused to pay up. Palmer now had no means of repaying Pratt and decided to insure the life of a stablehand called George Bates to raise the money. Bates was invited to lunch with Palmer, his friend John Parsons Cook and Palmer's solicitor. They explained to Bates that the policy, with the Sun insurance company, would enable Palmer to raise a loan of £500 and they persuaded him to sign the papers with the sum assured left blank. Palmer later filled in £14,000.

The Sun, however, had an office locally and had misgivings about insuring anyone on Palmer's behalf. They contacted the Prince of Wales'. The two companies decided to investigate and sent retired Inspector Field, late of the Detective Department at Scotland Yard, to Rugeley. Bates had been represented to the insurance company as a man of some means. Field was surprised to find him at home hoeing turnips and six months behind with his rent. Field visited Palmer and told him outright that he believed he had poisoned Walter for the insurance money. He also questioned him about his wife's death and told him he might have to account for himself in a court of law. As a consequence, Palmer gave up the idea of insuring Bates, but he was still deep in debt, with no hope of getting clear.

He owed £11,500 to Pratt, and in addition had borrowed another £440 off him using two of Cook's horses, Polestar and Sirius, as collateral, claiming that the loan was on Cook's behalf. The loan was in the form of a cheque payable to Cook. Palmer had forged Cook's signature and cashed the cheque. The loan was due to be repaid on 2 December, so if Cook had lived a few days longer, the fraud would have been exposed. The penalty for forgery was transportation. Not only did Palmer owe Pratt £11,500, but he had put up all his property, including his house and horses, as collateral for £10,400 owed to Herbert and Edwin Wright, solicitors in Birmingham. They were pressing Palmer for payment in November.

On Tuesday, 13 November, Cook entered his mare Polestar for the Shrewsbury Handicap, betting heavily on the event. The mare won, unfortunately for Cook as it turned out. His winnings came to about £2000 and he received between £700 and £800 on the course, the rest to be claimed from Tattersall's in London. Consequently, he had a lot of money on him when he and Palmer returned to the Raven Hotel in Shrewsbury to celebrate the win.

The following day Cook became very ill, although this was not unusual, he being of a sickly disposition. At about 10.30 that evening, just before Cook's illness began, Mrs Anne Brooks called at the Raven to see Palmer. She was a racecourse follower, and was anxious to ascertain the chances of Palmer's horse, Chicken, for the next day. She saw Palmer on an upstairs landing, standing at a small table. He had a glass of what looked like water in his hand and was turning it round, shaking the fluid in it, then holding it up to the light. Soon afterwards, Cook took a sip of brandy and water and complained to the men in his racing party that his drink had something in it. It burnt his throat. He was very sick with vomiting and handed his course winnings for safe keeping to Ishmael Fisher, a wine merchant and his betting agent, claiming 'that damned Palmer has dosed me'. Fisher called for a doctor who proposed to give Cook an emetic, but Cook managed to make himself sick with a toothbrush handle and was evidently better the next day.

Mrs Brooks, at Palmer's trial, said that many people had complained of being ill at Shrewsbury, so there is a slim chance that this early illness had nothing to do with what was to follow. On the other hand, 1 to 3 grains of antimony, as tartar emetic, would easily dissolve in brandy and water, and the drink would to some extent disguise its metallic taste. Tartar emetic, given medicinally to induce vomiting, produces a burning sensation in the throat and stomach.

On Thursday, the 15th, Cook and Palmer, with the other members of the racegoing party, went to see Palmer's mare, Chicken, lose her race, before they repaired back to Rugeley. Palmer went home and Cook retired to the Talbot Arms, across the road. For the next few days, Palmer was forever sending food and drink across the street for Cook. On the Sunday, he sent over some broth. The chambermaid, Eliza Mills, tasted it before taking it up to Cook and was suddenly so ill that she took to her bed for the afternoon. John Cook also became ill after eating the soup and Palmer called in the useful Dr Bamford, suggesting to the aged physician that his friend was having a bilious attack.

On Monday, Palmer sent over some coffee in the morning before leaving for a trip to London. Cook, without Palmer's ministrations, felt a lot better during the day. By the afternoon he was up and dressed, and was well enough to discuss racing with his jockey and trainer.

As Cook was ill, Palmer had gone to London to collect his winnings for him from Tattersall's. While in town, he saw George Herring, another betting man, and explained Cook's absence by saying that Cook's physician had advised him not to go out, it being damp. He asked Herring to collect Cook's winnings and to pay out certain sums from them, including the £440 to Pratt, which he coolly passed off as a joint debt of Cook's and Palmer's. Herring said he would write to Cook at Rugeley to confirm that the debt was settled – a letter that Palmer would have to intercept.

On Palmer's return to Rugeley that evening, he visited Mr Salt's druggists shop and obtained 3 grains of strychnine from the assistant, Charles Newton, a young friend of Palmer's, asking him, as a blind, how much strychnine would kill a dog.

After seeing Newton, Palmer went to visit Cook at the Talbot. Eliza Mills (the chambermaid) saw him sitting by the fire between 9 and 10 o'clock that evening. There was a pillbox from Dr Bamford on the dressing table, supposedly containing a preparation of mercury and morphine. At about 10.30 Palmer gave Cook some pills and must then have gone home. At about 11.45, Eliza Mills and Lavinia Barnes, the waitress at the inn, rushed to Cook's room on hearing him screaming. He was sitting up in bed, flailing about and beating the bedclothes. He said, 'Oh, fetch Mr Palmer.' He kept throwing himself back on the pillow, and had great difficulty in breathing. He cried out 'Murder!' and had Eliza rub his hand; he was stiff all up one arm. Palmer came in and Cook said, 'Oh, Palmer, I shall die.' Palmer reassured him, and gave him some pills with a drop of something from a wine glass. He vomited the drink into the chamber pot immediately. Palmer said he hoped the pills were not returned, and poked about in the vomit with a quill, looking for them. Cook was ill for over an hour, but survived.

Cook told the chambermaid he thought the pills that Palmer gave him at half past ten had made him ill; but although he cried 'Murder!', apparently he didn't think Palmer was really trying to kill him as he was quite happy to send the boot-boy over to Palmer's house next morning to fetch him a cup of coffee. But he didn't see Palmer in Mr Hawkins' druggists shop not an hour later.

Palmer was in the process of buying 2 drachms of prussic acid when who should come in but Newton, the other druggist's assistant. Palmer took him by the shoulder at once and steered him outside on the pretext of wanting to talk to him. Fortunately for Palmer, another acquaintance came up and engaged Newton in conversation, enabling Palmer to make the rest of his purchases without Newton seeing – 6 grains of strychnine and some Battley's solution, a sedative containing opium. Palmer, however, failed to take into account Newton's suspicious and curious mind. As soon as Palmer's back was turned, Newton went back into the shop to find out what had been going on.

Later on the Tuesday, another surgeon friend arrived in Rugeley to see Cook. This was William Henry Jones, from Lutterworth, Leicestershire. Palmer had sent for Jones on Sunday, but Jones himself was ill and was unfit to travel until Tuesday. Palmer told Drs Bamford and Jones that Cook was suffering from a bilious attack. Jones found Cook's tongue clean and doubted the diagnosis. Dr Bamford was officially in charge of the case and at about 7 p.m. the three medical men conferred over Cook's condition out of the patient's hearing. Palmer suggested that Bamford should make up some morphine pills as on Monday, but not tell Cook, as he had objected to the drug the night before.

Palmer gave Cook two of these pills at about 11 p.m. in Jones' presence, making sure that both Cook and Jones saw the sealed pillbox and Dr Bamford's writing on the label. Cook immediately vomited and again Palmer searched the chamber pot. He and Jones were both satisfied that the pills had been retained. Cook seemed easier, and Palmer went home, leaving Cook with Jones, who had arranged to stay the night in his room. At about midnight Cook called out: 'Doctor, get up; I am going to be ill; ring the bell for Mr Palmer.' Jones rubbed the back of his neck, which he said was stiff. Palmer came over within three minutes, claiming that he had never dressed so quickly in his life. He gave Cook two further pills, which the sick man swallowed. Almost immediately he screamed loudly and threw himself back in the bed with violent convulsions. Jones tried to lift Cook up, but his body was so rigid that Jones could barely move him. He died about ten minutes later.

Jones declared death to be due to what he termed 'tetanus', or 'lockjaw'. He did not mean to imply that Cook had caught tetanus from an infected sore or wound to the skin; the term was used loosely at that time to refer to the kind of convulsions that were only sometimes caused by the disease of tetanus. Cook was lying on the bed on his side when he died, with both hands clenched. His head was arched back in an unnatural position, bent like a bow, so that if he had been lying on his back he would have rested on his head and his heels.

Eliza, who had been ill after tasting the broth some days before, was the only other witness to the death of Cook. Shortly afterwards, she observed Palmer going through Cook's pockets. He also hunted under the bolster and the pillows. He handed Jones a watch and a purse containing five sovereigns, saying 'You, being his nearest friend, had better take possession of his effects.' He then complained, untruthfully, that it was a bad thing for him that Cook had died, because he was liable for his debts of about £3000 to £4000 and was likely to have all his horses seized.

Jones went to London to call on Cook's stepfather, William Vernon Stevens, to tell him the news and bring him back to Rugeley. Stevens was a retired London merchant with a sharp intellect. He had never liked Cook's association with Palmer, though the two men had never met, and he was suspicious of him now at their first meeting at the Talbot, especially when Palmer told him that Cook owed him £4000 and that his family were morally, if not legally, obliged to pay him the money. Stevens sent Jones to look for Cook's betting book, but it wasn't in Cook's room. It had last been seen in Palmer's possession in London. Stevens asked Palmer if there were any debts owing to Cook, and wanted to know what had happened to his stepson's winnings at Shrewsbury, insisting that the book be found. Palmer lied glibly that the bulk of the money had been paid on the course and that he knew of only £300 of debts to Cook. Stevens was furious, and incredulous that Cook's betting book couldn't be found. Palmer was offhand, saying that in any case, a man's bets died with him, so the book would be of no benefit to anyone.

On his return to the capital, Stevens determined to have a post-mortem done on Cook and approached Dr Alfred Taylor at Guy's, with an introduction from a mutual acquaintance. Taylor asked his colleague, George Owen Rees, to assist him when he learned that a fellow medical man was the suspect, as he wanted a witness to the proceedings. Taylor and Rees didn't perform the post-mortem; that wasn't the analyst's role. They waited in London for Cook's organs to be sent to them in jars.

Meanwhile, as a medical man, Palmer was permitted to attend the autopsy in Rugeley. It was conducted by Dr John Harland, with the assistance of Mr Devonshire of London University and Charles Newton, who were both employed to cut open the body. During the post-mortem, according to Harland, 'while Mr Devonshire was opening the stomach a push was given by Palmer which sent Mr Newton against Mr Devonshire and shook some of the contents into the body'. So when the jar reached Taylor in London, the stomach was cut open and turned inside out, and was lying on the intestines with no contents, these having somehow drained away. Seeing the damage, Taylor and Rees sent for the other viscera. They received a second jar at the beginning of December with liver, kidneys and spleen, plus a small bottle of blood from the heart.

Their summary report read:

Parts examined for strychnia: coats of stomach, and two ounces of bloody fluid from the jar containing it. Heated with dilute sulphuric acid and alcohol, filtered, evaporated; neutral-

ized by carb. potash, evaporated, and digested in alcohol; alcoholic liquid evaporated and tested by taste, as well as by
sulphuric acid and bichromate of potash, a slight purple
colour produced, but no satisfactory evidence of strychnia.
Antimony found in these parts. Two drachms of blood (the
whole quantity sent), antimony found therein. Liver, spleen,
kidneys and lungs, examined only for mineral poison. Antimony alone found in small quantity, in all the parts submitted
to examination.

Strychnine, tested with sulphuric acid and bichromate of potash (Otto's
test), gave a blue colour changing through violet and purple to red on
further exposure to the air. All the colour tests relied on the extract from
the body being pure, as even the slightest contamination could falsify the
test. A tiny trace of cod liver oil, for example, could give the same colours
as strychnine. If it were strychnine, its presence could have been confirmed
by looking for the distinctive needle-shaped crystals under the microscope
– the crystal test. Taylor's and Rees' result was negative for strychnine, so
they didn't do the confirmatory tests. And, of course, they had discovered
antimony. Antimony, though a poison, was often taken in small doses as a
medicine, and they couldn't tell for sure whether it was innocent or the
cause of death.

The analysts' report to their client concluded: 'We have no evidence
before us to enable us to form a judgment as to the circumstances under
which antimony was taken by deceased, and whether it was or was not the
cause of death.' This encouraging news was relayed to Palmer by the
Rugeley postmaster, who intercepted the report on its way to Stevens' solicitor. Palmer wrote with the news to the coroner, another friend, with a gift
hamper and a suggestion that Cook had died a natural death.

Taylor went up to Staffordshire in December to attend the inquest.
He met Cook's doctor friend, Jones, and his stepfather, Stevens, before the
hearing, when he learned of Cook's symptoms for the first time, and of
Palmer's purchase of strychnine, prussic acid and Battley's solution. Taylor
coached Jones, before his court appearance, on the answers to various questions which he then prompted the coroner to put. In his own testimony he
now gave his opinion that Cook had died in tetanic convulsions caused by
strychnine.

Taylor was a tall and imposing figure in the witness box. His portrait
shows a kindly face with a shock of dark hair falling over his forehead. Born
in 1806, he would have been 49 at this time. He explained to the inquest
jury that his failure to discover the strychnine was because it had been
given in a very small dose and had been quickly absorbed into the bloodstream, so that none remained in the body at the time of death. The jury

returned a verdict that William Palmer had murdered Cook with poison, but they were not specific as to the poison used. Palmer was arrested and taken to Stafford gaol.

This was the first case in England, if not the western world, of murder by strychnine, though there had been some accidental cases and suicides. Strychnine was discovered in 1818 in France. It can be extracted from several plants, the best known being *Strychnos nux vomica*. (Curare, used in poison arrows, is from another plant in the *Strychnos* family.) In Victorian England, strychnine, or strychnia – the terms were interchangeable – was sold as colourless salts, easily soluble in water, or as a liquid, its main characteristic being a bitter taste, detectable in a 1 in 70,000 solution.

After Palmer's arrest, the bodies of Ann and Walter Palmer were exhumed and Taylor was asked to analyse their stomach contents over Christmas 1855. At the inquests in January 1856 he reported that he had found antimony in Ann. Palmer was charged with her murder, the trial to commence after the trial for Cook's murder, should he be acquitted.

Although Taylor found no poison in Walter Palmer, the analyst had taken to the inquest a bottle containing 25 drops of prussic acid and stated that the smell would be disguised in a drink of brandy and water, such as Walter was known to take. The jury returned a verdict that William Palmer had murdered his brother with prussic acid. The *Illustrated London News* sharply criticised Taylor's performance at this inquest:

> Dr Taylor offered no distinct opinion of his own, but so spoke on the general facts as rather to urge the jury, eager to push the case to the utmost against William Palmer, to find a verdict of wilful murder. Dr Taylor will be told that, speaking as he does with such great authority, he should speak with more precision or remain silent.

Palmer was not charged with Walter's murder.

The affair caused much excitement and fervour in the illustrated press – the Victorian equivalent of modern tabloids – and in February 1856, three months before the trial, Taylor was tricked into an interview 'after the American fashion' for the *Illustrated Times*. As he later complained:

> Mr Mayhew called on me with an introduction from Professor Faraday. He represented that he was connected with some insurance company and wished for information about a number of cases of poisoning that had occurred during many years. He went away without telling me he was connected with the Illustrated Times or any other paper. It was the greatest deception that ever was practised on a scientific man.

 Taylor as good as told Mayhew that strychnine couldn't always be detected in the body of the deceased, and William Dove, of Leeds, poisoned his wife with strychnine three weeks later. It was clear, from Dove's trial, that he got the idea from the newspapers.

The rumours around Staffordshire that Palmer had many more victims made it unlikely that he would get a fair trial at a local court, and the Trial of Offences Act 1856 was rushed through Parliament to enable the case to be tried at the Central Criminal Court in Old Bailey, in the City of London. It was this trial which started the tradition of hearing the most serious criminal cases there.

Taylor's evidence was heard on the fifth day of the trial. He explained how strychnine worked: 'It is first absorbed into the blood, then circulated through the body, and especially acts on the spinal cord, from which proceed the nerves acting on the voluntary muscles.' Blood took only four minutes to circulate round the system. Taylor had experimented on some rabbits for the trial. They died within a few minutes, but if the poison were taken by a human being in pill form it would take longer to act, because the pill would need to be broken up in order to release the poison into the stomach.

If the minimum lethal dose of strychnine were given (about half a grain to 3 grains had been reported as a lethal dose) Taylor didn't believe he would be able to find it because, as Orfila had discovered, it would have been absorbed into the blood and then into the tissues, and would therefore no longer have been in the stomach. Apparently not having heard of Stas's process, he added: 'There is no process with which I am acquainted by which it can be discovered in the tissue.'

Before the trial, Taylor and Rees had analysed Dr Bamford's pills found in Cook's room. They contained mercury and morphine. At the trial, Taylor said that he had found no trace of mercury in Cook's stomach. This may or may not have been significant, bearing in mind that the stomach contents were gone and he had only the 'coats' to work with. Nor did he look for either mercury or strychnine in the other tissues, only antimony. He couldn't go back and test them for strychnine, or anything else, as the tissues had been destroyed in the search for mineral poisons.

Serjeant Shee, for the defence, tried to discredit Taylor in cross-examination by criticising a letter the analyst had written to *The Lancet* in February on the effects of antimony. It was only too clear from this letter that Taylor believed Palmer guilty. The letter ended:

> During the quarter of a century which I have now specially devoted to toxicological inquiries, I have never met with any cases like these suspected cases of poisoning at Rugeley. The mode in which they will affect the person accused is of minor

importance compared with their probable influence on society. I have no hesitation in saying that the future security of life in this country will mainly depend on the judge, the jury, and the counsel who may have to dispose of the charges of murder which have arisen out of this investigation.

Shee accused Taylor of making remarks prejudicial to Palmer's case, but Taylor was unrepentant.

Dr Robert Christison took the stand, and confirmed Taylor's experience with strychnine, adding that colour tests were not to be relied on for strychnine in an impure condition and because, even when it was pure, the colour reactions could be given by other substances. Christison had found failures in testing for strychnine which he had reported in the fourth edition of his toxicology textbook, published in 1845, when Palmer was a medical student in London.

William Herapath, professor of chemistry and toxicology at Bristol Medical School, and Henry Letheby, who taught forensic medicine and chemistry at London Hospital Medical College, were the medical witnesses for the defence. These two were old adversaries of Taylor and would oppose him on principle. Herapath claimed to be able to detect the 50,000th part of a grain of pure strychnine.

Letheby had never seen such a long interval between supposed administration of strychnine and its effect. This was about an hour, or one and a quarter hours, if we count Monday night's sickness as well. The longest, in his experience, was three-quarters of an hour, the shortest five minutes, with the average at fifteen minutes. Letheby was confident that he could find strychnine in an animal whatever the state of decomposition, and had never failed.

The medical evidence as to antimony and strychnine, however lengthy, and given with whatever authority, amounted to very little. No strychnine was discovered in the remains, and it was never proved that the antimony discovered was a fatal dose. The implication was that Palmer had given Cook antimony to make him vomit, and thereby establish the fact that he was poorly. When he died, therefore, it would come as no surprise. But Palmer acted so suspiciously throughout that the medical evidence was hardly necessary.

Once Cook's horse won at Shrewsbury, his fate was sealed. Palmer had to get his hands on the winnings, and to do this he needed Cook's betting book. He gave Cook antimony soup on the Sunday to make him feel too ill on Monday to go to London. Palmer's trip would therefore have been with Cook's permission and on his behalf. What Cook couldn't know was that Palmer was paying off his moneylender with Cook's winnings, using the betting book as his authority to act, supposedly, for Cook. Cook's winnings wouldn't clear the half of Palmer's debts but he could buy a little time with them. When Palmer returned to Rugeley on Monday night, his friend would want his money, and his book. Cook would have to die on the Monday night and the betting book would have to disappear, as it contained a note of all the London transactions.

Palmer had already set up Dr Bamford as a witness to Cook's sickness. He had also telegraphed Dr Jones to come. Jones' role was to witness Cook's tragic death on Monday night, but Jones himself was ill. Palmer couldn't afford to wait. He went to see Newton in the druggists as soon as the carriage from Stafford station arrived in Rugeley, sometime after 9 p.m., and acquired 3 grains of strychnine. It was dispensed in the form of a powder finer than salt. Three grains could easily be rolled by someone with medical training into, say, three pills.

Palmer visited his sick friend that evening and palmed Bamford's pills, substituting his own, which he gave Cook at about 10.30. Cook was desperately ill at 11.45. Palmer rushed over and gave him some other pills with a drink. These were antimony, to make Cook throw up. Palmer wanted Cook to vomit, not just to give the impression to the world that he was ill, but more importantly, to vomit up any poison left in the stomach before he died. Palmer knew there could be a post-mortem and Cook's stomach contents analysed. He wanted the stomach empty. Strychnine was known to be quick acting, so he needed to judge it finely. The poison had to affect the system, then the antimony had to induce vomiting, then Cook had to die.

But he got the dosage wrong and Cook survived. So he tried again on the Tuesday. This time he would make no mistake. He bought double the amount of strychnine, 6 grains, from the rival druggists. It was ill luck that Newton saw him in the shop, but fortunate that Dr Jones was better, and arrived to play the role intended for him the previous evening.

The Monday performance was repeated again on Tuesday evening, in front of credible witnesses. Palmer gave Cook the strychnine at 11 o'clock. Cook unfortunately vomited immediately from the effects of repeated antimony doses and Palmer anxiously searched the chamber pot for the strychnine pills. At midnight, when Cook became very ill, he got the call he was waiting for, rushed over and gave him two more pills, probably antimony; but Cook didn't vomit this time, and died a few minutes later. Palmer couldn't be sure that Cook had vomited up all the poison this time, which is why he slashed the stomach wall when it was lying in the jar in the mortuary and tipped out the contents.

William Palmer was executed in front of Stafford gaol on 14 June 1856, declaring – a liar to the last – that he was innocent of poisoning Cook by strychnia.

Once the execution had taken place, the knives came out and Letheby used the pages of *The Lancet* to accuse Taylor of not keeping up to date with chemical extraction methods, that of Stas in particular. Taylor answered this criticism, and made a few of his own, in a paper published later in the year in *Guy's Hospital Reports*, an in-house annual that was nevertheless widely read in the medical profession. It appears from this paper that if Taylor had heard of Stas, it was as the discoverer of yet another mediocre extraction process. Taylor kept abreast of the continental literature, and read everything that Orfila had written, putting it into English for the readers of his *Manual of Medical Jurisprudence*. But Orfila barely mentioned Stas's extraction method in the latest edition of his toxicology textbook, published shortly before his death in 1853. Taylor, however, claimed to have read about Stas's process in *Traité des Poisons* by Ch. Flandin, Paris, 1853. Flandin's report was rather vague. Stas had extracted nicotine from a dead body, it was true, but had extracted strychnine only from *nux vomica*. Taylor noted in his paper: 'Facts of this description have a pharmaceutical interest, but until the results have been verified by repeated trial in the dead body, they are of very little interest to the medical jurist.'

Nevertheless, Taylor and Christison had independently experimented, using Stas's process, in June 1856 (i.e. after Palmer's conviction), and both men had found that although it seemed to be a good extraction method, it was indeed difficult to detect strychnine. Taylor concluded that it was possible for an animal to die of strychnine poisoning and for it not to be found in the tissues.

By the time that Taylor's textbook, *On Poisons*, was published in 1859, he had come down firmly in favour of Stas's extraction process as the best, and this method, recommended in all his textbooks, became the standard extraction method for over a century.

Despite Palmer's obvious guilt, Taylor's performance as an analyst and medical witness was appalling. He interfered with a witness at Cook's inquest, he displayed partisanship towards the prosecution before the trial, and he stopped looking for vegetable poisons once he had found antimony – the search for which had, in any case, used up all the available material. A court of criminal appeal, had there been one in 1856, would have recorded an unsafe conviction. Yet the case did little to damage Taylor's career. He was called in three years later to perform the analyses in the Smethurst case.

Dr Thomas Smethurst, like Taylor, was born in 1806, but his medical career was more humble than that of his contemporary. He practised in Richmond-upon-Thames, where he lived with his bigamous wife, Isabella Bankes. In April 1859 Isabella became ill with diarrhoea and vomiting, and died a week later. Smethurst was arrested and the Richmond police sent some bottles of medicine and some pillboxes to Taylor for analysis, plus the viscera of the deceased, who was discovered at post-mortem to be five to seven weeks pregnant. This was an unexpected finding as she was 42 years old.

Taylor failed to take the advice given in his textbook – which was not to rely on one test alone – and performed only Reinsch's test on Isabella's remains and the medicines. Reinsch's test, like Stas's process, was an extraction method. It gave a metallic deposit on a piece of copper gauze dipped into the experimental solution. Further tests were required to determine which metal had formed the deposit. Taylor found antimony in Isabella's remains to about half a grain, not usually a fatal dose. But when he moved on to the medicine and pills, he discovered, not antimony, but arsenic, in a bottle of potassium chlorate. There was a grain of arsenic to every ounce of potassium chlorate. Taylor gave evidence at the police court that repeated doses of antimony and arsenic from this bottle would produce chronic inflammation and ulceration of the bowels and stomach (which corresponded with the post-mortem findings) and would lead eventually to death by exhaustion.

Smethurst was committed for trial. While he was waiting for the case to come up, Taylor continued to experiment with potassium chlorate and copper, having been alerted by a colleague to the possibility that copper contained arsenic as an impurity. The arsenic found in the bottle of potassium chlorate could conceivably have been a contamination from the test materials, released by the action of the chemicals. Taylor alerted the authorities, but the trial went ahead. Smethurst was convicted despite Taylor's admission in court that he might have made an error, and despite the fact that this was the sole hard evidence pointing to Smethurst's guilt.

Medical controversy, led by Henry Letheby, forced the home secretary, in the absence of a court of criminal appeal, to call in the queen's physician, the eminent Sir Benjamin Brodie, for an opinion on the case. He concluded: 'There is not absolute and complete evidence of Smethurst's guilt' and the prisoner was pardoned. He was rearrested immediately, and spent a year in gaol for bigamy. He inherited Isabella's money meantime, and returned to live with his original wife when he came out.

Antimony was still being used to simulate sickness in 1860 when Taylor gave evidence in *Reg. v. Winslow* at Liverpool Autumn Assizes. The victim, Winslow's wife, was suffering from disease of the caecum and it was alleged that antimony given by Winslow had hastened her death. The bodies of three other members of the family were exhumed and a small quantity of antimony was found in the viscera of each. The jury failed to convict.

Taylor was also responsible, in 1864, for obtaining a conviction, as in Palmer, when no trace of the poison was found in the victim. This was the case of Catherine Wilson, a case in which even Taylor's obituarist admitted: 'Taylor was seen at about his worst.' Catherine Wilson was employed by several people as a live-in help and eventually it came to light that the people with whom she had been living had a knack of dying with peculiar symptoms. Four bodies were disinterred but no poison was found. Taylor gave evidence that in all likelihood they had died of the effects of a vegetable poison, most probably *colchicum*, the autumn crocus, but medical evidence was almost nil. Nevertheless, Wilson hanged.

Taylor retired from Guy's in 1870 and died in 1880. He was succeeded by his protégé, Thomas Stevenson, about whom there was never a breath of scandal. Stevenson's first major case was that of Dr George Lamson, in 1882, although he appeared at many others at the Central Criminal Court until his death from diabetes in 1908.

CHAPTER SIX

DR GEORGE HENRY LAMSON
The poisoned pill

On 14 March 1882, George Henry Lamson, a 29-year-old American doctor and morphine addict, was sentenced to death at the Central Criminal Court for the murder of his crippled brother-in-law, Percy Malcolm John. Barely a month later, as a result of controversy arising from the toxicological analysis, two 'independent' official analysts were appointed by the Home Office. They were Dr Thomas Stevenson of Guy's Hospital and Dr Charles Meymott Tidy of the London Hospital, in Whitechapel.

Lamson was the son of an American minister working in Europe and claimed to have received his MD at the University of Paris in 1870, although he would have been only 17 years of age at the time. His first appointment was, by his own account, as a surgeon with the Ambulance Corps in the siege of Paris in 1870-1. A few years later, in 1876, he surfaced again, this time working for the Red Cross with the Serbian Army, and the following year became chief surgeon at Costaforo English Military Hospital in Bucharest, Romania, during the Serbian War. Here he was in charge of the hospital and worked alongside his father, who was the chaplain. According to his submission to the British *Medical Directory*, he was decorated with the Order of the Star of Romania, fourth class, and the Order of Medjidieh, fifth class, for his work at the hospital.

He had been wounded in the chest at some point during the campaign and it was at this time that he first used morphine. Initially, a colleague had injected him, but afterwards he took it himself, 'having considerable work to attend to, and in order to brace myself for my professional duties when in pain'. After a short time it became necessary to repeat the injections more frequently and the habit set in. He used a combination of morphine and atropine, stating later that this was because the atropine enhanced the effects of the morphine and almost overcame the sickness that the morphine caused. Sometimes he resorted to aconitine. This was originally for the symptomatic relief of neuralgia. Although poisonous, it was used in tiny quantities in medicine at that time to reduce fevers and in an ointment for its anaesthetic qualities.

He came to England in 1878 via Edinburgh, where he became a licentiate of the Royal Colleges of Physicians and Surgeons of Edinburgh. The qualification made him eligible for an entry in the official *Medical Register,* and gave him the right to practise – and, of course, to obtain drugs.

In the same year he married heiress Kate John, one of four surviving children of a Manchester merchant. The parents had died some years earlier and the children had been made Wards of Chancery. This meant that they would come into their parents' estate when they reached the age of 21 or married. Kate's share was about £2250 and most of this went directly into her bridegroom's hands. Before 1 January 1883, when the Married Women's Property Act came into force, almost everything a woman possessed on marriage (except freehold property) automatically belonged to her husband unless a legal settlement was made to the contrary.

The following year, Kate's young brother Hubert died while staying with the Lamsons. As he had not yet attained his majority, two-thirds of his inheritance was distributed effectively to his two brothers-in-law, while the share of the other brother, Percy (about £750), was still held in trust. If he, in turn, should unfortunately die before reaching 21, then the Lamsons would inherit half the jackpot, in total around £3000.

Hubert's windfall enabled Lamson, in late 1879, to set himself up in medical practice in Poole Road, Bournemouth. At first he played the part of a prosperous doctor and family man. A daughter was born, and the household consisted of a nurse, a coachman and other servants, but it later came to light that all was not well.

Lamson's coachman, who doesn't appear to have been too kindly disposed towards his employer, stated after the trial that immediately on entering his service, in October 1880, he found Lamson out of his senses, subject to the most childish fears and fancies, and quite unable to talk reasonably:

> His whole appearance showed that he was a lunatic. One morning he came out of the house and said to me, 'Taylor, I shall summon you. I am an officer of the Army, and I have had threatening letters that they are coming here to kill me.' This was said earnestly and in anger... On another morning my master fired a loaded revolver out of the second floor window, and afterwards could not give any reason for having done so... I could give innumerable instances of the insane conduct, appearance and speech of Mr Lamson, for in the kitchen we used to talk them over... Mr Lamson never behaved or acted like a master towards us servants, and we paid little attention to what he said or did.

Lamson was not so much of a lunatic, though, as to be unaware of what he was doing, as it must have been at this time that he conceived the idea of murdering the remaining brother, Percy. Percy was then around 18 years old and at boarding school in Wimbledon, in south London. The possibility of using aconitine as the murder weapon may have occurred to Lamson a few years earlier in Edinburgh where Robert Christison, who must have been about 80 years of age, was still lecturing. Christison livened up one of his lectures with a courtroom anecdote. During his evidence in a certain case he had turned to the judge and said: 'My Lord, there is but one deadly agent of this kind which we cannot satisfactorily trace in the human body after death, and that is —'. Here, the judge sharply interrupted him with: 'Stop, stop, please, Dr Christison. It is much better that the public should not know it.' Christison then recklessly revealed to the class – and to Lamson – that the poison was aconitine, the deadly poison extracted from the root of the *Aconitum napellus*, or monkshood. But Lamson still had the problem of how to administer the poison without arousing suspicion, while at the same time disguising its bitter taste. Fiction gave him the answer.

Lamson's father was now a clergyman in Florence, and on his way to visit him, from time to time, Lamson passed through Paris, where he had almost certainly read or seen the popular French novel *Le Docteur Claude* by Hector Malot. This, at least, was the opinion of Dr Thomas Stevenson, who wrote an account of the case from the analyst's point of view shortly after the trial. The murderess in Malot's novel, Nathalie, decides to kill her rival in love with a little known tropical arrow poison called strophanthus, from the seeds of the inée or onay plant. This actually does exist, according to the 1911 *Encyclopaedia Britannica*, and was used at that time as a heart tonic. Nathalie's victim is already taking digitalis for a weak heart, and the murderess reflects: 'Suppose that in her pill box were placed not one of digitalis but one compounded of the extract yielded by the seeds of onay – a pill exactly like the others in weight or shape so that one of these latter being removed, the substitution would not be noticed.' Nathalie plants the poisoned pill in the box, then goes to visit a sick aunt twenty leagues away. The tragic hero, Doctor Claude, not only loses his wife, but is very nearly guillotined for her murder. Fortunately, Nathalie commits suicide at the last moment by taking one of her own pills, leaving a confession for the authorities.

One can easily imagine the eyes of Le Docteur George alighting on a novel in Paris whose hero was, like himself, a medical man. Murder at a distance sounded like a very good idea to Lamson's fuddled mind. By the spring of 1881 his sins were beginning to catch up with him. His patients were losing confidence in him due to his strange manner, and his practice had declined. He had opened a bank account in Bournemouth in November 1880, but in January 1881 the bank refused to honour any more cheques. He owed money for his furniture, and the rent on his house in Poole Road was paid only until December 1880. In April 1881 his furniture and effects were seized by the sheriff to pay his debts and he was obliged to leave his home, having spent his way through two substantial inheritances since

October 1878. He sailed alone to New York on 7 April, lying to a fellow passenger that he had sold his practice due to ill health.

While in the States, his behaviour was becoming obviously deranged, despite the efforts of friends and his father to get him off his habit and back to medicine. A friend in New York State, Frank Philips, said that he had found Lamson in the middle of the street with no coat on, his left arm bared, a hypodermic syringe in one hand, and the thumb of the other pressing on the place where the injection had been made. Philips said Lamson took drugs frequently, at times as often as every hour.

He was staying with Irving McIlroy, rector at Rouse's Point, New York State, who took him up to Montreal on a trip towards the end of April. It was in a drug store there, McIlroy recalled, that Lamson

> wrote a prescription for a morphine mixture, the proportions being so large as to give the clerk cause to question him as to the use he intended to make of it and his knowledge of medicine. He answered the clerk, telling him that he was a physician, that he would find his name in the Medical Directory, and that he intended the medicine for his own use. While returning he told me that he used the morphine to inject under the skin to relieve the pain in his lung and to counteract sleeplessness. After reaching home I went with him to his room, saw him warm the preparation over the lamp, and inject a portion of it under the skin. In a few moments I noticed the symptoms which had so often alarmed us, namely, dilated pupils, flushed face, incoherence of speech, a confusion of ideas, and a drowsy uncertainty of movement that resembled intoxication... He was under the effect of the morphine mixture almost constantly while with us... I frequently went into his room to awaken him, and found him on his bed, littered up with books, clothes, papers surgical instruments, bottles of medicine, and a bottle of morphine mixture.

Even so, Lamson managed to rise from his torpor and get down to the mail office to despatch a poisoned pill to his crippled brother-in-law at school in the London suburbs, with a convincing note for the headmaster.

Percy John suffered from a lateral curvature of the spine, below the waist. This meant that although he was well developed and muscular in the upper part of his body, his legs were no use to him and he was confined to a wheelchair. He attended Blenheim House School, in Wimbledon, where, in the spring of 1881 he received a box of quinine pills from America, each wrapped in silver foil and in a tin box to protect them against the sea voyage. With them was a message to William Henry Bedbrook, the principal, that Dr Lamson had met someone in America, with a similar complaint to Percy's, who had derived great benefit from them. The principal dutifully gave a pill to Percy, but next morning the boy complained of feeling unwell and refused to take any more. The pills lay forgotten at school until they were rediscovered after his death.

No doubt frustrated by Percy's continued survival, Lamson tried again a few months later. The whole family, it seems, migrated to the Isle of Wight, off the southern coast of England, in the summer and autumn of 1881. His parents, the Revd and Mrs William Lamson, were holidaying there, having come all the way back from sunny Florence to do so. George and Kate, with their little daughter, were staying with them at Ventnor, while Percy was staying about four miles away at Shanklin with his other sister and her husband, Margaret and William Chapman.

Lamson's health was still giving cause for concern. His doctor on the Isle of Wight found him emaciated that summer, with abscesses on both arms from hypodermic abuse, and urged him to abandon the practice. A futile exercise. On 27 August, a day or so before he left again for America, Lamson went to tea with Percy at Shanklin. Now, recklessly abandoning Plan A – murder from a safe distance – he gave the unsuspecting boy a quinine powder. This time he had more success, and Percy was very ill, although he survived. (The fictional murderess, incidentally, had the same problem until she got the dosage right.) Later, Lamson gave Percy a whole box of quinine powders, some of which were afterwards proved to be laced with aconitine.

By December Percy had still not taken a fatal powder and Lamson was in desperate financial straits. His wife and child were living in hotel accommodation in Chichester while Lamson himself was staying at a seedy hotel in London. He spent the latter part of November urgently raising money, some of it fraudulently. He pawned his surgical instruments and a gold watch for £5, and borrowed £5 on 24 November, the day he spent 2s. 6d. on two grains of aconitine from a pharmacist in Lombard Street. On 28 November he tried unsuccessfully to cash a cheque for £15 at the American Exchange in the Strand. Two days later he travelled all the way to the Isle of Wight for four minutes, just the time he needed to cash a rubber cheque for £20.

On Friday, 2 December, not only did he leave his hotel without paying his bill but he tried to borrow £5 off the landlord. He left his portmanteaus behind to look as if he were returning, and went off carrying only hand luggage. He would have had about £37 in cash on him. This was a good sum in 1881 and was roughly Lamson's quarterly rent for his substantial family house in Bournemouth. It should surely have financed his journey to Florence, where he was heading after paying a flying visit to Wimbledon to say goodbye – a final goodbye – to his brother-in-law. He went to Wimbledon on that Friday evening, but returned unaccountably to

London without calling at the school, some said because his courage failed him at the last minute.

He returned there the next day, and while he was there, on the evening of Saturday, 3 December 1881, a curious scene took place in the school dining room which was to form the centrepiece of his trial a few months later.

Lamson was shown into the room by Bedbrook, the headmaster, and Percy was carried in by a fellow pupil and placed on a chair. Lamson greeted his brother-in-law with 'Why, how fat you are looking, Percy, old boy', to which the boy replied, 'I wish I could say the same of you, George.' Bedbrook offered Lamson some sherry in a large claret glass and Lamson asked him for some sugar, saying that these wines contained a large amount of brandy and that the sugar would destroy the alcoholic effects. Bedbrook didn't believe this, but nevertheless rang for Mrs Bowles, the matron, to bring some caster sugar. Lamson put a small spoonful of sugar into his drink and stirred it with his penknife. Then he took from his black leather bag a Dundee cake and some sweets. It was Bedbrook's recollection that he cut the cake there with his penknife and handed the pieces round.

At about 7.15 Lamson remarked, 'Oh, by the way, Mr Bedbrook, when I was in America I thought of you and your boys; I thought what excellent things these capsules would be for your boys to take nauseous medicines in.' He then produced from his bag two boxes of American capsules. A novelty at the time, they were the forerunner of what is quite commonplace now – bullet-shaped gelatine capsules that pull apart in the middle. Bedbrook chose one himself from the box, at Lamson's request, to demonstrate to his pupils how easily they could be swallowed and then watched him fill another with sugar from the bowl. Bedbrook was unable to say from where Lamson had taken that particular capsule, as he hadn't noticed. Lamson shook the capsule in front of his audience, saying, 'If you shake it the medicine will come down to one end.' He then passed the sugared capsule to Percy, with, 'Here, Percy, you are a swell pill taker; take this and show Mr Bedbrook how easily it may be swallowed.' Percy took the capsule, and immediately Lamson said he must be going and left to catch the next train to London, explaining that he was going to Florence via Paris on the 8 o'clock train from London Bridge. He left the two boxes of capsules behind.

It can't have been more than half an hour later that the boy became violently ill. In fact, he told the head that he had not felt so sick since George had given him a quinine pill on the Isle of Wight the previous August. He was in great pain, with the sensation that his throat was closing, and complained that his skin seemed to be 'drawn up'. He vomited on the floor, in his bed and in a basin, and was in a most wretched state. Dr Berry, Percy's usual doctor, was called for, and by chance there was already a doctor in the house as a guest, Dr Little. Dr Berry, prompted by a comment from the principal, asked Percy, 'Did your brother-in-law ever give you a quinine pill before?' When the boy confirmed that he had felt ill on the Isle of Wight, the doctor asked, 'Did your brother-in-law know that it had made you ill like this?' He answered, 'I cannot say.' The two doctors suspected that the boy had been poisoned but were unable to help him. All they could do, practically, was to give him two injections of morphine to ease his pain and writhing. The first seemed to help, although the second had no effect, and he died at about 11.20 that night.

The following morning, Sunday, Bedbrook went straight to the police at Wimbledon and the wheels of the law were set in motion. Inspector Fuller called at the school on the same day and removed several items of possible evidence. These included the American capsules, the tin box sent from America containing two pills wrapped in silver paper, the box of twenty quinine powders bought on the Isle of Wight, some sweets, sugar, sherry and the remains of the Dundee cake.

The first task to be performed was the post-mortem. Before the Edwardian era, post-mortems in sudden deaths, in London, were usually done by the police surgeon, although his main role was the health and welfare of the police officers in his division. It was carried out on the Tuesday by Thomas Bond, police surgeon to 'A' Division of the Metropolitan Police, assisted by Drs Little and Berry. 'A' Division of the Metropolitan Police was still stationed at police headquarters in Great Scotland Yard, off Whitehall. (New Scotland Yard, on the Embankment, would become headquarters in 1890.) Bond was the leading police surgeon of his day and functioned in much the same way as a present-day forensic pathologist. He was based at Westminster Hospital Medical School, where he lectured in forensic medicine. The results of the autopsy showed some small greyish spots, or patches, in the stomach, the result possibly of an irritant poison. Bond suspected a vegetable alkaloid.

On the Wednesday, the items collected by Inspector Fuller from the school were given by the police to Dr August Dupré, lecturer in chemistry and toxicology at Westminster Hospital, and a close colleague of Bond. Dupré was not a medical doctor, but a chemist with a PhD from the University of Heidelberg. He had studied under Bunsen (of Bunsen burner fame) in the 1850s, although he had been a naturalised Englishman since 1866. Among other appointments he was public analyst for Westminster and was chemical adviser to the Explosives Department of the Home Office.

While Bond and Dupré were conferring at Westminster Hospital, Lamson was reading the papers in Paris and decided that he had better return home to brazen things out. He wrote to his now only surviving brother-in-law, William Chapman, a civil service clerk living in Willesden:

I was so prostrate at the sudden, awful and most unexpected news that I became delirious very soon. I was obliged to remain in bed all day yesterday. Early this morning I saw the Evening Standard. I read therein the dreadful suspicion attached to my name. I need not tell you of the absolute falsity of such a fearful accusation. Bedbrook was present all the time I was in the house, and if there was any noxious substance in the capsule it must have been in his sugar, for that was all there was in it. He saw me take the empty capsule and fill it from his own sugar basin. However, with the consciousness that I am an innocent and unjustly accused man, I am returning at once to London to face the matter out... I shall arrive at Waterloo station about 9.15 tomorrow.

Unknown to Lamson, however, the pharmacist who had sold him the aconitine was also reading the papers and, on seeing Lamson's name in connection with the crime, got in touch with Scotland Yard. So when Lamson arrived there on Thursday morning, with his wife, he was arrested and taken straight away to Wandsworth police station in a cab. When Inspector Butcher of Scotland Yard searched him at Wandsworth, he found a book on him containing a note of the effects of acrid vegetable poisons when swallowed.

In *Study in Scarlet*, Sherlock Holmes is called in by the humble Inspector Gregson, but the real-life consultant to the police was called in by a letter from no less a personage than her majesty's permanent under-secretary of state for the Home Office, Sir Adolphus Liddell, KCB (a relative of Alice Liddell, the original 'Alice in Wonderland'), who wrote on Friday, 8 December 1881, asking Stevenson to make an analysis of the viscera of the deceased.

Thomas Stevenson was a bluff, bearded farmer's son from Yorkshire who, unusually for a professional man in Victorian times, retained his northern accent all his life. He was lecturer in chemistry and forensic medicine at Guy's Hospital and examiner in forensic medicine for the University of London. Dr Alfred Taylor had retired from court work about ten years earlier and since then Stevenson had been called in occasionally by the Home Office on poisoning cases. He operated from the chemistry laboratory of the Medical School at Guy's – a modest affair with a glass partition separating Stevenson's domain from the students, which allowed their supervision but probably not much privacy for the lecturer.

Stevenson combined his forensic and teaching roles with appointments as public analyst for various London parishes and the counties of Bedfordshire and Surrey, and he was medical officer of health for St Pancras. This was his first major case, though many others would follow. He and Dupré knew each other quite well, both being founding members of the Society of Public Analysts in 1874.

Because medical students learned their science at the several London teaching hospitals, forensic medical expertise was scattered over the capital. So when Stevenson was called into the case, replacing Dupré, Bond had to take the items currently at Westminster across London to Stevenson at Guy's, together with some sinister jars of body parts removed at post-mortem. Stevenson, however, asked the Home Office if Dupré could assist him in the analysis, and the chemist was back on the case.

Lamson pleaded not guilty when the trial came up at the Central Criminal Court on 8 March 1882 before Sir Henry Hawkins. The solicitor-general, Sir F. Herschell, prosecuted and Montagu Williams spoke for the defence. After evidence had been given as to the circumstances surrounding Percy's death, Thomas Stevenson was called to the stand and described his analysis. Stevenson and Dupré had made extracts from the different parts of Percy John's internal organs, although by the time he received the jars, Stevenson noted, the small intestine and colon were 'already somewhat green from decomposition', a fact that was to assume importance later.

The extraction process, a variation of Stas's, was lengthy, cumbersome and complex. It is difficult to imagine that a nineteenth-century jury could understand Stevenson's explanation at one hearing. There was no separate test yet for aconitine, as Christison had disclosed. Stevenson, and others, relied on the unique sensations that arose from tasting each substance. Aconitine gave rise to a very peculiar sensation, as Stevenson described it in court:

> Though placed upon the tongue, there was a sensation of a burning of the lip, although the extract had not touched the lip. The sensation was a burning tingling, a kind of numbness difficult to define; a salivation creating a desire to expectorate, and a sensation of swelling at the back of the throat, as if a hot iron had been passed over it or some strong caustic applied.

Stevenson added, under questioning, that he had fifty to eighty vegetable preparations in his possession and had tasted most of them. In this particular case the sensation 'lasted upon the tongue for four hours'.

Aconitine is so poisonous that even one-sixteenth of a grain is enough to kill, so Stevenson had to be very careful how much he tasted. To verify his findings, he injected a solution of each extract under the skins of laboratory mice, all of which died. He compared their symptoms with a similar extract of Morson's aconitine, the brand which Lamson had purchased shortly before the murder, and noted that the mice died in the same way. Traces of aconitine were found in Percy's stomach contents, urine and vomit, with some less conclusive findings from an extract of liver, spleen, kidneys, stomach and contents tested together.

Dupré, not being medically qualified, was set to work on the analysis of the foodstuffs and the medicaments. The batch of twenty quinine powders from the Isle of Wight contained three in which the quinine was mixed with aconitine. Dupré had spotted that some powders were a different colour from the rest. They should all have been pure white, but these three were a very pale fawn colour, indicating a contamination. A piece out of one of the two remaining pills that had crossed the Atlantic was cut out with a penknife for analysis. It contained nearly half a grain of aconitine. The other pill was harmless. No quinine, by the way, was found in the body extracts, which showed that Percy had not taken one of the poisoned powders sent to him earlier.

Stevenson thought that the poison was in the American capsule which Lamson had sugared before handing it to Percy. He demonstrated how invisible a grain of aconite was by putting one into an empty capsule and showing it to the jury. The capsule would also disguise its bitter taste.

Montagu Williams brought no evidence or witnesses for the defence, medical or otherwise, but made a brave, though unsuccessful, attempt to discredit the scientific evidence. In this endeavour he was briefed by Charles Meymott Tidy, lecturer in forensic medicine at the London Hospital Medical College in the Whitechapel Road, a stone's throw from what would be Jack the Ripper's gruesome beat six years later. Tidy did not appear in the witness box, but was at Williams's side throughout the trial, advising him.

Traditionally, the Home Office had come to use the lecturer at Guy's for toxicological work, and the main centre for defence had become the London Hospital, due to the long-standing rivalry between Alfred Taylor of Guy's and Henry Letheby at the London. Now Letheby's pupil, Tidy, was opposed to Taylor's pupil, Stevenson, although, fortunately, this lacked the acrimony that had featured so strongly in the past.

Tidy, like Stevenson, was an analytical chemist as well as having medical qualifications. He also combined his teaching role with being a public analyst and a medical officer of health, at one time for the City of London. His book, *Legal Medicine*, was published in 1882.

Williams' defence contained the elements of a debate against the introduction of novel scientific evidence. With an untried technique, it can be claimed that there is no body of knowledge in which the expert can demonstrate expertise; the trial of the accused is also the trial of the technique, with the life of the accused hanging in the balance. These arguments are better known to us now, but in 1882, when the medical expert had god-like qualities, they broke new ground.

'Who knows anything about aconitine?' Williams asked the court, 'and echo answers "Who?" ... up to the present day, with the exception of one single case, there is no authority of any kind or sort upon the subject.' This was the case of Dr Pritchard, in Glasgow in 1865, who poisoned his mother-in-law with antimony and aconitine mixed in with Battley's sedative solution (for headaches). There was actually an earlier case in Ireland in 1841, *Reg. v. McConkey*, but in neither case could any trace of the poison be discovered in the body.

Williams pointed out to the jury, quite rightly, that of the four medical witnesses, only Stevenson had any first-hand knowledge of aconitine and its effects. The possibility of the poison being a vegetable alkaloid was first raised at the post-mortem by Bond, but Bond had candidly admitted that he had seen no deaths from aconitine, adding cautiously, 'unless the present is such a case'.

Williams then moved on to attack Stevenson's tests. He took the jury again through the very complicated steps of Stevenson's extraction procedure, which had taken several days, and asked the jury to agree with him that the test was not altogether reliable. His implication was that ether had killed the mice. One of them had actually died 'under the process of pricking ... and the injection of mere water will kill them. Yet because these mice die within fifteen minutes of these injections you are to come to the conclusions that this was due to aconitine. Is it safe to rely on such a test?' The subjective taste test was likewise dismissed as unsound.

A more serious point raised by the defence was the question of cadaveric alkaloids. There was a current theory that the decomposing body produced poisonous alkaloids, also called ptomaines (from the Greek, *ptoma*, a corpse) that could have given rise to the positive results. The point was made that there had been a delay of five days before Stevenson had received the jars of body organs. Stevenson had said that he was inclined to believe the cadaveric alkaloid theory but that it was unproven, with the implication that therefore it was not appropriate to bring it up in court. So, in effect, he was saying that the prosecution's untried scientific technique was allowed, but that the defence's was not.

The speculative nature of the scientific evidence for the prosecution was the reason given by Williams for not calling scientific evidence in rebuttal. He could have called Tidy, but said that if he was in a position to place before the jury contrary opinion, it would come to exactly the same thing – speculation. What he had wanted, he declared, and what Lamson himself had suggested to him, was for an analyst on behalf of the defence to have been present at Stevenson's analysis:

> If the evidence of medical experts was to be taken against him,
> why, in the name of common fairness and common humanity,
> did you not allow him to have an analyst present to speak as
> to the means by which the analysis was conducted? We

complain, and that bitterly, of this. Was there ever a greater piece of red-tapism than the letter which has been read from the Home Office? Says the Home Office, 'The presence of a third medical man at an official analysis ordered by this Department is contrary to all practice'. If it is contrary to all practice, the sooner the practice is remedied the better... To try a man upon speculative theories on the one hand and upon an analysis taken behind his back on another is trifling with life.

Despite Williams' valiant attempts, the jury took only thirty minutes to find Lamson guilty and he was sentenced to death. No matter how strong the defence had been, Lamson was damned by the fact that he had bought two grains of aconitine only days before the crime.

As soon as the trial was over, the home secretary, Sir William Harcourt, was asked in the House of Commons 'whether, in cases of suspected poisoning, when an analysis is directed to be made, he would consider whether it would not be more satisfactory that the suspected person should have an opportunity of being represented professionally'. The home secretary side-stepped the issue and replied that he quite under-stood the sentiment that the analysts who carried out the experiments should not be appointed by the Crown as the prosecuting body, and that he 'proposed to ask the president of the Royal College of Surgeons and College of Physicians yearly to appoint two independent experienced men of science to refer to in cases of this kind for the purposes of performing these experiments.' In April 1882, therefore, the Royal College of Physicians appointed Thomas Stevenson and the Royal College of Surgeons appointed Charles Meymott Tidy. The fees and expenses for the analysts would be paid by the Home Office. But what made the home secretary think that he was appointing two 'independent' men of science when the Home Office was paying their fees? The answer can only be that independence here did not imply impartiality, but was more akin to the independent or freelance status of barristers who were, and are, free to take cases either for the pros-ecution or the defence. Normally the Home Office analyst was called in by the Home Office, as one might suppose, but at least one instance is recorded of a case where the analyst was engaged for the defence, as Tidy appeared against Stevenson in the Maybrick trial in 1889.

The colleges naturally nominated their own members, which left Dupré, with a non-medical degree, out in the cold – a slight which his obit-uarist thought worthy of mention some twenty-five years later. Seven Home Office analysts in all were appointed between 1882 and 1927 and only one of these men, analytical chemist John Webster, had no medical degree. Webster was based at St Mary's Hospital, Paddington, from 1900 to 1927. When Dr J. H. Ryffel, the last senior analyst, retired from Guy's in 1955, the role was abolished. By then, toxicology had to some extent become mechanised and the work was taken over by the Home Office Forensic Science Service (or, in London, the Metropolitan Police Laboratory).

Lamson, in the condemned cell at Wandsworth, was granted a stay of execution after intervention from the US president so that affidavits swearing to the prisoner's insanity could be despatched from the United States to the home secretary. There was considerable comment in both British and American newspapers that Lamson was obviously insane, and the Revd Lamson regretted that insanity had not been used by Williams as his son's defence. These protests, however, cut no ice with the home secretary and the execution took place on 29 April 1882. The *Daily News* spoke for informed opinion: 'If Dr Lamson had been reprieved on the ground of insanity it would be impossible hereafter to punish any criminals who could show that indulgence in sedatives and narcotics had weakened their physical and mental condition.'

Deprived of his drugs in prison, Lamson regained his senses and was full of remorse for his actions. He left behind a moving account of the effects of his morphine habit and gave the chaplain his confession before being led out to the scaffold.

Lamson was followed as a student at Edinburgh a few years later by Robert William Buchanan, a Canadian who eventually settled in New York. Buchanan got the idea of murdering his shrewish wife with morphine from the case of Carlyle Harris, a medical student who had despatched his girlfriend with the drug a few months earlier. The two cases have several echoes of the Lamson affair, which may have inspired them. Harris's trial was the first occasion in the United States that morphine had been detected by chemical analysis.

CHAPTER SEVEN

HARRIS AND BUCHANAN
The pinprick pupils

O n the south side of West Fortieth Street, New York, in 1891, stood a fashionable seminary for girls, the Comstock School for Young Ladies, principal, Miss Lydia Day. One of its pupils was Helen Nielson Potts, a tall, quiet girl from Ocean Grove, New Jersey, whose father was in railroad construction. She was 19 years old.

On 31 January, a Saturday, some of the young ladies ventured out to a symphony concert, and invited Helen, but she said she felt unwell and stayed behind. She spent a cosy evening in the principal's sitting room before retiring early to bed in a room which slept four. At about 11.30, her room-mates returned from the outing and found Helen breathing in great distress. They tried to shake her awake but found this difficult. Helen said drowsily that her limbs felt numb but that she was having pleasant dreams. Then she sank back on her bed, exhausted, saying: 'Oh, girls, I think I am going to die; I never felt like this before.'

Frances Carson, her room-mate, was beside Helen's bed, rubbing her head. Helen said wearily: 'Frances, I can hardly see you; I can hardly feel you; rub harder.' Then she added: 'If anybody else but Carl had given this to me I would think I was going to die; but of course Carl wouldn't give anything to me but what was right.' She repeated; 'Oh, Carl, Carl, Carl,' as though she was crying, her voice choked with emotion. Her friends tried to get Helen to sleep, saying that she would be all right in the morning, but she replied: 'If I do, it will be the sleep of death.' 'You go to sleep, Helen,' Frances said, 'and I will be right here, and you can call me if you want me.' The dying girl answered: 'All right; only look every few minutes and see if I am still breathing.' They were her last words.

Her room-mates sensibly sent for Miss Day and the school physician, Dr Edward Fowler, who lived nearby. Fowler realised immediately that the matter was serious. He found Helen in a coma with a cold, pale skin, of a bluish tinge. She was breathing slowly and in a very laboured manner, perhaps only twice a minute. The pupils of both eyes were so contracted that they were hardly visible. There was a pillbox on the table beside the bed, from which the last capsule had been taken. Fowler made some enquiries of her schoolmates and discovered that she had been complaining of sleeplessness and had been taking morphine prescribed by her boyfriend, Carlyle Harris, a medical student. The doctor didn't suspect foul play at this time, just an unfortunate overdose.

Harris was called to the school during the night. He was distressed, and explained that he had prescribed capsules containing four and a half grains of quinine and one-sixth of a grain of morphine. This was not a fatal dose. Harris was sent to fetch the prescription. When he brought it, he asked anxiously if the druggist could have made a mistake. By then it was early morning and Fowler advised him to go to the pharmacist to check if the proportions of the drugs had been reversed by mistake. Harris soon returned, lying that he had been to the pharmacy and that they had declared there was no error.

By now, Fowler had been joined by two colleagues, and the three men attempted desperately to save the girl's life. They tried black coffee, artificial respiration, digitalis and other opium antidotes, but were unable to rouse her and she died just before midday. Fowler was not impressed by the future doctor's bedside manner. After her death the physicians moved away from the bed so that the young man could say farewell to his fiancée. He didn't take the opportunity offered, nor did he show her any signs of affection. He seemed more afraid of being blamed for her death and announced that the capsules must be all right because he had prescribed six but had kept two for himself, excusing his actions by saying that it would be injudicious to put a grain of morphine into a girls' school.

Carlyle Harris was still not under suspicion. He was the son of respectable folk. His mother was a lecturer at the Women's Christian Temperance Union and wrote under the pen name of Hope Ledyard. Harris's grandfather was a distinguished physician, Dr McCready of the College of Physicians and Surgeons, and was paying for his grandson's medical education. However, Helen Potts' mother was also a woman of indomitable character, and a few days after her daughter's funeral – which Harris didn't attend 'for fear he might break down' – she contacted *The World* newspaper with her suspicions that he had done away with her daughter.

The two youngsters had, in fact, been secretly married. Only Mrs Potts knew, and she had been trying to persuade her son-in-law to acknowledge his wife in public. Harris feared his grandfather would withdraw funding for his medical education if he learned of the marriage. Helen's mother believed that Harris, caught between these two opposing pressures, had taken the desperate measure of poisoning his young bride. Mrs Potts knew that he had prescribed the capsules. Helen had complained to her mother that they were doing her no good and had made to throw the box away. Tragically, Mrs Potts herself had persuaded Helen to take the last one, which her daughter promised to do.

The newspaper seized on the story with gusto and unearthed enough information to publish a sensational accusation in the paper which led to Harris's arrest and trial on a charge of murder.

The couple had met in the summer of 1889 when the Potts family had been at their summer home near the ocean. Mrs Potts was against a marriage or engagement at that time as she felt her daughter was too young, and Carlyle was still a student, but she did not prevent them seeing each other. She was inclined to be more tolerant of Harris at that time than Mr Potts, who disliked him. Potts knew that the previous summer Harris had operated the Neptune Club, an entertainment establishment at the seaside which had been raided by the police as a gambling house. Harris had been arrested as its keeper. Mr Potts did not know of the wedding the following February in New York. Harris and his brother, McCready, called on Helen at her home, ostensibly to take her on a visit to the Stock Exchange. Instead, they were married in a civil ceremony. According to a friend of Harris, this was 'because he could not accomplish her ruin in any other way'. Harris was later heard to boast that he had 'married' at least two women before Helen.

By August she was pregnant. Harris bungled an attempt at an abortion and Helen, by then very ill, was despatched to her uncle, Dr C. W. Treverton, of Scranton, Pennsylvania, to repair matters. Treverton wrote to Harris demanding money to finish the job. But he wasn't home. Instead of spending this difficult time with his wife, Harris was being thrown out of a hotel where he had been discovered in the room of his companion, Miss 'Queenie' Drew. He had met her on a train, given her $10 and promised to find her a situation in New York. Once he had persuaded her into a hotel, he had pressed home his advantage.

Knowing nothing of the seamier side of her son-in-law's activities, Mrs Potts insisted that he make their union public. Harris refused, saying that he would rather cut and run to the West. Mrs Potts feared that if this happened, her husband would blame her. Nevertheless, she kept up the pressure, and on 20 January 1891 she was finally able to persuade Harris to go before a minister with his wife on the anniversary of his civil wedding, 8 February. She was able to convince herself that a mere civil wedding didn't count for anything. Harris, who had no intention of confirming his marriage, went straight to a pharmacist, where he was well known, and wrote a prescription for six capsules of quinine and morphine. The total morphine contained in them amounted to one grain, or half an average lethal dose. No other purchase of morphine was ever traced to him.

The following day Harris saw Helen and persuaded her to accept a box containing four sleeping pills; then he left town on a trip. This was deeply suspicious. He had probably spent the previous evening adding a fatal dose of morphine to one of the capsules and had then absented himself from the scene.

The crime was surely inspired by the Lamson case in England. What medical student, even ten years later, could fail to have heard of this case? The accused man's lecturer, Dr George L. Peabody, at the College of Physicians and Surgeons, testified not only that Helen had died exhibiting symptoms of morphine poisoning, but that he had lectured on its effects only ten days before her death. Harris might have been able to make his supply up to a lethal dose when the drug was passed around the class.

Following Harris's arrest, poor Helen was exhumed, three months after her burial. Dr Allen McLane Hamilton oversaw the exhumation. She was in an excellent state of preservation, according to Hamilton, 'a beautiful young girl who, notwithstanding the fact that she had been buried for several months, looked almost lifelike in her simple grey dress embroidered with silver and her tiny slippers'. Hamilton found some congestion in the brain which he said was a sign of narcotic poisoning, but no clots, ruptures or haemorrhages.

The toxicological expert at the trial was Dr Rudolph August Witthaus, a celebrated analytical chemist at City University, New York, and the University of Vermont. He was a small, dapper man with sandy hair and spectacles. His manner was crusty and his delivery was as dry as dust. He read his testimony from a large memorandum book. The description of his analyses was long and intricate. There was absence of quinine in detectable quantities, echoing the Lamson case. Morphine, on the other hand, had been found in appreciable amounts by sixteen different tests. He had injected some frogs with the extract made from the exhumed girl's organs and had injected other frogs with a harmless substance as a control. When prodded with a sharp instrument, the frogs with the narcotic failed to hop about like the control frogs, and lay comatose until they died a day or so later. The foreman of the jury closed his eyes and lapsed into slumber.

William Travers Jerome, for the defence, decided to attack Witthaus on the absence of quinine. He recalled the toxicologist to the stand and, in another echo of the Lamson case, suggested that ptomaines had been present in the residue that Witthaus tested with his reagents for morphine. Witthaus cautiously refused to swear that ptomaines would, or would not, produce reactions similar to morphine. But under cross-examination by Assistant District Attorney Francis Wellman, he stated that there was no known ptomaine that would give the reactions determined in his analyses. When the body had been buried and then exhumed, as in Helen Potts' case, there was time, the defence contended, for these to have been produced.

By the time Professor Theo Wormley, author of *The Microchemistry of Poisons*, had taken the stand for the defence, the jury foreman was asleep again. Wormley criticised Witthaus's bromine test for quinine. This was a colour test. If quinine was present, under certain stringent conditions the solution would turn a definite green. Wormley showed that there must be an exact relation between bromine, ammonia and quinine for there to be a quinine reaction. The quinine, in a case like this, would necessarily be of an unknown quantity. Wormley took two slender vials from his satchel in court, each containing 5 cc of a 1 per cent solution of quinine. To the first he added one drop of saturated aqueous solution of bromine and to the second he added two drops. Then he added one drop of ammonia to each. The vial with one drop of bromine produced no reaction, whereas the vial with two drops went green.

The jury were far from convinced by these chemical prestidigitations for the defence. There were no signs of a pre-existing disease in the victim, and the symptoms of poisoning by a powerful narcotic were overwhelming, particularly her pinprick pupils. Harris was found guilty in just over an hour.

After the conviction, Harris's grieving mother, closely followed by the press, got busy in Scranton, Pennsylvania, where she was active among Helen's coterie, trying to prove that she was a morphine eater. In fact, Mrs Harris did manage to scrape up some dubious affidavits to this effect from persons claiming Helen's acquaintance. Of the sly abortionist, Dr Treverton, there was no sign. His house had been burnt down a short time after the trial and he was said to have moved to Chicago with the insurance money of $2000.

District Attorney Delancy Nicoll claimed that the affidavits were rank perjury. An appeal was denied, and on 31 March 1893, Recorder Smyth, the trial judge, sentenced Harris to death. On this same afternoon in March, Smyth opened another trial, that of Dr Robert William Buchanan, for poisoning his wife with morphine.

Buchanan was Canadian, from Nova Scotia, who had studied medicine at Edinburgh in the 1880s. Here, by the way, he might well have come across a postgraduate student called Arthur Conan Doyle who was working on his MD thesis on syphilis. Buchanan returned to Nova Scotia in 1886 and the following year settled with his wife in Greenwich Village, New York, where he started a modest medical practice. In 1890, aged about 30, he was granted a divorce, not so common in those days, on the grounds of adultery. His wife had abandoned him for someone else, he said, leaving her small daughter behind.

On Thanksgiving Day, only fifteen days after the divorce, Buchanan asked Richard Macomber, a restaurant keeper and friend, to go with him to Newark, New Jersey, to witness a will which was to be drawn up by a woman friend. She was a widow, Annie B. Sutherland, a grateful patient of Dr Buchanan's and, at the age of 50, a good twenty years older than he. The will, needless to say, was in Buchanan's favour – provided she did not remarry. If she did remarry, then all her estate was to go to her husband. Buchanan expected to be her heir, and to make sure of this he married her two days later, on 29 November. Mrs Sutherland gave her age, mendaciously, as 41.

The couple did not live together right away. Mrs Buchanan, as she now was, remained in Newark and the doctor returned to his practice, not only as if nothing had happened, but telling friends that he had had enough of women and marriage. After a time, Annie sold her house in Newark, which enabled Buchanan to buy the rented house in Greenwich Village, 267 West Eleventh Street, and she moved in, at first telling people that she was the housekeeper. Macomber and Buchanan's other intimates knew the truth, however, and after a time the fiction was dropped.

Buchanan confided too much in Macomber, a smug and ready witness. He sat in the witness box, sleek, with his legs crossed so that the pointed toe of one of his patent leather boots swayed back and forth over the head of the court stenographer. Annie had an insufferable temper, he said. She used vile language in front of Buchanan's daughter. She made constant scenes. Buchanan spoke to Macomber about 'dumping the old woman'. Macomber reminded his friend of the money she had given towards the house purchase, around $9000. She would certainly cut him out of her will if he treated her badly, and could sue him for the return of the money. The scandal would ruin him.

Relations between Buchanan and his wife deteriorated after about January or February 1892, and the doctor asked Macomber to take in his daughter, away from her stepmother's violence. Shortly after this, Buchanan said that Annie had made a terrible scene and had threatened to poison herself. He had laughed and said, 'Go ahead. You know where the poisons are kept.' Buchanan became afraid, not that she would poison herself, but that she would poison him, and he started to eat with the Macombers. The doctor ran his practice from his own house and slept there, but otherwise he was at the Macombers with his daughter. The doctor and his wife regarded each other with the darkest suspicion, and seldom spoke to one another.

At about 9 o'clock on the morning of 22 April 1892, Dr B. C. McIntyre was called to the Buchanan home to see Annie, who had been taken ill an hour or so before. The doctor found hysterical symptoms and constriction of the throat, and prescribed sedatives. He returned later in the day to find her much worse and, at Buchanan's suggestion, called in another doctor, H. P. Watson. Further sedatives were prescribed and the physicians went away. They called in the following morning and were there when she died at about 10 o'clock. They signed a death certificate stating that she had died of a cerebral haemorrhage – a stroke. After the funeral, Buchanan closed up his house and went back to Nova Scotia to his old home for a rest and a change of scene, or so he told Macomber.

No one was suspicious that he shed no tears for his harridan of a wife. He inherited between $30,000 and $50,000. Why should he weep? However, a couple of weeks later, history repeated itself. This time it wasn't the victim's mother who made contact with the press, but a certain James M. Smith, aged about 60, from Newark, who visited a local newspaper and, motivated purely by spite, told them what he suspected. The second Mrs Buchanan was by no means the daughter of a Philadelphia banker and a respectable widow, as she had been represented. She was a brothel keeper, and owned several 'houses' in Newark, where Buchanan had met her as a client. The doctor had won Annie away from Smith, who had been her associate for about eleven years before Buchanan had dislodged him.

This would suggest that Buchanan had wooed her long before his own divorce and had planned the will in his favour, probably even the murder, a considerable time back. The paper investigated, and Smith's story was borne out by their own research. But when they came to interview the two doctors who attended Mrs Buchanan they came across a brick wall. Watson and McIntyre reiterated that there was no question of anything but a natural death. Thwarted by this, a reporter went to Halifax and discovered an odd fact: Buchanan had remarried his first wife when the second had been dead for only four weeks.

The press attention alerted Buchanan to the fact that he was under suspicion and he panicked. He denied his remarriage to the reporters. He tried out the idea on Macomber that his wife was a morphine eater and that an exhumation would implicate him in a murder of which he was innocent. He considered flight and set a private detective to watch Annie's grave. He was arrested, however, while he was walking along Broadway with his lawyer, having been under surveillance for some days.

The talkative Macomber, who did much to hang his friend, also had an excellent and accurate memory. Buchanan had scoffed at Harris for bungling Helen's death, he said. He had told Macomber that Harris should have given her a little belladonna with the morphine. Although the two substances were both alkaloids, morphine contracts the pupils, while belladonna, from the deadly nightshade (*Atropa belladonna*) expands them, and this would have confused the morphine symptoms. When Drs McIntyre and Watson were called to the stand they admitted that they had not thought of this and that such a double drugging might have escaped their notice.

As in the Harris case, the toxicological evidence was – or should have been, if the jury could have stayed awake – of major importance. But Witthaus was again the analyst; and once again his testimony fell far short of what was claimed for it by the prosecution. After elaborate experiments lasting six weeks, one-tenth of a grain of morphine had been extracted from the deceased's viscera. William J. O'Sullivan, for the defence, asked Witthaus to show it to the jury, but he was unable to oblige. He would not commit himself to stating that he had found belladonna in the stomach and intestines. There was another drug present, but he could not identify it with certainty. The jury nodded drowsily. Witthaus had experimented on a cat, dropping diluted residue of the unknown drug into its eye. The pupil enlarged. It could have been belladonna. O'Sullivan suggested that the ptomaines produced in the body after death were responsible for enlarging the cat's pupil. He called to the stand Professor Victor C. Vaughan, dean of the Medical Faculty at Michigan State University.

Vaughan took fifteen minutes to recite his qualifications. He had studied poisons for the last twenty years and for the last ten years had made ptomaines his special study. He passed vials of them among the jurors, who looked at them wisely. Vaughan turned the courtroom into a laboratory, taking up a table with his apparatus and announcing that he would replicate Witthaus's tests. The latter sat with Assistant DA Wellman, looking nervous and cross, taking notes. Vaughan had two small bottles. One, he said, contained one-tenth of a grain of morphine and some decomposed matter, or ptomaines. The other apparently contained only water and some ptomaines. The results were somewhat inconclusive. Both bottles showed a colour reaction, one more pronounced than the other. In the end Vaughan came clean. Neither contained morphine. The colour reactions were both obtained from ptomaines alone.

The case was all but won for the defence. Then Buchanan went into the witness box. In England this would not have been allowed. The defendant was not considered a competent witness in his own defence until the Criminal Justice Act 1898 came into force. In the Harris case, it was thought that Harris's non-appearance in the witness box had counted against him. It showed an evasion of questioning which helped to hang him. Buchanan, therefore, and against the advice of his lawyer, elected to be questioned.

He presented a sorry spectacle in court during what the press, begging the question, called 'the Buchanan wife-poisoning trial'. He was a short, frail-looking man with a thin drooping moustache and unhealthy pale skin. The *New York Times* described him as a 'middle-aged, undersized man with a countenance as devoid of expression as a blank page'. His small eyes, in gold-rimmed spectacles, looked at nothing. His testimony was shredded under Wellman's formidable cross-examination. When asked if he had put a watch on his wife's grave to ensure that the body was not dug up, he said nothing. Wellman also asked him if it was true that he had enquired of his lawyer which countries had no extradition treaty. Again, he had no answer. The State permitted a letter to be brought into evidence which had no bearing on the case but which was sent by Buchanan to Macomber shortly after Annie's death, written from Halifax. It was not read out in court but was passed silently from juryman to juryman, with the obvious intention of shocking them by its tone and bad language. Did he speak ill of the dead?

The jury reached a guilty verdict of 'murder in the first degree' after being out all night, and Dr Robert Buchanan was hanged in July 1895.

Thomas Stevenson had indicated in the Lamson case that the jury was still out on ptomaines. The Buchanan jury was having none of them, but where was toxicology on the subject? Since the Lamson case in 1882, Stevenson, in London, had taken some trouble to investigate these substances and published his findings in the 1894 edition of Taylor's *Principles and Practice of Medical Jurisprudence*, which he now edited. Several ptomaines had been isolated, some of which were poisonous and some of which were chemically inert. They were produced in buried corpses, a class of objects which, for Stevenson, included sausages and tinned foods, by the action of micro-organisms. They could readily be confused with vegetable alkaloids like veratrine, morphine and codeine. However, Stevenson's own experiments under rigid test conditions showed that the existence of poisonous cadaveric alkaloids in human viscera, even when putrid and diseased, was very rare.

The defence might have scored a point in both the Harris and Buchanan cases if they had questioned Witthaus's confident assertions that he had found morphine in appreciable amounts. This case was probably the first to attempt quantitative analysis on a morphine extract. Neither Harris nor Buchanan denied that morphine had been taken – only that a fatal dose had been given. The quantity found in the remains should therefore have been of vital importance. The slumbering jurymen (noticed by the *New York Times* correspondent) raises the suspicion that the chemical analysis counted for less with the juries than the other circumstantial evidence.

Toxicology was still very much feeling its way at the end of the last century, in the States as much as in Britain. There were very few experts. In England there were the two Home Office analysts and Scotland had Henry Duncan Littlejohn, professor of forensic medicine at Edinburgh University. In New York there were Professors Witthaus, Doremus and Mandel. Specialist laboratory facilities for toxicology in the States were pitiful. The chief medical examiner's office in New York City was not instituted until 1918, but at least it began with a toxicological laboratory. There was a medical examiner's office in Boston as early as 1878 but a laboratory there for routine toxicological analysis was only provided after the Jessie Costello trial in 1933.

Toxicology was better served in France, where it was taken seriously in Paris from the time of Orfila. But the focus of legal medicine, and the attention of the press, shifted south from Paris in 1889 to Lyons — and to morbid anatomy — when Professor Jean Alexandre Eugène Lacassagne, at the Lyons University Medical Faculty, was able to identify a rotting corpse found in his district as that of the missing Parisian bailiff, Gouffé, simply from his skeleton.

CHAPTER EIGHT

EYRAUD AND BOMPARD
An essay in decomposition

Toussaint-Augustin Gouffé, a Paris bailiff, was reported missing on 27 July 1889 by his brother-in-law, M. Landry. The bailiff, a 49-year-old widower who lived with his two daughters, was a well-known woman-iser and the police were not particularly worried. However, when he still had not returned by 30 July, the case was referred to the Sûreté chief, Marie-François Goron.

Goron visited Gouffé's office in rue Montmartre and discovered that, although the safe was still locked, there was a quantity of burnt matches by it on the floor. The concierge at the offices said that on the night of Gouffé's disappearance a man had come to the office and opened the door with a key. As he was leaving, the concierge surprised him, and he fled, hiding his face. Goron concluded that someone had obtained the bailiff's keys and tried to rob him. The safe contained 14,000 francs in notes. A description was sent out to all police stations. Gouffé was born in 1840, weighed 80 kg (176 lbs), was 1.78 m (5 feet 10 inches) tall and was foppishly dressed with thick chestnut brown hair and a neatly trimmed beard.

No progress had been made by 17 August when Goron learned that a sack containing the body of a man had been taken to the Lyons morgue. A country road-mender in Millery, near Lyons, had made the gruesome discovery. He was walking home from work on 13 August through a wood, in the depths of the country, when a most unpleasant odour assailed his nostrils. He traced the smell to a clump of brambles and cleared his way through to discover a large burlap sack. When he slit it open, the half decomposed head of a black-haired man fell towards him. The Lyons police took the remains to the city morgue. A large key was found in the bushes near the body.

The concept of the 'morgue' had spread down the country since its origins in Paris. As early as the seventeenth century, the public had been encouraged to visit the Petit Châtelet prison, near the River Seine, to iden-tify bodies which were washed ashore from time to time. Relatives would peer into the basement, where the bodies were displayed, from a window opening on to the courtyard above. The French for 'to peer' at something in this way is *morguer*. The public morgue in Lyons was connected physically and institutionally to the Medical Faculty of Lyons University, next door, presided over by Professor Jean Alexandre Eugène Lacassagne. Lacassagne, however, did not perform the initial autopsy, which was done by Dr Paul Bernard on 14 August.

The body in the sack was naked, wrapped in oilcloth and tied with 25 feet of cord. The victim was male, measuring about 1.75 m tall, weighing about 75 kg, 35–45 years old, with black hair and a beard. There were two breaks to the larynx, indicating strangulation. This didn't fit Gouffé's description and nothing, at first, connected the two cases. Then a peasant gathering snails near the river in the next village to Millery found some odd pieces of wood. The local gendarme saw that the wood was part of a damaged trunk and was giving off the typical smell associated with cadavers. Thinking that it might be connected with the discovery of the corpse in the sack, he took it to Lyons. The key found near the body fitted the lock. The trunk lid was dated 27 July, either 1888 or 1889, and was labelled: 'From: Paris 1231 – Express train 3. To: Lyons – Perrache I'.

Despite the discrepancies in the description between the chestnut-haired bailiff and the black-haired corpse, Goron thought they might be one and the same, and sent Landry, Gouffé's brother-in-law, to Lyons. Landry failed to recognise the corpse, but had taken barely a glance at the rotting face before fleeing from the sight. The officer accompanying him telegraphed Paris that the man was not Gouffé after all. On the other hand, he had news for Goron about the trunk. A cabman, Laforge, said that on 6 July in the previous summer he had been waiting at the railway station when three men asked his help to load a heavy trunk on to his cab. He drove the three passengers and trunk to Millery and waited while the men unloaded it and went off with it. They came back without the trunk and Laforge drove them back to Lyons. The police showed him the Lyons rogues' gallery and he picked out three villains who, it turned out, had been in jail for almost a year charged with robbery and murder. The case appeared to be solved.

In September, 1889, however, Goron learned from an associate of the dead man that on 25 July Gouffé had been seen in a Paris brasserie with a shady character called Michel Eyraud, a dealer and conman. Eyraud had his mistress with him, Gabrielle Bompard. The couple disappeared from their usual haunts at about the same time that Gouffé vanished. Goron had the Lyons police send him the luggage labels from the trunk. It was obvious to the Sûreté chief that the date referred to 27 July 1889, not 1888, the very day that Gouffé disappeared. He cross-checked with the luggage registry at the Gare de Lyon. Yes, the trunk had left Paris on the 11.45 a.m. train to Lyons on 27 July 1889, weighing 105 kg.

Goron went down to Lyons and soon discovered that the cabman, Laforge, was a police time-waster, the sort who always turns up in sensational cases with some eye-witness account. His story was a tissue of lies. Goron demanded an exhumation of the corpse.

The second post-mortem took place on 12 November 1889 and was performed by Professor Lacassagne, one of the most brilliant medico-legists of his time. Born in 1843, he studied medicine at the Ecole Militaire at Stras-bourg and then spent some time in Africa. His interest in criminalistics stemmed from a study he had made on tattoos there. He founded the chair of legal medicine at the Medical Faculty at Lyons in 1884 and was just begin-ning to make his name. From their point of view, the murderers of the bailiff couldn't have dumped the body in a more unfortunate spot.

Lacassagne carried out the post-mortem in his tiered lecture theatre, attended by, among others, his former pupil, Bernard, who had done the first autopsy, and Goron. It took him eleven days. Before he began, he had been given a description of the dead man. On examining his teeth, he esti-mated him to be about 50 years old. Gouffé was 49. It was impossible, now, to measure the height and before he could proceed Lacassagne had to sepa-rate the flesh from the bones. Having done this, he called in his colleague, Dr Etienne Rollet. Rollet had just established a way of approximating height from the measurement of the long bones of the skeleton. The Millery corpse was subjected to the new method and his height was judged to be 1.785 m. Gouffé was 1.78. The skeleton's head measurements accorded with infor-mation supplied by M. Gouffé's hatter.

While cutting into the flesh and muscle, Lacassagne had noticed discrepancies between the right and left legs. He asked Dr Gabriel Mondan, an eminent osteologist, to examine the bones. Their condition suggested that the dead man had suffered muscular atrophy on his right leg. He also had traces of water on the knee – an inflamed accumulation of fluid – and his big toe carried the marks of gout.

Goron was able to track down Gouffé's doctor, who had sent the bailiff to a specialist at Aix-les-Bains for treatment to his leg and foot. The specialist was contacted and said that he had treated Gouffé for gout in his right big toe, and he confirmed the physical changes in the right leg.

Goron telegraphed the Sûreté to send someone to Gouffé's apartment for his hairbrush, and Lacassagne asked Hugounenq, professor of chem-istry at Lyons, to analyse a sample of hair from the corpse and a sample from the hairbrush. Meanwhile, Lacassagne discovered that hair cut from the corpse's head, after repeated washing, lightened to chestnut brown. Hugounenq's analysis revealed none of the chemicals that were present in hair dye, and Lacassagne concluded that the changes were a phenomenon of decomposition. Under the microscope the thickness of the two samples showed that they could have come from the same head.

The Sûreté chief was now certain that he had Gouffé, and stepped up his effort to find the killers. A replica of the trunk was made and was put on display at the Paris morgue in November. It was given widespread news-paper coverage, and a Parisian trunk maker soon came forward to say it was of English manufacture. At the same time, a letter was received at the Sûreté from a Frenchman living in London, Chéron, who took in lodgers. In June

85

1889 his new lodgers, M. Michel and his daughter, had bought a large trunk from Zwanzigers in the Euston Road and had taken it with them when they left in July.

Goron went himself to London and interviewed Chéron, who led the detective to Madame Vesprès, the couple's previous landlady. She knew very well that the young woman was not M. Michel's daughter but his mistress, Gabrielle Bompard. Michel was Michel Eyraud, Madame Vesprès' lover of fourteen years earlier.

Back in Paris, Goron discovered more about Eyraud from a police informer. He was 56 years old and was something of a Don Juan, wearing a wig to hide his balding head. He had lived in Spain as a child and spoke fluent Spanish. Later, when apprenticed to a dyer, he had run away from his master and joined the French Expeditionary Force to Mexico, where he had deserted. After an amnesty in 1869, he thought it safe to return to France, where he married a wealthy woman, squandered her money, then abandoned her and her child to go to South America as a textile trader. When this failed, he returned to France and ran a distillery until it went bankrupt.

In 1888 he had taken up with Bompard, a streetwalker. She was pretty and unscrupulous and capable of any crime. The daughter of a widowed metal merchant of some standing in the north of France, she had been educated at the best schools in Belgium and France before she was expelled. Disliking the governess her father had provided for her at home, and discovering, moreover, that she was his mistress, Gabrielle left for Paris. Once she had run out of her father's allowance, and his good will, she had taken to prostitution.

A hue and cry was set up for Eyraud with pictures obtained from his abandoned wife. Then, in January 1890, Goron received a long rambling letter from Eyraud himself, the first of three, written in New York. Eyraud claimed that he had fled the country due to 'economic reverses'. Bompard had brought him to the brink of financial ruin. He knew Gouffé as a friend and claimed that Bompard could have had him murdered by one of her many lovers.

Even stranger was the arrival in Goron's office on 22 January of Gabrielle Bompard herself, accompanied by her new protector, George Garanger, an American businessman. On a trip to Vancouver, Garanger had met a French businessman named Vanaert, travelling with his daughter, Berthe. Garanger foolishly entered into a business deal with the plausible Vanaert, and was only too willing to escort the lovely Berthe to Paris for her father, while Vanaert, needless to say, was making off with Garanger's investment.

By the time the couple arrived in Paris, Garanger had become Berthe's lover and had discovered that she was Gabrielle Bompard. Her story was that she was an innocent dupe of the vicious swindler, used by him to lure

Gouffé to his death. Eyraud had installed Bompard in a Paris apartment, where she invited Gouffé, among others, at Eyraud's request, in order to procure money for him. On the evening that Gouffé disappeared, she was expecting the bailiff, but Eyraud told her the rendezvous was cancelled. When Bompard arrived at her apartment some time later, she found Eyraud there with a red-haired man who was putting on his overcoat and who left shortly afterwards. The trunk was in the corner. The following day, Bompard said, she and Eyraud took the trunk to Lyons and handed it over to the same red-headed man at Lyons station before the pair set off for a new life in the States. Garanger believed every word and Bompard expected Goron to do the same. But the police chief wasn't such a fool and arrested her immediately. Eventually, he prised the whole story out of her.

Behind the divan in her apartment – in villainous tradition – was an alcove concealed by a curtain. Eyraud fixed an iron ring to the ceiling above the bed and drew a rope through it with a hook attached to one end. He stood in wait behind the curtain, holding on to the rope, while Bompard, wearing a simple robe tied with a sash, entertained Gouffé. In a supposedly seductive mood, Bompard untied the sash and placed it round Gouffé's neck. Eyraud then let down the hook and quickly fastened the sash on to it, drawing the rope upwards before the victim had time to realise what was happening.

When Bompard started to scream, Eyraud dropped the rope and strangled Gouffé, using his bare hands. He then stuffed the body in the trunk and left Bompard to guard it while he took the bailiff's keys to his office to rob him. Unable to break into the safe, he had returned, furious, beaten Bompard and forced her to have sex with him a few feet from the trunk. There was no red-haired man. Bompard and Eyraud alone had dumped the trunk and the body in Millery before making good their escape.

The arrest caused a great sensation in Paris and crowds went to the rue Tronson-Ducoudray to see the murder apartment, where Goron discovered the iron ring still in the ceiling. When Bompard was despatched by train to Lyons in a reconstruction of the summer's events, the cavalry had to be called out to hold back the crowds. As to Eyraud, he was spotted in Havana by a resident Frenchman and was arrested leaving a brothel.

The trial took place in Paris in December 1890. Bompard claimed that she had been hypnotised by Eyraud, hypnotism being the latest fad. Professor Liégeois, of Nancy, for Bompard, argued for four hours with the Parisian expert, Professor Brouardel, for permission to hypnotise Bompard in court. Liégeois lost. The couple were found guilty; Eyraud was sentenced to the guillotine and Bompard received twenty years' forced labour.

It was generally thought in France that consciousness was retained for a short time after death by guillotine, as demonstrated in experiments with dogs. Dr Laborde, a follower of the Italian criminologist Cesare

Lombroso, and president of the Société d'Autopsie, had repeated these experiments by injecting dog's blood into the arteries of the heads of guillotined criminals and believed that he had indeed observed a resurrection of consciousness, though for the most part this was a reddening of the complexion after the transfusion. Laborde needed fresher heads – his best result had been on a head only five minutes' decapitated – but the authorities wouldn't let him set up a laboratory in the prison. Fearing that he would become one of Laborde's experimental subjects, Eyraud's last wish was that his body would not be handed over to science, and a bizarre verbal battle took place at the Ivry Cemetery when the penal authorities refused Laborde's demands for the murderer's head. The press blamed the authorities for standing in the way of scientific progress.

Lombroso, born in Italy in 1835, served in the early part of his career as an army physician and, in peacetime, measured and observed 3000 soldiers passing through his hands. It was during this time that he developed the idea of the criminal man which bore fruit in his book, *L'Uomo Delinquente* (1876). His general theory was that criminals are distinguished from non-criminals by the manifestation of atavistic features, *atavus* being the Latin for ancestor. The more primitive the features, the more 'savage' the inborn temperament. So those modern men with ape-like features were throwbacks and could be expected to behave contrary to the rules and expectation of nineteenth-century society. Charles Darwin was initially to blame. In the *Descent of Man*, he had written: 'With mankind some of the worst dispositions which occasionally ... make their appearance in families, may perhaps be reversions to a savage state.' *L'Uomo Delinquente* was never published in English, so its effect in Britain and the United States was limited, but it had a great impact on the Continent from the time of the second edition in 1878.

Lombroso's ideas of the criminal man were much opposed by Lacassagne, who believed that society had the criminals it deserved. While Eyraud and Bompard were lugging trunks around Paris in July 1889, Lombroso and Lacassagne were engaged in verbal battle in another part of the city. Together with their colleagues, the two medico-legal giants were attending the Second Congress of Criminal Anthropology and Legal Medicine at the Universal Exhibition in the shadow of the newly built Eiffel Tower. One major problem with Lombroso's work was his lack of control subjects. He had made many thousands of observations, but they were on soldiers, and more lately, on prisoners. Lacassagne and his team challenged Lombroso to make a series of comparisons between a hundred criminals and a hundred honest persons. A commission was set up to conduct the research which included the two protagonists, and the result was to be presented at the next congress in 1892. The research was never presented. Lombroso and his team took umbrage and failed to turn up.

France had always been more advanced in legal medical research than Britain and the USA. The first department, at the University of Paris, had been set up in the French Revolution, when there were plenty of bodies to practise on. It was largely French research with which Alfred Taylor filled the pages of his *Manual* and *Principles and Practice of Medical Jurisprudence.* The laboratory at the University of Lyons in 1884 was a new departure for the south, but led to the setting up of the first dedicated police laboratory in France, in 1910.

The young Edmond Locard was assistant to a bone surgeon, Professor Ollier, at Lyons in 1900, but when the professor died, Locard transferred to Lacassagne's department. Shortly afterwards, the two men found themselves sheltering from a storm in a bus shelter. While they stood there, Lacassagne asked Locard to read through some papers he handed him and make a report to him before the storm abated. Locard was hooked. In January 1910 he branched out from Lacassagne to establish the first *laboratoire de police criminelle* in Lyons in a room the police found for him in the attics of the Palais de Justice. It was five floors up, and then a ladder. He ran the laboratory, still in the same premises, until 1951. Although situated in Lyons, it dealt with cases nationwide.

A great fan of Sherlock Holmes, Locard's lasting contribution to forensic science was his instruction to the police not to touch anything at the scene of the crime until the technician arrived because 'every contact leaves a trace.'

His greatest scientific achievements were in the field of dust analysis and in poroscopy, the study of microscopic sweat pore marks left behind with fingerprints.

CHAPTER NINE

THE STRATTON BROTHERS
The thumbprint on the cash box

Fingerprinting did not evolve in the nineteenth century specifically for 'forensic' purposes. That is, it wasn't created in order to link a suspect to a crime, nor did it develop as an aid to detection. These applications came later, after the turn of the century. Photography, anthropometry and fingerprinting – the three associated police sciences – developed alongside the need to keep track of prisoners released from prison on to the streets of London on licence or 'ticket-of-leave'.

Originally, when prisoners were transported, this wasn't a problem; they were released directly into the penal colony. But in the middle of the nineteenth century Van Diemen's Land and Australia began to raise objections with the British government to being populated by prisoners. Van Diemen's Land even went so far as to change its name to Tasmania. The result of all these objections was the Penal Servitude Acts 1853, 1857 and 1864, which gradually abandoned transportation and substituted a prison term in England followed by a period on ticket-of-leave. If prisoners reoffended they had to serve the rest of their original sentence as well as any new term of imprisonment imposed. But first, of course, they had to be identified as reoffenders. This was done by the Habitual Criminals Register, introduced in 1869. Photographs of prisoners were added to the record sheet in 1871 but the register was useless and police relied on personal recognition, making thrice-weekly visits to prisons to check the remand prisoners. Mistakes were made, and by the 1880s the whole system was in disarray.

In Paris, at his famous Bureau d'Identité Judiciaire, Alphonse Bertillon had introduced a system of measuring prisoners in 1882 on the basis that no two adults would have exactly the same measurements on certain key bones. A photographic section was added in February 1888 instituting for the first time the 'mug shot' – the two views, full face and profile (to show the ears), with which we are so familiar today.

In Bertillon's bureau, the measurement records were found by a process of elimination. First the individual was matched to head-size – small, medium or large. Then, within that category, there were drawers for left middle finger – small, medium and large – and so on. (Here, undoubtedly, is the origin of the classification system later used for fingerprints.) As a check, the individual would be matched for photographic likeness, scars and other distinguishing marks.

The idea of Bertillonage, more properly called anthropometry (man measurement), was taken up by Sir Francis Galton in London. He set up an anthropometrical laboratory as early as 1884 in Kensington as part of the Health Exhibition and measured visitors for a small fee. This continued after the exhibition had closed. To add some substance to a lecture on Bertillonage, in 1888, Galton remembered some correspondence in *Nature* about finger-marks and wrote to the journal. He received a reply from Sir William Herschel, who had used fingerprints in India as a means of preventing impersonation when Indian pensioners came to collect their money. Herschel, now retired, loaned Galton two sets of his own prints, taken at twenty-eight-year intervals, for the lecture. This partially solved one of the questions that Galton had about fingerprints: was the pattern persistent over time? Galton identified three facts that had to be established before it would be possible to advocate the use of fingerprints for criminal or other purposes. Not only had fingerprints to be constant throughout life, but it had to be proved that the variety was very great, and they had to be retrievable from a classified storage system.

Galton devoted a great deal of his time in the latter years of the South Kensington laboratory to investigating these factors. His book *Finger Prints*, the first of its kind, came out in 1892 and the three conditions appeared to be met. He had proved persistence through life (even reforming exactly after injury) and that each pattern was unique. Moreover, the book contained the author's attempts at a classification system based on drawers for arches, loops and whorls.

Galton, among others, wanted anthropometry to be established in Britain, following some notorious cases of mistaken identification, and a select committee on anthropometry was set up by the government in 1893. When the committee discussed what information should be on the prisoner's record card, Galton suggested the addition of fingerprints, as a distinguishing mark, and this was agreed, the new system to start in July 1894.

Galton recommended an associate of his, Dr George Garson, to be in charge of the new service. Garson was a vice-president, along with Galton, of the Anthropological Institute, and an assistant in the Anthropological Department of the Royal College of Surgeons' Museum in Lincoln's Inn Fields. He was engaged for three years from 4 July 1894 at a salary of £600 via the Home Office. The office was at New Scotland Yard and Garson had a sergeant and a constable to assist him. His duties were to train male and female warders to take measurements and fingerprints in prisons throughout England. A few years later, this work done, Garson was retained as an adviser at a reduced salary. Unfortunately, no one asked his advice, and the work in practice was taken over by the police.

E. R. Henry, Inspector General of the Calcutta Police, had met Galton in the 1890s and corresponded with him on the subjects of anthropometry and fingerprinting for use in India. By 1897 he had developed a finger-printing classification system for India which was better than Galton's, being able to accommodate a larger number of prints. Henry was the coming man.

In 1900 Henry published the first edition of his book *Classification and Uses of Fingerprints.* The 1900 Belper Committee on the Identification of Criminals was convened as Henry's book was being printed, and in 1901 anthropometry, and the now disgruntled Dr Garson, were discarded in favour of fingerprinting. Henry was appointed assistant commissioner in charge of the CID the same year, and the Fingerprint Branch was established on 1 July with officers from the Anthropometric Office – Detective Inspector Charles H. Stedman, Detective Sergeant Charles Stockley Collins and Detective Constable Frederick Hunt.

With the introduction of Henry's system of classification came a radical change in the use of fingerprints. Instead of using the system as an aid to identification in criminal records, the system now began to be used as an aid to detection. The fingerprint, or a photograph of it – compared with the authenticated fingerprint of the suspect – was produced in court as scientific evidence, with the police officer concerned as the expert witness. To use fingerprints in this way in England added yet another hurdle to the three conditions of use raised by Galton of persistence, individuality and adequate classification: it had to be accepted in court.

The trial of Harry Jackson for a burglary committed in June 1902 was the first test case in England. Detective Sergeant Collins, a keen amateur photographer, and his colleagues had searched through thousands of record cards to match a left thumbprint found in fresh paint on a windowsill. Collins took into court photographs and tracings that showed corresponding ridge countings, and together with other circumstantial evidence, Jackson was found guilty, thus setting a court precedent.

The precedent for accepting a fingerprint as evidence in a murder case was established in the Stratton case in 1905, when Albert and Alfred Stratton were tried for the killing of Thomas and Ann Farrow, an elderly couple who kept a paint shop in Deptford.

The first hint that all was not as it should be at the shop, early on a March morning in 1905, came when Jennings, the milkman, and his young assistant saw two men hurtle out of the shop and run hell for leather up the road, leaving the door open. They didn't investigate, but continued on their round. A few minutes later, a workman standing at the bus stop opposite, glanced across the road. He was disturbed to catch sight of an old man in the doorway with blood streaming down his face. The workman wondered if he ought to go for a policeman, but just then his bus arrived and, like the milkmen, he did nothing.

It was left to 14-year-old Willy Jones to get help. When he arrived for work at 7.30, he discovered his employer lying in a pool of blood and alerted a passer-by. The police found that Mrs Farrow had also been attacked. She was sprawled across the bed upstairs, having been savagely beaten. She was still alive, but only just, and died a few days later. The police discovered two masks made from women's black stockings at the scene and found that the cash box, kept under the bed, had been rifled. It looked as though Farrow had come downstairs with trousers and jacket over his nightshirt to attend to an early customer. He was attacked in the shop and had gamely tried to prevent the assailants from climbing the stairs to where his wife was guarding the money.

Melville Macnaghten, the new assistant commissioner of CID (Henry had been promoted and was now the commissioner), had gone with Detective Inspector Fox and several detectives to the scene of the crime, and it was Macnaghten – a keen fan of fingerprinting – who examined the money box for prints and noticed a smudge on the smooth inner surface. The box was wrapped and taken immediately to Detective Inspector Collins. Macnaghten also had the fingerprints taken of young Willy and the two victims. This was the first time that a fingerprint had been taken off a corpse.

In the course of their enquiries, one of Fox's detectives overheard mention in a Deptford pub that Alfred and Albert Stratton were capable of committing the crime. They were known to the police but had never yet been arrested. Aged 22 and 20 respectively, they were layabouts who lived off women. Fox tracked Albert Stratton down to a shabby lodging house and interviewed his landlady, Mrs Kate Wade. Mrs Wade said she had found several black masks made from stockings under Stratton's bed, and told Fox that Albert's brother Alfred had a girlfriend named Hannah Cromarty.

Fox found Hannah at her single-room lodging. She showed signs of a recent beating and was ready to tell the police what she knew. Late on Sunday evening a man had come to the window of the ground-floor room and had spoken to Alfred through the window. Early the next morning there had a been a knock at the window and Alfred got up and dressed. When she next awoke it was broad daylight and Alfred was standing in the room, having let himself out and in again by the window, a regular habit. He told her to say that he had been with her all night.

The evidence was not very good – a landlady's gossip and the word of a loose woman. The milkman, Jennings, had been found, but was unable to recognise them as the villains. The fingerprint on the cash box, which was proved to be Alfred Stratton's thumb, was really all there was.

Collins stated at the trial that there were between 80,000 and 90,000 sets of fingerprints at New Scotland Yard, representing 800,000 to 900,000 digits. In his experience he had never found any two such impressions to correspond. His search in this instance had been unsuccessful until he had fingerprinted the suspects and found ten points of resemblance between the mark on the cash box and Alfred Stratton's thumbprint.

The detectives from the Fingerprint Branch were now well established as the expert witnesses in fingerprint cases, a fact which was highlighted in the Stratton case by the behaviour of Garson, whose evidence for the defence was thoroughly discredited. Garson had written on one and the same day to offer his services both to the director of public prosecutions and to the solicitor for the defence, mentioning to the latter that the way fingerprints were being used by the police would bring them into disrepute. Garson's offer was taken up by the defence, and he tried to throw doubt on Collins's and Stedman's evidence. Counsel for the prosecution, Richard Muir, read out Garson's letters to both defence and Crown, and successfully discredited him when it became known that he had not seen the fingerprint in question before he had written. When Garson argued that he was an independent witness, he was interrupted by the judge who interposed: 'An absolutely untrustworthy one I should think.'

Garson wrote an indignant letter to *The Times* after the case, putting his view that the judge 'assumes my evidence would have been adapted to suit the requirements of either side'. He was ready to give his views on the points of identity or difference to either side. The judge, he continued, 'does not condemn the barrister who is ready to take fees to defend any case'. Finally, he gave his opinion that 'the whole subject demands accurate scientific training and absolute independence of testimony that would be hopeless to look for in a partially educated investigator'. In other words, a medical man was required, a point echoed by *The Lancet*:

> It seems to us that the person called upon to examine and to
> advise as to identity or non-identity should possess thorough
> and practical knowledge as well as trained mental powers of
> discrimination. To intrust the duty to partially skilled persons
> is in the highest degree dangerous from a public point of view.

This assumption that only the medically qualified were competent to be expert witnesses in police and Home Office prosecutions continued to influence government thinking with regard to twentieth-century forensic science in England. Garson never regained his public standing. He appears to have taken a country practice shortly after the case and he disappears from the *Medical Directory* after 1932.

The development of fingerprints had a knock-on effect both within New Scotland Yard and around the country. Within the CID, in 1903, a register was started entitled 'Visits with camera to photo fingerprints'. The first entry, indicating the official birth of the scene of crime work, was dated 20 February 1903, and was to an address in Wimpole Street. In August a photographic outfit was sanctioned for the Fingerprint Office. Detective Superintendent Carter wrote many years later that 'one officer was detailed to photograph wanted persons, scenes of crime, small items, jewellery etc., and documents'. The accounts showed that the system was rudimentary in 1905, when expenditure was £43. It had risen to £86 in 1914 and by 1974 it was £30,000 per annum on consumable materials alone.

A small police laboratory was set up in Cardiff in 1902 with fingerprints and photography as its basis, and in 1906 the West Riding Constabulary sent Sergeant Oliver Cromwell to New Scotland Yard to study fingerprinting and photography, which skill he passed on to his own divisions.

Behind the introduction of anthropometry and fingerprints was Sir Francis Galton, who persuaded those in authority that his criteria for the acceptance of fingerprints – persistence, individuality, and a retrievable classification system – had been met. The difficulty over classification, which Galton recognised, diverted attention to the fact that Galton had failed to demonstrate the individuality of fingerprints. His actual words, on tentatively suggesting that there was a 1 in 64,000 million chance of two fingerprints being alike were: 'I always fear these large numbers; I merely give those figures as a perfectly reasonable result after very careful experiments; but I do not cling to them at all.'

Galton's 'very careful experiments' were described in detail in his 1892 *Finger Prints*. He devised three experiments based on reconstructing masked areas of enlarged fingerprints by guesswork. He assumed that 'any one of these reconstructions represents lineations that might have occurred in nature'. This assumption would have got him poor marks in a twentieth-century statistics examination. For one of these experiments he obtained a success rate of seven correct reconstructions out of sixteen, a little under half. Yet it was from this experiment that he claimed there was a 1 in 64,000 million chance of two fingerprints being exactly alike. The fact that he was successful nearly 50 per cent of the time should have shown him that there was something wrong with his reasoning.

Fortunately, Richard Muir, prosecuting the Stratton brothers, would have none of this, realising that a much more powerful impact on a jury would be achieved by Collins's statement that he had looked through 900,000 fingerprints without ever having found a match.

That the individuality of fingerprints had not in fact been proved passed everyone by – and still does. The publicity campaign was more successful than it should have been, and even the villains didn't think to challenge fingerprints in court. When first offender Green of Gloucester was proved by his dabs to be none other than old lag Brown of Birmingham in 1903, he said, 'Bless them fingerprints, I knew they'd do me in.'

Fingerprinting in the United States had a difficult beginning. In 1896, the International Association of Chiefs of Police (IACP), i.e. for the USA and Canada, recognised the need for a central identification bureau in the States and considered that the Department of Justice was the right authority. Unfortunately, the attorney general of the day rejected the plan and so the IACP established its own National Bureau of Criminal Identification in Chicago, based on Bertillonage. Any police force could apply to this bureau for identification of a suspect. A little later a similar series of records began to be kept at the US penitentiary at Fort Leavenworth.

Although New Scotland Yard adopted fingerprints from 1901, the USA was not convinced of their infallibility until 1903. In that year a new prisoner, Will West, was admitted to Fort Leavenworth. His measurements were taken and the chief records clerk recognised him, saying that he had been there before. He found West's record card, with a convincing photograph, which stated that Will West had been committed to that same institution on 9 September 1901 on a charge of murder. Unless he had by then escaped, Will West was still down in the cells. The two cards matched even to the Bertillon measurements. The other Will West was brought up from the cells and confronted with his namesake, and the two men were fingerprinted. The patterns were different. Fingerprinting was adopted at Leavenworth the following year and Bertillonage was discontinued.

Police Commissioner McAdoo, of the New York Police, was impressed by the Will West story and sent Detective Sergeant Joseph A. Faurot over to New Scotland Yard to learn about fingerprints from Inspector Collins. But by the time Faurot returned, McAdoo had been replaced by a successor unsympathetic to the system and Faurot had to continue pretty much on his own.

The use of fingerprints to catch a criminal, rather than to identify a recidivist, was sensationally demonstrated by Faurot in 1906. He was on patrol in New York on the night of 16 April, and decided to make an inspection of the Waldorf-Astoria Hotel, a magnet for thieves and burglars. By chance, he came across a man creeping out of a suite wearing evening dress, but no shoes. Faurot arrested him and took him to police headquarters. The man, an Englishman, claimed to be one James Jones, engaged in an *affaire* at the hotel which was none of the police's business. He demanded to see the British consul and generally caused a fuss. Faurot wasn't taken in by his bluster and sent a copy of his prints to Collins at New Scotland Yard. The reply took two weeks to arrive. Jones was Daniel Nolan, alias Henry

Right: Professor Robert
Christison.

Below: The discovery of
Mary Docherty's body.

Left: Hare's house in Tanners Close.

Left: Marie Lafarge in the dock.

Left: James Marsh's apparatus.

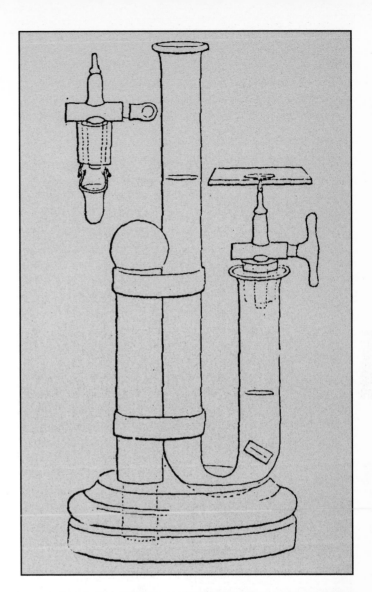

Below: Improvements made by Berzelius.

Professor M. J. B. Orfila.

Above: 'This time Professor Webster was ready for Dr Parkman'.

Right: Professor John Webster.

Left: Dr Alfred Swaine Taylor.

Below: Drs Alfred Taylor and Owen Rees analyse Cook's remains.

Below: French police take
Gabrielle Bompard's anthropometric measurements.

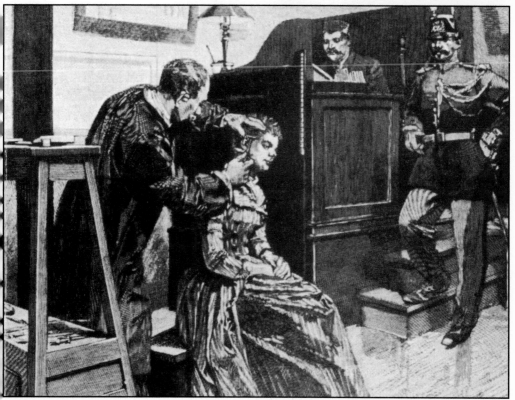

Right: Professor Rudolph August Witthaus.

Right: The Comstock School for Young Ladies, building in 1997. (Jeffrey Bloomfield)

Right: Dr Hawley Harvey Crippen.

Right: Sir William Willcox. From a miniature in the Society of Apothecaries of London, painted by Isabel Saul

SIR WILLIAM HENRY WILLCOX, K.C.I.E., C.B., C.M.G., M.D., F.R.C.P.
MASTER 1935-36.
1870
1941

Below: Sir Bernard Spilsbury.

Below: 'If the cap fits ...'
Sacco tries on a cap found at the scene.

CAP PICKED UP AFTER HOLDUP

NOW USE THE SAME FORCE YOU USED PULLING ON THIS ONE!

DIST ATT'Y

CAP TAKEN FROM SACCOS HOME

"TOO TIGHT - NOT HIS CAP" SAID SACCO

Above: Charles Henry Schwartz and his family.

Below: Vanzetti (left) and Sacco at Dedham courthouse, 1923.

Left: Sir Sydney Smith

Below: 'Young John', Professor John Glaister Junior.

Left: Jeannie Donald.

Below: Plan of Urquhart Road, Aberdeen, showing No. 61.

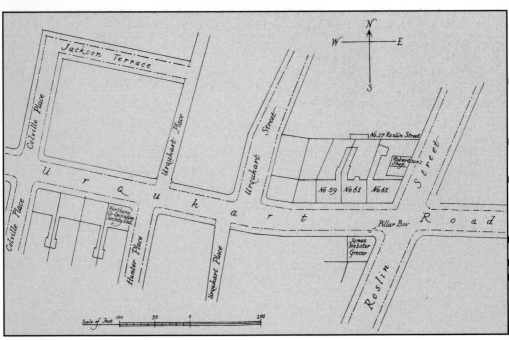

Right: Dr Buck Ruxton.

Below: Ruxton's bath, now used as a horse trough at Lancashire Constabulary HQ. The plaque reads: This bath was used by Dr BUCK RUXTON when mutilating the bodies of his wife and his maid on an unknown date between the 14th and 29th September 1935 at 2 Dalton Square, Lancaster. (Anthony Rae)

Left: 2 Dalton Square, Lancaster.

Below: Mark Wilde and Cornelius Howard, the look-alike defendants.

GORSE·HALL·MYSTERY

CORNELIUS·HOWARD

·MARK·WILDE·

Johnson, with twelve convictions for hotel theft. Wanted for burglary of a well-known writer's house and the theft of £800, he was believed to have fled to America. Two photographs were enclosed. Faced with this evidence, Jones confessed.

Fingerprints in New York made slow progress, despite the publicity surrounding this case, and it was not until 1911 that they made their first successful court appearance. Caesar Cella, a notorious burglar, was accused of breaking into a milliner's in the heart of New York. His friends raised $3000 for his defence, and five witnesses were found to substantiate his alibi. This was that he had spent the evening at the Hippodrome on the night of the burglary and had afterwards gone home with his wife, where he had stayed until morning.

Faurot gave evidence that there were several dirty fingerprints on the window of the shop, where Cella had entered, and a match was made to his file. After he had given his evidence, the defence was poised to cross-examine when the judge called out 'Stop!' and ordered court attendants to take Faurot to the judge's office and keep him there under guard.

While he was out of the court, the judge asked fifteen spectators and court personnel to step forward and touch their right index fingers to one of the windows of the room, noting the spot carefully. In addition, one of the fifteen was asked to press the same finger to a glass desk top. Faurot was brought back into the room and the judge asked him to show the court which of the prints on the window matched the one on the desk top.

Pulling out his magnifying glass, Faurot had the right answer in four minutes. Some spectators applauded, and Cella changed his plea to guilty, hoping for a lighter sentence. It seemed that he had waited for his wife to go to sleep, then slipped out of the house, returning before she woke.

Fingerprint records in the USA were patchy for many years and there was no central system. A Fingerprint Bureau had been established by the Department of Justice in 1905, but in 1907 this was transferred to Fort Leavenworth, where cheap prison labour was used, enabling the convicts to tamper with the files. This was far from satisfactory. As time went on, Congress agreed that fingerprints should be kept centrally in Washington and two Bills were introduced, one to have the records at the Department of Justice, and one at the Department of the Interior. The attorney general (in charge of the Department of Justice) was impatient, and acted ahead of the legislation, sending for the records for his Department. But because Congress had not authorised the expenditure, the comptroller general refused the funds to set up the service. When J. Edgar Hoover took over the Bureau of Investigation in 1924, the system was in chaos, with 800,000 fingerprint records in storage together with 200,000 Bertillonage record cards.

Hoover quickly got things moving. With the support of the attorney general and Congress, the government put up $56,320 on 1 July

1924 and the service was fully in operation by the end of August. The scattered records were sent to Washington and the location was finally endorsed as a permanent Division of Identification and Information within the bureau in June 1930.

Barrister Richard Muir, who prosecuted the Stratton brothers in 1905, played an important, if not unique, role in proving the evidential value of fingerprints. He made an even greater impact a few years later during the trial of Dr Crippen for the murder of his wife, when he promoted a young Bernard Spilsbury to a position of unwarranted prominence in the trial in order to destroy the pathologist for the defence. In doing so, he launched Spilsbury on his path to fame, and established pathology as a courtroom discipline which would gradually overtake toxicology in importance.

CHAPTER TEN

DR CRIPPEN

The London cellar murder

Dr Hawley Harvey Crippen (Peter to his friends and family) was unhappily married to a loud and blowsy music-hall singer, professionally called Belle Elmore. They lived at 39 Hilldrop Crescent, north London, with a dog, a cat and a caged bird. The house was one of those three-storeyed semi-detached houses with steps up to the front door and a basement which provided a coal hole to the street at the front and a door straight on to the garden at the back.

Crippen was a 48-year-old American doctor from Michigan. Although he appeared in the American *Medical Directory* for 1896 as a homoeopathic practitioner, essentially he was a quack, dispensing mail order medicines and tooth remedies from an office in New Oxford Street with the help of his lady 'typewriter', Ethel le Neve. Actually, Ethel was the daughter of a coalman named Neave, but she was pretentious.

On the night of 31 January 1910, the Crippens had their friends, the Martinettis, over for a meal. They were the last people to see Belle alive. Crippen put it about that she had left him and gone back to America. We now know, of course, that he had given her a fatal dose of hyoscine hydrobromide that evening, probably in a glass of stout.

A few weeks after his wife's disappearance, Crippen attended a dance with Ethel, who was wearing Belle's furs and jewellery. She moved into Hilldrop Crescent shortly afterwards, and Crippen told Belle's friends that his wife had sadly died of pneumonia in Los Angeles. But tongues were wagging, particularly those of the Music Hall Ladies Guild, of which Belle was the treasurer. The Ladies made enquiries in the States, couldn't trace Belle, and alerted the police.

Inspector Walter Dew called at the house in early July to make routine enquiries. Crippen, a small, balding man with protuberant eyes behind gold-rimmed spectacles, confessed to him in this interview that he had lied to Belle's friends. His wife had left him for another man; he had made up the story of her death to save face. Dew went off satisfied that Crippen was telling the truth, but when he came to write his report he realised he needed a few more details and returned to Hilldrop Crescent.

The house was deserted. Crippen and Ethel had fled. Now suspicious, Dew ordered a search. His first finding was a revolver and some ammunition in a drawer. Two days later, a mound of human flesh, covered in lime to decay it, and wrapped in a pair of men's pyjamas, was found under the coal cellar floor. The remains of the household pets were found, similarly limed, in the garden.

A hue and cry went out for the missing couple. Everyone, everywhere, was looking for them. Then the famous Marconigram was sent to New Scotland Yard by Captain Kendall on the SS *Montrose* bound for Canada. 'Have strong suspicion that Crippen London cellar murderer and accomplice are among saloon passengers moustache taken off growing beard accomplice dressed as boy voice manner and build undoubtedly a girl both travelling as Mr and Master Robinson.' The message was sent, curiously, from a place called Crookhaven, on the south coast of Ireland.

Inspector Dew caught a faster ship, the *Laurentic*, and set off in hot pursuit, accompanied by hordes of reporters. The story was a gift for the newspapers. It unfolded like a novel, gaining suspense as the *Laurentic*, with Dew, gained on the *Montrose*. The case is famous for being the first time that radio caught a murderer, but the use of the Marconigram did not end there. As soon as he was in reach of Canada, Captain Kendall used the radio to send reports of his passengers to the Canadian newspapers. These were picked up as fast as technology would permit and relayed to Britain and the Continent. So whereas everyone in the Northern Hemisphere knew what Crippen and Ethel had for breakfast, the couple themselves were blissfully ignorant that they had been discovered.

The *Laurentic* caught up the *Montrose* at Father Point, in the St Lawrence. According to Inspector's Dew's letter home, this was a 'lonely little place ... with scarcely more than a dozen cottages and a Marconi station to it'. Dew borrowed a pilot's uniform as a disguise, and, with Chief McCarthy and Officer Denis of the Canadian Police, set off in a tender to board the *Montrose.*

'I saw Crippen pacing the deck about two yards away. I sent Mr McCarthy and Denis to bring him in. I said "Good morning Dr Crippen", and he replied, "Good morning." He made no attempt to dispute his identity.'

The press had bought tickets to travel on the *Montrose* from Father Point to Quebec, but Dew had arranged for their launch to set off in a different direction. Consequently, by the time they were allowed to board the ship, Crippen and Ethel were secured in separate cabins. The reporters were furious. Dew was indignant at their close attention: 'I throughout was subjected to the utmost annoyance by them, as they were peering through cracks and adopting the most extraordinary tactics to obtain information... Fabulous sums were offered me for information and permission to take photos of Crippen and especially le Neve in boy's clothing... My life has been made a perfect burden. I am followed and my every movement is watched. They even intrude into my hotel and force their questions upon me at meals and every possible ruse has been adopted to break through the reserve I have maintained from the first.'

Ethel was treated kindly in Canada, and went to stay with Chief McCarthy and his wife, but she became ill, and spent some time in the prison infirmary in Quebec before the party returned to Britain on the *Megantic.*

Crippen was tried first, at the Central Criminal Court in October 1910, with Richard Muir prosecuting and the Lord Chief Justice, Lord Alverstone, presiding. The Home Office analyst, William Willcox, was chief medical witness for the prosecution. Willcox, a chemist and toxicologist attached to St Mary's, Paddington (where penicillin would later be discovered), had regularly travelled across London to Guy's in the early part of his career to learn toxicology from Thomas Stevenson, and had become junior Home Office analyst in 1904. He took over as senior analyst on Stevenson's death in 1908. It was discovered in August that Crippen had purchased 5 grains of hyoscine from a pharmacy in Oxford Street in late January; Willcox extracted a fatal dose of hyoscine from the remains a few weeks later.

The nature of pathology had changed radically during the late Victorian and Edwardian periods. For many years it was taught as morbid anatomy in the London teaching hospitals, usually by someone in a junior, or stepping stone, position, but once pathological tests developed to diagnose diseases such as leukaemia, tuberculosis and cholera, the role increased in importance and status. A contributory factor in this was the fact that the emphasis in pathology was changing from the dead to the living – there was no money to be made from the dead – and by the 1880s the pathologist was no longer regarded as a morbid anatomist, but a student of disordered function.

Notwithstanding the current emphasis on the living, diagnosing the cause of death was still a vital part of the pathologist's function, and a small corner of this new pathology, as with the old, was occupied by the medicolegal autopsy. The pioneer, in London, of this kind of work, initially called 'special pathology', was Augustus Joseph Pepper, who, like Willcox, worked at St Mary's. Pepper had been called in occasionally on medico-legal cases by the local coroner, Dr George Danford Thomas, from about 1883; they were both members of the Pathological Society. Pepper's main work, though, was as a surgeon and lecturer in operative surgery, from which he retired in 1908. He was called out of retirement in 1910 to perform the autopsy on the victim of the 'London Cellar Murder', as the press dubbed it, assisted by his junior colleague, Bernard Spilsbury.

Spilsbury, at that time, was the hospital's morbid anatomist, as well as being lecturer in pathology and curator of the pathological museum. He had investigated thirty-three deaths under anaesthetic there by 1910. It was the Crippen case, more than any that had gone before, which established special pathology as an indispensable courtroom discipline and made Spilsbury's name both as a special pathologist and as an expert witness. Yet this reputation was undeserved. The medical profession and the public were swept along by the publicity given to the trial. Spilsbury was really quite inexperienced compared with the defence pathologists, Turnbull and Wall, from the London Hospital, and to win his case, prosecutor Richard Muir deliberately and artificially enhanced Spilsbury's expertise in order to humiliate the defence experts. The ploy succeeded brilliantly.

The public, who had queued in the street outside Number 1 court, were not disappointed in their quest for gruesome detail. A piece of flesh from the cellar, quite leathery by the time of the trial in October, was handed round the court on a tray to demonstrate that it contained an old abdominal scar where Belle had had an operation. Pepper was the first medical witness. Both he and Spilsbury, who followed him into the witness box, were sure that this piece of flesh was from the abdomen and contained an old scar. If this hadn't been challenged by the defence medical witnesses, then Spilsbury might have played a more minor role. However, the leading defence witness, Dr G. M. Turnbull, director of London Hospital Pathological Institute, made a poor showing in the witness box.

Turnbull was an experienced pathologist – he had supervised over a thousand post-mortems each year since 1907 as against Spilsbury's thirty-three deaths under anaesthetic in total – but he was a poor witness, and he was genuinely unable to determine whether the flesh, which had pubic hair attached, was from the abdomen or the thigh. It depended on whether a particular tendon was present. If the tendon was there, then the flesh was from the abdomen. Richard Muir humiliated Turnbull by asking the less experienced Spilsbury to point out the tendon to him in court, which he did. At first Turnbull was hesitant and said he didn't think Spilsbury had actually identified the tendon. Then he became confused and changed his mind, to the irritation of the judge, who made an arbitrary decision to proceed on the hypothesis that the flesh had come from the abdominal wall, as the St Mary's men had suggested.

Turnbull and his colleague, Dr R. C. Wall, were really inclined to think that the 'scar' was simply a pressure mark caused when the flesh was buried folded. Their evidence for this was that they had found five hair follicles and a sebaceous gland in the slides that Spilsbury had prepared for the court. These don't occur in scar tissue. Spilsbury simply denied that these were present and offered to show the jury the slides. He said it only looked as if there were hair follicles and a sebaceous gland in the section because in stitching up the flesh during the operation the surgeon had included the edge of the outer skin into the stitch. Turnbull felt that Spilsbury had made a mistake: 'Such an inclusion might be mistaken by somebody unaccustomed to the microscope.' This gave Muir, now evidently becoming a little heated, a further opportunity to humiliate Turnbull:

> We are not talking about people unaccustomed to the micro-scope. We are talking about people like Dr Spilsbury; that is the person I am talking about. Do not talk about people unaccus-tomed to the microscope. I am talking about people accus-tomed to the microscope.

Turnbull was bullied at this time into agreeing that the much less experienced Spilsbury was right. When he was re-examined by defence counsel, he reverted to his original opinion that the mark was not a scar. Muir's speech to the jury, at the end of the trial, returned to Turnbull's poor performance:

> Dr Turnbull has examined the piece microscopically, so have Dr Spilsbury, Mr Pepper and Dr Willcox. All Dr Turnbull can do is to say, in answer to me, that a person unaccustomed to the use of the microscope might make a mistake about it. As though I were talking about a person unaccustomed to the microscope! Did he mean to suggest in that innuendo that Dr Spilsbury was unaccustomed to the use of the microscope? Was that the suggestion? I hope not.

Competence as a pathologist is not the same as self-confidence as a witness. Turnbull's professional competence was demonstrated by his appointment as director of the Pathological Institute and by the fact that he had a disease named after him; but he was a hopeless witness. Spils-bury's confident manner in the box, as first demonstrated at the Crippen trial, would often be remarked upon in future years, yet his skills as a pathologist remained to be proved. Indeed, his reputation as a competent pathologist and microscopist was successfully, although artificially, enhanced by Muir who presented him in a glowing light in order to destroy the evidence of the main defence witness, regardless of the truth. The outcome was that Spilsbury became the only full-time forensic medical specialist in England until his death in 1947. Yet the foundation for his successful career was very shaky.

What hanged Crippen, though, was not so much the medical evidence as the label on the pyjama jacket, an apparently insignificant item. Embroi-dered in red on a white background, it read:

SHIRTMAKERS.
JONES BROS (HOLLOWAY) LTD
HOLLOWAY N.

103

Crippen's defence, poor as it was, was that the body must have been buried in the cellar before his tenancy began in 1905. Unfortunately for him, Jones Brothers became a limited company only in 1906, and Jones's buyer gave evidence that the label on that particular jacket dated from 1908.

Crippen hanged at Pentonville on 23 November 1910. Ethel was tried as an accessory at the Old Bailey shortly after her lover's trial, and was acquitted.

Willcox, the analyst, and Spilsbury, the pathologist, appeared on an equal footing in many cases in the following years, such as the Seddons (1912), G. J. Smith (Brides in the Bath 1915) and Armstrong (1922). Their prominence coincided with what might be called the golden age of the domestic poisoner. The role of the Home Office analyst died out in the 1950s, as the methods became instrumentalised and routine to a large extent; the fact that written evidence was allowed from the 1960s also served to push the analyst out of the limelight, leaving the forensic pathologist to shine in his place.

The question that still remains to be answered is why did Crippen choose hyoscine as the murder weapon. Crippen was a homoeopathic doctor, and it was natural for him to choose a poison from the range of homoeopathic remedies available at that time. But he also had access to cyanide, aconite, conium, cantharides and arsenic, among others, so why plump for hyoscine?

Hyoscine comes from the plant *Hyoscyamus niger*, or henbane. It is used as a sedative, a painkiller and an antispasmodic. Today, it can be bought over the counter in tablets for period pains and as a motion sickness remedy. In fiction, although hyoscine was used by Ngaio Marsh in *The Nursing Home Murders* (1941), it usually appears in its American guise as scopolamine, the truth drug. Philip Marlowe is given a shot of it in *Farewell My Lovely* (1940).

The theory put about by the prosecution in the Crippen case was that Crippen gave his wife a sedative to keep her asleep while he entertained Ethel in another room of the house. If this theory were true, then the death would have been an accident and the cover-up a result of panic. Perhaps he gave her too much, by mistake. The therapeutic dose for hyoscine hydrobromide was 100th to 200th of a grain. Half a grain would kill. The symptoms of a lethal dose were at first some delirium and stupor, with dryness of the throat and paralysis of the pupils. Very soon complete unconsciousness and coma, with paralysis, would follow, and death would occur in a few hours.

Willcox recovered an estimated 2.7 grains from Belle's remains. This doesn't sound like a sedative dose. A correspondent to the *British Medical Journal* in October 1910 may have stumbled across the solution. His letter suggested that Crippen had got the idea from the novel *A Wingless Angel*, by Dick Donovan.

In the book, first published in 1878, a young woman, Mary Leslie, dies dramatically while being attended by the hero, Dr John Ashton, and her virtuous friend, Ruth Rivers, the 'wingless angel' of the title. Mary dies accusing Ruth: 'Aarrgh,' she cries, 'you have poisoned me', as she falls back on the pillow. Dr Dudley, an eminent physician, is called in and finds a white powder about the cork and neck of Mary's medicine bottle. He takes it away with him for analysis, suspecting some powerful vegetable poison. 'This powder,' says the author, 'was a very active and peculiar poison, and was known in the profession as Hyoscyamia. It was an alkaloid extract of Henbane. But it was a very rare poison... The great peculiarity in this poison was that it left no trace in the human body... The symptoms were almost identical with phrenitis, or inflammation of the brain; and if he had no reason to suspect the presence of poison, he should most certainly have certified that Miss Leslie's death was ascribable to phrenitis.'

In his evidence at the fictional inquest, Dr Dudley said that the poison, although well known in India, was unobtainable in the United Kingdom. Crippen, having homoeopathic qualifications, knew differently. It was one of the standard remedies in homoeopathic medicine and appears as such in books as early as 1885.

There are two villains in the book. One is a Mrs Belmore, a name uncommonly like Belle Elmore, and her Indian Ayah, a woman called Woonah, who stands behind Mrs Belmore for most of the story. This Woonah is actually a man, disguised as a woman. He has Mrs Belmore in his power and wants Mary Leslie out of the way, for reasons that needn't concern us. However, once his plans have gone wrong and the poison is discovered, he puts plan B into operation. He throws off his woman's disguise and *as a man* takes passage on a P&O steamer bound for Calcutta. Unfortunately, while on board some incident takes place which results in his being recognised and he is arrested on ship and brought back to England to stand trial.

It seems plausible enough. Crippen is known to have read *The Four Just Men* on board the *Montrose*. Suppose Ethel came into the office one day with her latest detective story, *Wingless Angel*, from the public library, and they discussed it.

There is some rather iffy evidence that Crippen was interested in undetectable poisons. Author William le Queux wrote a book called *Things I know about Kings, Celebrities and Crooks* after the Crippen case (which is why his story is a bit iffy). According to Le Queux, he had found a rare book called *Secrets of the State of Venice* (1869), written in Latin and old Italian with formulas for ancient and undetectable poisons. He had mentioned this in a novel which Crippen had read. Crippen had looked for the book in vain and wrote to Le Queux in March 1908 for an appointment, calling himself Dr George Adams (unless of course it was someone else altogether). They met at the Devonshire Club for a drink. Le Queux said that the book was in his study in Florence. 'Dr Adams' asked him for details of the formulas that left not the slightest trace. Le Queux said that they probably weren't quite so undetectable now if subjected to toxicological analysis.

Crippen decided he might pick up some extra money by contributing a plot for a mystery story and selling it to Le Queux. In fact, Le Queux did use one of them in the novel *Red Widow*. Crippen had apparently immersed himself in volumes on poisons. He read practically everything in print on the subject of toxicology and became an authority on the manual of fellow American Dr Rudolph August Witthaus. Crippen, still calling himself Dr Adams, met Le Queux again, later in 1908 or 1909. He told the novelist the formula of certain secret poisons, one of which, when given hypodermically, would cause almost instant death, as though from heart failure. 'If the body were discovered at once,' Adams continued, 'poison might be suspected because of a peculiar smell, which, however, would disappear after about four hours. To obviate that, the puncture or scratch, should be rubbed with menthol. And I defy any pathologist to discover the true cause of death.'

Le Queux claimed to have forgotten all about Crippen until he saw his picture in the *Daily Mirror*. Although the story sounds quite questionable, what is striking is the physical resemblance between Witthaus and Crippen – as if Crippen had modelled his looks, or at least his moustache, on his hero and role model.

But what does Witthaus say about hyoscine in his toxicology text-book? He says some very interesting things from the would-be murderer's point of view. Although the symptoms include dilation of the pupils, giddiness and delirium, there is 'usually no pain'. And should the patient recover, 'he has usually no remembrance of anything that transpired while he was under the influence of the poison.' How very convenient.

What was more to the point was that Witthaus seemed to confirm what the novel suggested, that the poison was undetectable. He says:

> The chemical identification of atropin, hyoscyamin and hyoscine, in the small quantities in which they may be expected to be present in a cadaver, may easily fail... This group of poisons undoubtedly suffers some degree of decomposition in the presence of putrefying material and particularly in substances undergoing fermentation.

He recommends Vitali's test, a colour test. Witthaus's book was published in about 1906.

Willcox indeed used Vitali's test. In the presence of vegetable alkaloids, the substance turned purple when Vitali's preparation was added to it. But Witthaus was out of date. Willcox was able to narrow down his search for hyoscine by adding bromine solution to his extract to make hydro-bromic acid. He obtained spheres from this, but no crystals. Atropine and hyoscyamin gave needle-shaped crystals and hyoscine formed spheres.

Yet if Crippen spent such a lot of time looking for a poison that was undetectable in the human body, why did he cut Belle into bits and bury her in the cellar? The likelihood is that plan A was to copy the novel and have Belle die tragically at home from phrenitis, but something went wrong. The papers at the Public Record Office in Kew contain some statements from neighbours that never found their way into court. One of these neighbours remembers hearing shots in the early hours of possibly 1 February. Another neighbour heard screams at midnight a few nights later.

These statements didn't fit in with what the police already knew and they were a bit vague, so they were never brought into court as evidence. But suppose that Belle did not pass peacefully into paralysis and coma. Suppose she raged around the house in a frightened delirium and Crippen shot her in the head in a panic. This theory was put forward many years ago by one of the barristers on the case in his memoirs. He would have seen all the statements. Belle's head was never found and is supposed to be at the bottom of the English Channel, having been dropped there from a ferry on a visit to France at Easter 1910. Does it have a bullet hole? Perhaps the screams heard by the neighbour were those of Ethel, discovering Crippen sawing up the dear departed in the middle of the night. Once things had started to go wrong, as in the novel, the pair fled on board ship, Plan B, and life imitated art.

Willcox was hard pressed in October 1910. Crippen's trial finished on 22 October, and on the 24th he was needed at Chester, where he was required to give evidence in the Wilde case, the first major case which used a biological test to distinguish human blood from that of other species.

CHAPTER ELEVEN

CORNELIUS HOWARD / MARK WILDE

The double acquittal

Gorse Hall, in 1909, was an imposing mansion overlooking the sooty mill town of Stalybridge, near Manchester. At one time it belonged to Beatrix Potter's grandparents, and the writer and naturalist wrote of it in her journal in 1884, after her grandmother's death. The house then stood empty, until George Harry Storrs moved there in 1891 following his marriage to local girl Maggie Middleton. Storrs, born in 1860, had recently taken over the family business, including Aqueduct Mill, from his father, a local magnate. The couple were childless, but adopted a niece of Maggie's, Marion Lindley, who was left an orphan when she was 9. In 1909, at the time of Storrs' murder, she was an observant 26-year-old.

Marion was away on the evening of 10 September 1909, when a curious incident took place at Gorse Hall, which had no telephone installed. Despite its name, the house wasn't set in the deserted countryside. Although it had its own grounds, it wasn't far from the town centre, and across the road from the main gate was the local Liberal Club. Sometime after 9 p.m., James Worrall, the coachman, appeared at Stalybridge police station, having run all the way from the house without stopping to use the Liberal Club telephone. Panting and sweating, he told police that there had been a shooting at the house. The inspector sent a sergeant and four constables straight away.

Eliza Cooper, the housemaid, let in the uniformed party and led them into the parlour-cum-dining room. George and Maggie Storrs were in the room with Georgina McDonald, a widowed friend of Maggie's, who had come over from Leeds for a few days. George explained to the police what had happened. At 9.30, the two ladies were sitting at the dining table waiting for dinner to be served, and George was reading in an armchair by the fireplace. He looked up from his book, and saw a shadowy form outside the window. As he went across the room to investigate, a man's voice shouted: 'Hands up, or I'll shoot!' As he spoke, a pane of glass was broken and the barrel of a gun protruded into the room. Storrs continued, somewhat ill advisedly, towards the window, and pulled down the blind. Two shots were fired, and Storrs made for the door. At this point, his wife caught him by the arm and begged him not to leave the house. Eliza, by this time, had heard the noise and had run from the kitchen into the parlour. Storrs told her to open the front door a few inches and ring the handbell that was used to summon Worrall from his flat over the stables.

Storrs couldn't describe the man. The police, reinforced by officers from neighbouring Dukinfield, searched the house and grounds. At daybreak, the police made a closer inspection of the window and the parlour. There were no signs of a bullet, bullet hole, or shotgun pellets; nor was there any trace of powder. The blind was clean, its only blemish being a cut in the shape of a 7. Storrs told police that 'the shots must have been discharged outside, and not through the window'. Although Maggie Storrs backed up her husband's assertion that shots had been fired, the police weren't convinced. The purpose and motive for the incident were never explained. Storrs said he suspected no one. He hadn't recently sacked anyone from the mill who might have had a grudge against him.

In response to the incident, Storrs arranged, not to have a telephone installed, but to have a large bell, supplied by a church-bell foundry, placed on the roof, which could be heard a mile away at Stalybridge police station. The two constables who patrolled nearby Albert Square extended their beats to take in the grounds of Gorse Hall. Storrs, obviously worried, got Worrall to make sure that the window shutters were all closed and that the kitchen door was locked at nightfall each evening.

At midnight on Friday, 29 October, seven weeks later, the whole town was woken by the urgent ringing of the bell. The two beat policemen dashed up the drive, and at the station a sergeant and a constable ran all the way to the house, joined on the way by other constables. When the two beat policemen arrived at the front door, they found Storrs standing in the open doorway looking at his fob-watch by the light of the oil lamp behind him. Then he entered the house and called upstairs, and the tolling stopped. He returned to the front door and told the police that he had decided to try out the bell, to see if it would produce the desired results. The reaction of the police who had gathered at the house was not recorded.

Monday, 1 November, was election day in Dukinfield and Ashton, both within walking distance from Stalybridge. The police didn't warn Storrs that his protection would be withdrawn for the whole of that day and evening, as all Stalybridge men would be needed elsewhere, to keep rival factions in order. At about 9.15 p.m., Storrs was playing patience at a small table in the parlour, while Maggie and Marion were at the table, waiting for the meal to be served. Eliza had just left the room and was in the hall heading for the kitchen when she met Mary Evans, the cook, coming up from the cool cellar with a can of milk.

Mary entered the kitchen first and saw a man standing, or possibly crouching, between the back door and the dresser. The light was poor, and at first she thought it was the coachman and remarked, 'Oh, Worrall, how you frightened me!' But it wasn't Worrall, and he was pointing a revolver at her head. 'Say a word and I shoot,' he said, in an accent recalled later as that of a 'superior workman', whatever that might mean, though it might be inferred that he was a local man. The cook dropped the milk and fled, trying to pull shut the kitchen door behind her. But the stranger was holding it open on the other side. She let go, and shrieking, 'There's a man in the house!', ran past Eliza into the parlour. Eliza stood dumbstruck in the hall as the kitchen door banged back on its hinges and a young man rushed past her after the cook. She could see by the oil lamp hanging near the foot of the stairs that he was wearing a dark cap and a dark tweed suit, had a muffler round his neck, and was holding a gun in his left hand. Eliza ran away, going through the kitchen and into the safety of the yard.

Mary, closely pursued by the intruder, ran into the parlour, screaming again, 'There's a man in the house!' The three occupants rose to their feet in alarm. The two women turned towards each other; Storrs made for the doorway. The women shouted to him, but he took no notice. They followed him into the hall, with Mary close behind.

The two men faced each other. George Storrs, 49 years old, was powerfully built, nearly 6 feet in height, with a large moustache and whiskers. The intruder could have been in his late twenties; he was fair and slim, with a slight fuzzy moustache, and stood about 5 feet 8 inches tall. He had the handle of what looked like a knife showing between his waistcoat and shirt. He looked at Storrs and shouted, 'Now I've got you!', or possibly, 'I've got you now!' Storrs lunged for the revolver and grabbed the intruder's wrist. Maggie edged past them and unhooked a shillelagh hanging on the wall for decoration; but, as her husband and the intruder were locked in combat, she hesitated to strike. The young man inched the revolver towards Maggie, saying, 'I will not shoot.' She snatched the gun away, and Storrs shouted to her to ring the bell. She passed him the shillelagh and dashed upstairs to the bell pull in the attic. On the way, she slipped the gun under a carpet out of sight.

Marion raced for the front door and ran outside to get help. The cook, a born servant, ran back to the kitchen and out into the yard where she found Eliza. The two servants searched for Worrall, but he was in the bar of the Grosvenor Hotel where he heard the bell tolling, and didn't hurry back, thinking it was another practice. Marion ran in the dark down the drive, out of the front gate and across the road. Knowing that women weren't allowed into the Liberal Club, she made for the Oddfellows Hall next door. Inside, she could hardly find her voice. When she did, it was barely a whisper: 'My uncle is being murdered!'

Women weren't allowed in the Oddfellows either, and her arrival caused quite a stir. Nevertheless, the gallant members – after hustling her into a private room – gave her some brandy, and eight bold Oddfellows braved the house where the four women had left Storrs to tackle an armed intruder alone.

The kitchen looked like an abattoir. Storrs was lying in the middle of the room covered in blood, but he was still alive. Oddfellow Henry Heald was first on the scene. He went over to Storrs and asked, 'Who attacked you?' Storrs ignored the question and enquired after his wife. Heald had the distinct impression that 'he could have said who the intruder was had he wanted to'. Heald cut off Storrs' butterfly collar with a penknife and doused a handkerchief in some water to bathe his face. He had a cut above his nose, but most of the blood in the kitchen must have come from deeper wounds that Heald couldn't see. Maggie was still in the attic tolling the bell. Two men went up the stairs and found her on her knees, clutching the tasselled bell pull so hard that they had to prise her fists from the rope.

Constable David Buckley, the most recent recruit of the force, was the first policeman on the scene. He also asked Storrs, 'Who was the man?' Storrs repeated several times, 'I don't know.' The dying man asked for brandy and Harry Barley, another of the Oddfellows, poured him a glass from a decanter in the parlour. More policemen arrived to trample over all the evidence. James Worrall was now outside the back door with Eliza Cooper and Mary Evans. He was crying. A local doctor reached the house, running, at about 10 p.m., but there was nothing he could do for Storrs, who died from loss of blood shortly afterwards. The chief constable, Captain Bates, also put in an appearance. All in all, there were between twelve and fifteen people milling about the place.

Superintendent Leonard J. Croghan examined the scene as best he could, finding bloodstains in the kitchen and the adjoining scullery. His notes ran:

> Marks were in evidence on the scullery floor; there were blood marks in the slopstone, on the wooden rail on the window sill, and on the wall at the side of the window. Also stains on glass above the catch (no marks on window catch). There were no bloodstains outside window. The scullery window was broken, and a tin wash-basin in scullery had apparently been used for the purpose, as it was outside the window in the yard with marks on it and badly dented.

It looked as if the fight in the hall had moved into the kitchen where Storrs had managed to overcome his assailant and lock him in the scullery. The man had then smashed the window with the tin wash-basin, climbed out and returned through the kitchen door to stab Storrs fatally before running away. The autopsy revealed that Storrs had fifteen separate stab wounds on his body.

The only lead was the assailant's revolver. This was retrieved from its hiding place under the carpet and passed to Alfred Pickford, a Manchester gunsmith, for his opinion. The gun was a small five-chambered 'American Bullock'. It was not actually of American origin, but was mass produced in Europe, probably in Belgium. It was rare in Britain, or, at least, Pickford had never seen one before. A cut-down rifle bullet had been jammed into one of the chambers to give the gun the appearance of being loaded, but it had been made intentionally useless by removing the swivel pin connecting the hammer and the main spring. The trigger spring was also missing, and the extracting rod was bent. It had not been carried to fire, only to threaten. There were seven neat and equidistant scratches on the barrel which had probably been cut there to identify it, rather than as a tally of victims. A photograph and description of the gun were circulated widely, asking for help in identifying the owner.

On 12 November, James Worrall hanged himself in the hayloft. Police did not consider his suicide as a sign of guilt. The servants would have recognised him, even in the lamplight. He had been crying for most of the time since the death of his employer, who had become more of a friend to him over the years, and no doubt he blamed himself for not hastening back to the house when he heard the bell.

The police rounded up the usual suspects, but no one seemed to fit the bill, until they found Cornelius Howard. Howard was born in 1878, younger than Storrs by eighteen years, and was a pork butcher by trade, as was his father. The Howards were related to the Storrs: Cornelius was Storrs' first cousin, but the Howards were the poor relations and the Storrs had little to do with them, even though they lived in the same small town. Cornelius joined his father in the shop after he left the local school and worked there until his mother died, after Christmas in 1898. Then he left Stalybridge to became a soldier-cook, after a short and unsuccessful career in larceny. He left the army in April 1909 and took to burglary to support him while he was job-hunting. He failed at both, and in July he was appre- hended in Sheffield, across the Pennines in Yorkshire, for breaking into a jewellers and stealing a glazier's diamond. He spent almost three months in gaol waiting for his case to come up – including the date of the alleged shooting on 10 September – and was given an unconditional discharge when he appeared in court on 7 October.

When Howard was picked up, in Oldham on 17 November, police found a pair of black socks, saturated in blood, in his pocket, as well as three penknives and an open knife with a black handle. It looked like a table knife with the blade ground to make it thin and sharp. His other pockets contained stolen tobacco. What was more interesting to the police was that his clothes were covered in blood. He had blood on his jacket and splashes on his trousers and left boot. They had apparently come from several lacer- ations to the outside of his left leg, just below the knee. He told Oldham police: 'That was done by some glass falling on my leg in Joyce's lodging-house on 10 November.' His landlord, he said, was putting in some windows and dropped a pane of glass. He also appeared to have a cut and a bruise on his other leg, and a scratch on his hand. They looked about the same age as the wounds on his left leg. They were about three weeks old, and could have been done on the night of the murder.

Howard was taken to Dukinfield police station, and his clothes were examined by Dr John Summers Park, the local medical officer of health and police surgeon. The doctor took the clothes back to his surgery and later reported that the stains were undoubtedly blood but he could not determine whether they were human or animal.

On closer interrogation, Howard changed his story about the blood. 'A large piece of jagged glass dropped on my leg while I was smashing a window last Thursday night at Tansey and Walker's, the wholesale grocers near the town hall at Stalybridge.' He also confessed to two other break-ins on 30 October (the Saturday before the murder) and denied that he had owned a revolver since leaving the army. His story checked out.

On 18 November, Howard was put in an identity parade at Dukinfield police station. (Although Gorse Hall was nearer Stalybridge police station, it was under the jurisdiction of Dukinfield police; the boundary between the two forces ran through the grounds.) Howard was given his cap to wear, and the four women in the Storrs' household were brought in one by one. Only Marion Lindley, the niece, picked out Howard without hesitation. Mrs Storrs picked out no one. Eliza Cooper pointed to Howard and said, 'That is most like the man.' Outside the room, she told police that Howard 'seemed a little taller' than the murderer, and he was clean-shaven, whereas the murderer had sported a fuzzy moustache. Mary Evans, the cook, walked back and forth and eventually pointed uncertainly at Howard, saying that he was most like the murderer, but she was not sure that he was the man.

The inquest was held in Dukinfield on 24 November. Howard was represented by two Manchester barristers, Percy Macbeth and Edward Theosophilus Nelson. Nelson was a West Indian from Demerara in British Guiana, and – being black – was something of a rarity in the English courts of 1909. The four women who had left Storrs to his fate now all identified Howard in court as the assailant, even Mrs Storrs, although smelling salts had to be administered to her during the identification evidence. She sobbed and cried out, 'I think he *is* the man. He knows.'

Howard's clothing and the knife had been sent to Dr Joseph Carter Bell, the Cheshire county analyst, for examination. The public analysts were established by an Act of Parliament in 1860; their main role was the stamping out of adulterations in food and drink, mainly through prosecutions in the police courts. They were so successful in this that by the beginning of the twentieth century most of their aims had been achieved. Their court work counts as 'forensic science' or 'criminalistics' just as surely as laboratory work done for a murder trial – the adulteration of food and drink is a criminal offence – but few regard the county analysts (successors to the public analysts) as 'forensic scientists'. Yet a prime mover in the Victorian Society of Public Analysts was Home Office analyst Thomas Stevenson, who was president in 1896. It was Stevenson who first devised examinations for would-be public analysts and he, and then William Willcox, were examiners. The exams were later made compulsory. Nowadays, the county analysts do laboratory work for police forces as a matter of routine. Dr Bell, however, did hardly any better than the police surgeon, except to say that whereas the stains on the trousers and socks were blood, the red stains on the jacket were paint. Traces of blood, grease and starch on the knife suggested that it had been used to cut meat.

Howard had given Joyce, his landlord in Oldham (a few miles away) as an alibi, but Joyce couldn't confirm that Howard had been there on 1 November. A fellow lodger told the coroner that Howard was absent that day and didn't return until Tuesday or Wednesday. The assailant had a light moustache, so police prevailed upon a barber near Howard's lodgings to give evidence that he had given a 'clean shave' (i.e. including the moustache area) to someone very like Howard on the day after the murder.

Howard eventually remembered that he was in Huddersfield, in Yorkshire, that evening, at a pub called the Ring o'Bells. Two Huddersfield witnesses therefore appeared before the coroner. The landlord, James Davies, said he remembered Howard in the pub on 1 November (even though his statement had said, 'It was November 1st or 2nd'), but the next witness, John Robinson, a watch and clock repairer – and serious drinker – thought the night was the Tuesday, because he was in the Dog and Gun on the Monday, trying to collect a bet. The inquest jury returned a verdict of wilful murder against Cornelius Howard.

His case came up at Chester Castle in March 1910 before Mr Justice Pickford, who, as a barrister, had defended Florence Maybrick in 1889. Francis Williams, KC, led for the Crown, assisted by Ellis Ellis-Griffith, but the defence lawyers had been replaced by Trevor Lloyd, who was more experienced. The four women repeated their evidence, and Lloyd tried to throw doubt on the efficiency of their memories, especially that of Maggie Storrs, who had failed to pick anyone out at the identity parade, but now identified Howard.

The prosecution came up with three witnesses to attest that John Robinson, the drunken clock mender, was in the Dog and Gun, not the Ring o'Bells, on the night of the murder and therefore could not alibi Howard. But the defence had found William Marmaduke Thompson, whom Howard remembered meeting outside the Conservative committee rooms in Huddersfield between 8 and 8.30 on the Monday, election night. Thompson had apparently been helping out at the polls. It was not possible to get from

Huddersfield to Stalybridge in time to commit the murder. Howard had greeted the idling Thompson, lounging about in the entrance to the building, with, 'I see you're busy, Billy.' Thompson was a bookie's runner, and the two men exchanged a few words about the success of Howard's horse, Razorbill, which had won at Wetherby that day at odds of three to one. Thompson owed Howard eight shillings, but as he didn't have the money on him, he arranged to meet him next day to pay him his winnings, which he duly did. Thompson added that Howard was invariably clean-shaven. It was Thompson who saved Howard's neck. The jury brought in a not guilty verdict after twenty minutes' deliberation and, amid cheers from the public gallery, rebuked by the judge, Howard was discharged.

Maggie Storrs had the house demolished that summer, and moved away to a village near the Lancashire seaside, still with her niece and the two servant women. But events were not over in Stalybridge. Late on Monday, 10 June, a moonlit night, courting couple James Bolton and Gertrude Booth were walking home along Early Bank Road, a wooded dirt-track lane near the Gorse Hall estate, when they saw a young man walking towards them. He was light complexioned with fair hair, was dressed in a dark suit and wore a dark cap and a black muffler, despite it being a summer's night. The man passed them and Gertrude and James quickened their pace. Gertrude, who didn't like the look of the young man, looked back, only to see him turn on his tracks and run after them. The man grabbed them, and offered to cut James's throat. James pushed the girl away, shouting 'For God's sake, run, Gertie!' and turned to grapple with their attacker. Gertrude ran off towards the town, sobbing hysterically, then tripped up and fell headlong. James was able to get the knife off the man and the two made good their escape.

The description that James gave to the police tallied with the description of the Gorse Hall murderer, and Detective Inspector William Thomas Pierce, from police headquarters in Chester, was sent up to investigate. The police found a young millworker, George Hayes, who had met an acquaintance, Mark Wilde, on Early Bank Road that night. He had asked Wilde for a light and in the flare of the match saw that his friend looked the worse for wear. 'Have you been in a scrap?' he asked. Wilde denied it. Police pulled him in for questioning. Aged 28, he lived with his parents and six sisters in Stalybridge. His father worked at the railway station and was a teetotaller and non-smoker. Wilde, like Howard, had been a soldier, and had left that year, in January. His army record stated that he was 5 feet $4^{1}/_{2}$ inches in his stockinged feet. He was fair-haired and light-complexioned with a small moustache. Until Friday, 10 September, the night of the first attack at the Hall, he had been working as a shunter's assistant at the railway station.

James Bolton and Gertrude Booth picked him out at once in an identity parade at Dukinfield police station, and he was charged with attempted murder. His clothes, which appeared bloodstained, were removed. Wilde was asked about his whereabouts on 10 September and 1 November. He remembered 10 September as he had got the sack for refusing to go into work on his night shift, which started at 9 o'clock. He had a row with his father, left the house and spent the evening across the road at the Astley Arms. He had slept on Mrs Ann Mason's sofa. On election night, 1 November, he went to Ashton intending to go to the Hippodrome, but spent the evening on a pub crawl instead:

> When I got to Scotland Brow, opposite the labour exchange that is now, a fellow was just coming out of the public house there as I was going in. He gave me a shove and knocked my hat off, and told me to get out of the road, so I struck him. He ran down the street by the Bluebell public house, and I followed and caught him just round the corner, and we had a fight.
>
> After we finished, I went home by way of Tame Valley and the generating station. I turned off there to go home, but stood at the corner of High Street and Binns Street, and there saw my cousin Thomas Lockwood. He told me about the affair at Gorse Hall. We parted, and I went home.

At some point after the murder, he took his two revolvers, which normally stood on the mantelpiece, pulled them both to pieces and threw all the parts away separately, for safety. He had bought one of the guns cheaply, he said, off a soldier in a pub because it was out of order. The story fitted. Police trailed round all the fields where Wilde said he had thrown bits of gun, to no avail, but a search of the house turned up a pair of trousers that Wilde said he was wearing on 1 November, and police found a clip of five rifle cartridges. (A rifle bullet had been cut down and jammed in the gun from Gorse Hall.) Wilde's street fight in Ashton couldn't be substantiated from policemen's notebooks, but that didn't mean it didn't happen. Police often arrived at fights too late.

Wilde was tried for the attempted murder of the courting couple at Chester on 12 July and, despite his denials, got two months. It was a light sentence, deliberately so. Police wanted time to prepare the case against him for Storrs' murder and they wanted to ensure that he was held at a local prison and not sent an inconvenient distance away to a gaol for long-term prisoners.

In the summer of 1910, the press were more entertained by the Crippen case than by the curious goings-on in Cheshire. The police, as well as the nation, were now coming alive, through the Crippen case, to the value of first-class scientific evidence, and sent Wilde's clothes to London to be examined by William Willcox, who, as readers of the newspapers would have recognised, was active in the London case. Willcox tested the clothes for human blood using the serum, or precipitin test.

This test was the culmination of over eighty years' research into bloodstain analysis. Orfila wrote a paper in 1827 on medico-legal tests for blood, but with such a limited repertoire of chemical reagents at the time, the tests were not very reliable. The most they could do was to show that a substance definitely was not blood. By the middle of the century it had become possible under the microscope to distinguish fresh mammalian blood, under good conditions, from bird and fish blood. But if the blood had to be reconstituted from a dried stain, using a liquid medium, there was no certainty that the cells would retain their original shape or size. Mammalian blood is disc-like and non-nucleated; the nuclei are left behind in the bone marrow, where the cells are made, when they squeeze through to join the bloodstream. Birds, fish and reptiles have oval cells with nuclei.

The spectroscope was sometimes used in forensic medicine in Victorian England to identify bloodstains. This apparatus had been developed in about 1860 by Kirchoff and Bunsen at the University of Heidelberg. They discovered that every chemical element would produce a unique spectrum of light when viewed through the prisms in the spectroscope. The first time this type of evidence was used in a murder case in England was in the very first railway murder in 1864. Franz Muller stabbed bank clerk Thomas Briggs on a train between Hackney Wick and Bow, east London. Henry Letheby, Taylor's old adversary, gave evidence for the Crown that the stains in the railway carriage were indeed blood.

The guaiac test, developed in 1863, was a chemical test which turned the substance under investigation blue in the presence of tincture of guaiac (from the *Lignis vitae* tree) and oil of turpentine. But it suffered from the problem that other substances, like bile, saliva, milk and sweat, could also turn the sample blue. It could prove only that the sample was not blood, if it did not turn blue. Corroboration was a problem if the blood was all used up for the test. The value of the microscope and the spectroscope was that these optical examinations provided such corroboration, while not destroying the sample.

The real breakthrough came in 1901 in Germany with the development of the serum test. This grew out of the work on anti-toxins that was being developed from 1890. In this year, Emil von Behring discovered that when animals were inoculated with small quantities of diphtheria toxin, their blood serum (the watery component of the blood) formed antibodies against that specific disease. This promoted recovery in diphtheria patients. A few years later, Paul Uhlenhuth, working in Berlin at the Institute for

Infectious Diseases, was experimenting with injecting protein (egg white) from chicken's eggs into rabbits. When he then mixed the blood serum from these rabbits with the egg white in a test tube, a cloudy precipitate fell to the bottom of the tube. If he mixed the rabbit serum with pigeons' or gulls' eggs, nothing happened and the test tube remained clear. When, however, he injected protein from a pigeon's egg into a rabbit and then mixed the rabbit serum and pigeon-egg protein together in a test tube, sure enough, it precipitated.

The forensic implications of this for detecting human blood were recognised immediately in Germany, and were used in a case as early as 1901, but in Britain Thomas Stevenson was more cautious, and it was several years before Willcox, his successor, felt confident enough to use the technique in a capital case. The Wilde case was the first major case in Britain in which human blood had been identified.

Willcox reported that he had found human blood on the right sleeve of Wilde's jacket and on the sleeve's lining. The analyst was more cautious about the stains on his waistcoat, and would say only that the blood was mammalian. He thought the stains on the front had been caused by contact with some bloodstained object thrust between the waistcoat and the wearer's shirt. Willcox found no blood on the trousers or the knife, which Wilde had denied ever having seen before. However, the value of all this for proving Wilde's part in the Gorse Hall murder was dubious, considering that he had already served a sentence for a bloody knife assault on a couple in June. The police concentrated on trying to prove a link between Wilde and the 'American Bullock'.

Inspector Pierce traced Wilde's army companions. Lance-Corporal Frank Fowles remembered – though we don't know with how much prompting – that Wilde owned a five-chambered American Bullock (which had a ring attached to the base of the handle). This gun had a defective mechanism and scratches on the barrel. Pierce also traced George Higley, a railway porter in the Midlands who had left the army at the same time as Wilde, and Constable Samuel Wellings, at Liverpool, who had likewise known Wilde in the army. Higley remembered that Wilde's gun had indentations on the barrel. PC Wellings recollected Wilde telling him that the spring was broken and that he had noticed other defects than the spring. He recalled the name 'American' something, perhaps 'Bulldog'.

As with Howard, the four women witnesses were called to a line-up, this time at the gaol where Wilde was doing time for the assault on the courting couple. All but Maggie Storrs identified him as the assailant. Eliza Cooper said: 'That man is more like the man I saw at Gorse Hall than Cornelius Howard.' As soon as Wilde was released from his sentence, on 30 August, he was rearrested, and was back in the same gaol by nightfall.

The case came up on Monday 24 October at Chester Castle, two days after Crippen's conviction. The judge at Chester was Sir Thomas Gordon Horridge. Francis Williams and Ellis Ellis-Griffiths were for the Crown and black barrister Edward Nelson defended Wilde. Nelson was quick to point out that this was the second time that the women had positively identified a man as the assailant in the lamp-lit mansion. Mrs Storrs had one of her fainting fits in the witness box and was revived by Dr Willcox, who had to get back to London for the next day, as he was due to give evidence in the trial of Ethel le Neve. Willcox was allowed to leave the court as soon as his evidence had been given. The three former comrades of Wilde firmly identified the gun as the defendant's. The full story of the attack on the courting couple came out in court, but – in Wilde's favour – it was obvious that there was no blood on his trousers despite the bloody struggle at Gorse Hall.

Emma Wilde, Mark's mother, gave evidence that he had come home at about 10 o'clock on the night of the murder looking as if he had been in a scrap. Nelson asked her if the two revolvers were on the mantelpiece that night: 'Yes, and they were for a week or two after then.' She had received a visit from the police about the guns in June and one of the detectives had remarked: 'Oh, we had Mark out last night, and he showed us where he had thrown the revolvers. By the way, is this one of them?' The detective then produced a gun, and Emma said, 'No, Mark's wasn't as big as this, and it hadn't a ring at the end.'

A surprise witness was Cornelius Howard. He had put on weight and looked much fitter than he had in his lean jobless months earlier in the year. The purpose of his appearance in court was to show the jury that the two men did, indeed, resemble each other, as shown by a newspaper sketch done in court. They were asked to stand side by side near the solicitors' desk, facing the jury box, and then faced to the side so that the jury could see them in profile.

Wilde gave evidence on his own behalf. He denied owning the gun, or the knife used in the attack on the courting couple. Wilde's girlfriend, Kate Kenworthy, had seen Wilde more than once on the evening of 10 September, though she was not with him that evening. She saw him going into the Astley Arms between 8 and 9 p.m. and at about 10 she saw him talking to his mother on the pavement outside. Other people saw Wilde on 10 September but no one came forward with an alibi for 1 November. On the other hand, police could not contradict Wilde's story in any detail. Nelson's summing up focused on the eye-witness identification, calling the women 'wicked' for coming to give evidence a second time. He said, 'Circumstantial evidence is not evidence upon which a jury should convict, especially in case of life and death, unless every single link in the chain is there.'

An odd thing happened during the judge's summing up: one of the jury interrupted to ask whether the army witnesses had been in contact with one another during the investigation. Francis Williams rose to say that their statements had been taken at separate times and in separate places, which rather side-stepped the question. Perhaps the jury were impressed with the men's amazing memories.

The jury were out for fifty minutes and returned a not guilty verdict. Wilde returned in triumph to Stalybridge, accompanied by family and friends, which now included Cornelius Howard, who took a meal with the family before departing.

No one was ever convicted of the murder. The incident on 10 September seems inexplicable. Jonathan Goodman, who wrote *The Stabbing of George Harry Storrs*, is very suspicious of this incident, and thinks it was a set-up. Why did George Storrs stupidly walk towards the gun barrel in the window, unless he knew he was in no real danger? Why did he start for the door to investigate? Where were the bullets and cartridge cases that were supposed to have been fired? Where were the holes? Why did it happen when the perspicacious Marion was absent from home? Goodman thinks the mysterious gunman was Worrall, the idea being to give Storrs a plausible reason to install the bell. Storrs was a frightened man, but of what, or of whom, we'll never know. He may have fabricated a reason for installing the bell and asking for police protection because he didn't want to reveal the real reason. Henry Heald, who was first on the scene, felt that Storrs knew who had attacked him, and the gunman's opener, 'Now I've got you!', suggests a prior grievance.

Goodman suggests two plausible reasons why both Howard and Wilde could have been the assailant. In 1907 a London store tycoon, William Whiteley, was shot by Horace Rayner, a young man claiming to be his son. He had gone into Whiteley's office and demanded money, and when it was refused had shot Whiteley and then turned the gun on himself. Despite shooting himself in the eye, Rayner did not die, and lived to be imprisoned for the murder. It was a sensational case and was reported in the Stalybridge newspaper. Perhaps Howard thought he was the bastard son of Storrs and intended to carry out a copy-cat crime. William Marmaduke Thompson had a poor reputation with the police, being a bookie's runner. A man he had dealings with said he would sell his soul for sixpence. Perhaps the conversation took place earlier, before the polls closed at 8 o'clock, and Howard's opening remark, 'I see you're busy', was not in friendly sarcasm, but was the truth.

Mark Wilde benefited from being the second person tried. Had he been first, perhaps he would have been convicted. If he really did attack the couple in the lane, maybe he was a psychopath and there was no logical reason for his killing Storrs. However, there is a motive of sorts. Kate

Kenworthy, Wilde's girlfriend, was given the sack from Storrs' mill in late summer 1909 for being a trouble-maker, and she was unable to find another job in the same district. When she left to find work elsewhere, her relationship with Wilde ended. Perhaps he blamed Storrs for this break-up. But real life isn't like a detective story, where the villain, according to the principle of fair play, has to be someone who featured earlier in the story. There could be any number of shady characters in Storrs' past who could have come back to haunt him.

I don't think the assailant meant to kill Storrs. I think he wanted to talk to him. The gun may have been his inarticulate way of catching Storrs' attention, perhaps after being snubbed. The oddest thing about the whole story is the assailant's almost gentle action in passing the gun to Mrs Storrs, saying, 'I will not shoot.' Suppose that, after the women had fled, the two men struggled and once in combat the attacker became the victim. Storrs was a much bigger man. Suppose he lost his temper with the intruder for whatever reason – outrage at the attack, or for some old grievance – and went after him with the shillelagh. Maybe the assailant tried to lock *himself* in the scullery and climb out of the window but Storrs pulled him back into the kitchen, and it was then that the younger man stabbed him several times during the fight, in self defence. After all, none of the women reported seeing him use the knife earlier. There were no witnesses to the actual murder.

If only the Dukinfield and Stalybridge police had had fingerprint departments. If only the police had had scene of crime procedures. If only half the world and his brother had not trampled over the house. But there were pockets of expertise, both in Europe and America, where criminalistics were slowly being nudged forward. In the United States, August Vollmer has a just claim to have founded the first police laboratory and training school there, in Berkeley, California. Other forensic work grew slowly, in cities such as Baltimore, Washington, Boston and Chicago. In the UK, the laboratories at Glasgow and Edinburgh, though designed for forensic medicine, came to be predominant in forensic science as well.

CHAPTER TWELVE

CHARLES HENRY SCHWARTZ
The burnt-out lab

The Police Department at Berkeley, California, started to give classes to police officers in about 1908. Topics studied over the next few years included police methods and procedure, anthropometry, fingerprinting and occasional lectures on criminology and psychiatry. The driving force behind this activity was police chief August Vollmer, a former mailman. By 1917, Vollmer had managed to interest the university in his work and a school for police was founded at Berkeley with Vollmer as director and Dr Albert Schneider, MD, PhD, as dean. Vollmer taught police methods, and Schneider took on physics, physiology, microanalysis and criminology.

The new department encouraged research and it was here that Dr John A. Larson, PhD, of the Police Department at Berkeley, was able to develop a prototype lie detector, in about 1921. Larson used it to discover some losses in a girls' dormitory at the university, with some success, and he continued to employ it extensively, with Vollmer's encouragement. Since it measured blood pressure only, it can't really be considered a 'polygraph'; if anything, it would have to be termed a 'monograph'. This was not the first laboratory-based development: Lacassagne's team at the University of Lyons had already done pioneering work on latent fingerprints and some early ballistics in the 1890s, but the lie detector must surely have an unchallenged claim to be a first for the USA.

One of the most notable of the early laboratory pioneers in the United States was E. Oscar Heinrich, who, from 1921 was professor of criminology at Berkeley. He lectured in chemical jurisprudence, photography, optics, chemical and physical evidence, and disputed handwriting.

Heinrich was born in Clintonville, Wisconsin, in 1881, the son of immigrant German parents. A determined youth, he had put himself through pharmacy school by studying at night and working in a drugstore by day. This didn't satisfy his intellectual aspirations and despite his lack of formal qualifications he persuaded the university at Berkeley to enrol him on the BS course in chemistry, which he took in 1908.

He married, and lived with his wife and two boys for nine years in Tacoma, Washington, where he practised as a chemist and sanitary engineer, eventually becoming city chemist. This role brought him into contact with the police and coroner from time to time in an investigative role. Always painstaking and thorough in whatever he did, he made himself an expert on ballistics for a gunshot case, spending all night reading the few textbooks available. But his main area of expertise was on altered documents. He was able to use his skills in chemistry and microscopy in both criminal and civil cases and his reputation spread.

In 1916, despite his obvious lack of background experience, he obtained the post of police chief in Alameda, across the bay from San Francisco and not far from Berkeley. Here he developed scientific aids to the police in the areas of fingerprinting and scene of crime work, particularly in the use of photography. He left this post in 1918 to move to Boulder, Ohio, to be city manager. But before long he left this administrative role to return to forensic work on the sudden death of Theodore Kytka, a San Francisco handwriting expert. Heinrich was persuaded to take over Kytka's practice, operating from his San Francisco office as well as maintaining a laboratory at Berkeley.

His first headline-hitting case was in 1923 when he helped to identify some train robbers from a pair of denim dungarees left at the scene. Just from the overalls he was able to inform police, in Sherlock Holmes style, that they were looking for a left-handed lumberjack accustomed to work around fir trees. He was, moreover, a white man, between 21 and 25 years of age, not over 5 feet 10 inches, weight about 165 pounds, medium light brown hair, light brown eyebrows, small hands and feet and fastidious in personal habits.

The explanation was simple, once you knew how it was done. Heinrich had found fir tree woodchips in the right-hand pocket. A left-handed lumberjack stands with his right side to the tree while chopping it down, and the chips fly into the right pocket, rather than the left. A strand of Caucasian-type hair gave his colouring and age. His height was indicated by the creases in the overalls from where they were tucked into boot tops. Heinrich concluded that the suspect was fastidious in his habits from a well-manicured fingernail found in the pocket.

After some prodding and probing, Heinrich found a small piece of paper right down in the pencil pocket of the bib. It was a registered mail receipt numbered 236-L. When this was traced, it led police to the D'Autremont brothers, twins Roy and Ray, and their brother Hugh. Roy was a left-handed lumberjack.

Shortly after this case, Heinrich found himself called in to investigate an explosion and fire at a Berkeley factory.

First World War flying ace Charles Henry Schwartz cut something of a dash in the social circles of Berkeley. He was a handsome man, always smartly dressed, and in 1925 was aged around 36, with a large house, a wife and three young children. He had come to California after the war and was fond of recounting his war stories to anyone who would listen, boasting a scar above his heart where a German machine-gun bullet had nearly cost him his life. Details of his early life, however, seemed somewhat sketchy. By profession Schwartz was a manufacturing chemist and claimed to have invented a new way of manufacturing artificial silk. This process was still under wraps at his new laboratory at Walnut Creek, outside town.

At the other end of the social scale was Gilbert Warren Barbe, an itinerant evangelist. He had returned from the trenches with his faith in humanity shaken but his faith in Christianity intact. His aim was to bring light and happiness into people's lives. Although the lifestyles of the two men were poles apart, Barbe had struck up a kind of friendship with Charles Schwartz through a mutual interest in chemistry. Then, in July 1925, the evangelist disappeared without explanation from the ramshackle hut he occupied. No one was unduly worried: doubtless he had moved on to spread his message further afield.

On 30 July that same year, Schwartz was working late at his laboratory – the Pacific Cellulose Plant – on one of his experiments. Walter Gonzales, his night watchman and handyman, arrived with his dog to do his rounds, and at 7 o'clock in the evening he took a bowl of hot soup to Schwartz in his laboratory, which was up a flight of stairs. The watchdog padded along with him and suddenly took a professional interest in a small cupboard under the stairs, growling and scratching at the floorboards. Schwartz, who had come to the door of the laboratory for the soup, spotted the dog and angrily gave it an abrupt kick on the flanks to knock it out of the way. He turned to the surprised watchman with a brief word of apology and returned into his laboratory, dismissing Gonzales for the night.

At 9.10 Schwartz telephoned his wife to say he was on his way home, but he never made it. About ten minutes later the neighbourhood was rocked with a terrific explosion that brought people out of their houses. The factory was ablaze. Firemen fought their way into the smoke-filled building but they were too late. A body was found on the laboratory floor, charred beyond all recognition. Mrs Schwartz was taken to the laboratory and, with barely a glance at the horrific sight, identified the remains as those of her husband. She was escorted from the scene, near to collapse.

Police soon learned that Schwartz had recently insured his life for $185,000 with a policy that covered accidental death; so when the insurance assessors told Sheriff Veale that the dead man was three inches taller than Schwartz, he decided to postpone the funeral pending further investigation. Curiously, the Schwartz home was broken into at about this time, but all that was taken were photographs of Schwartz himself and his family.

Despite the assessors' claims that the body was not Schwartz, it had been identified not only by the family physician but by a dentist who had recently removed a top molar. Faced with these contradictions, the sheriff decided to call in Professor Heinrich.

Heinrich examined the charred body, now reposing at the coroner's office, and read the autopsy report. His first question to the sheriff was what Schwartz had had for dinner on the night he died. This was a meal that included cucumber and beans. The stomach of the dead body contained only the remains of undigested meat. An examination of the skull revealed evidence of a blow to the back of the head with a blunt instrument. Heinrich had also obtained some of Schwartz's hair from his hairbrush and compared it microscopically with hair from the deceased. It was not the same. The clincher was that the right ear of the body was not so very badly burnt and was completely different from the ear in the one photograph that Heinrich had been able to trace.

But what about the missing tooth? Heinrich had examined the teeth at the coroner's office, and had spoken to the dentist. The dentist had said that, apart from the missing molar, Schwartz had a good set of teeth. Yet the teeth in the deceased's skull were not just blackened by the fire, they were discoloured and decayed in life, a poor set. Furthermore, on closer inspection, Heinrich was horrified to see that the tooth had actually been knocked out of the head quite recently with a chisel. The root was still embedded in the jaw. An even more cold-blooded act was that the dead man had empty eye sockets. These hadn't been burnt out by the fire. Heinrich believed they had been gouged out after death, presumably because they were the wrong colour.

Suspecting Schwartz now of committing a murder and setting the fire, Heinrich went out to examine the laboratory. He took several scraps of evidence from the scene to his laboratory at Berkeley and a few days later came back with interesting news. Chemical analysis of traces found in Schwartz's laboratory indicated the presence of carbon disulphide, a highly inflammable liquid. If the person found in the lab had battled for his life against the poisonous vapours given off by this burning substance, then a lung haemorrhage would have resulted. The autopsy showed no such haemorrhage.

The odd fact about the laboratory was that the windows were intact, but the doors had blown off. Heinrich found reddish stains both in the laboratory and in the stairs cupboard. He calculated that Schwartz had hit his victim over the head and stuffed him in the cupboard until he was needed. Once he had got rid of the night watchman, he had dragged the dead man into the laboratory, and spilt carbon disulphide in a stream from the doorway along the floor and then around the body. Schwartz had then dropped a match into the end of the stream and made a bolt for it. Heinrich found the match.

But this wasn't all. Heinrich's trained chemist's eye could see that the laboratory wasn't set up to manufacture artificial silk, or anything else for that matter, but was arranged showily, to give the impression of industry to financial backers. As Heinrich himself put it, 'It was all bunkum.'

The last question was the identity of the victim. Charred fragments showed that he had been wearing a blue denim shirt, overalls and a hunting jacket, not the kind of clothing that the natty Schwartz would have been seen dead in. Further investigation of some fragments of paper revealed that they were part of the *New Testament* and of a religious tract entitled *The Philosophy of Eternal Brotherhood*. Heinrich was even able to bring up to view some fragments of the victim's handwriting, using infra-red photography, and these were reproduced in the city newspapers. The handwriting was identified as that of Barbe, the itinerant preacher, by an undertaker and his wife who had helped him out in a nearby town. She had given Barbe a kit of needles and thread. This had survived the fire and she later recognised her gift.

The police now made up for their earlier lack of thoroughness by discovering that Charles Henry Schwartz was a well-known crook and philanderer who operated under several aliases, and was by no means a war hero. In fact, he had spent the war as a company barber. It turned out that Alice Schwartz had sunk all her money into her husband's business, believing his stories that he had perfected a secret formula to produce high-class artificial silk. Not only that, but she had even baled him out financially when another woman brought an action against him for breach of promise. Even to the suspicious detectives, Mrs Schwartz's tale rang true.

Schwartz's description was circulated throughout the country together with the information that he was known to walk stiffly erect, to jingle coins in his pocket and to smoke cheroots. Eventually, a Mr Hayward became suspicious of his reclusive new lodger, in Oakland, not far from Berkeley, and called on the police. Schwartz wouldn't open the door to the police when they called, and by the time they had shouldered their way in, the con man had shot himself with an automatic pistol.

A note was found among his belongings addressed to his wife, but it was full of lies:

My dear wife:
I am writing you without making any excuses; but one thing I will tell you, I am not guilty of the crime they accuse me of.

Last Monday a man called at the factory for work. I was in the lab. He came straight in. We talked a little while, when suddenly the man told me if I didn't give him work, I would have to give him money.

He attacked me. I gave him a blow on his head. He fell. I gave him another. Suddenly I knew he was dead. But I could not make up my mind to go to Bell [Schwartz's lawyer] and tell him.

I decided to run away, but made a dirty job of it. I put the man in the closet, got ready. Can you imagine how I felt all this time? Oh, God, how I suffered. If I had not this damned suit on of Miss Adams' I would have gone through with it, but it was impossible.

I wish to tell you, my dear little girl, I do not know the man, never looked how he was dressed, never touched him after that. The only thing I did was I tried to burn him, to wipe out and go – go. I do not know where. I went home to take all my photos and all I was in need of, hoping to have a few words with you.

I kiss this in bidding and kissing you goodbye. My last kiss is for you, Alice.

The motive was never clear. If it had been an insurance scam, then Mrs Schwartz would need to have been in on it, or Schwartz could never have claimed the insurance. The 'suit of Miss Adams' might be a clue. Perhaps this was the breach of promise suit. If all Schwartz's sins were coming home to him, perhaps he intended to start a new life from scratch, paying his debt to his wife by way of the recent insurance policy. If this was what he planned, it didn't work. Because he died at his own hand, he invalidated the insurance and left Alice penniless except for the $600 found on his body, all he had in the world.

The west coast didn't have a monopoly on expertise. Heinrich owed his knowledge of infra-red and ultra-violet light to the work of Robert Williams Wood, at Johns Hopkins University in Baltimore. But Wood was more than a leading physicist; he was called in from time to time by the Baltimore police.

CHAPTER THIRTEEN

LEROY BRADY

The candy-box murders

Robert Williams Wood, born in 1868, was brought up in the Boston suburbs in a well-to-do professional family and graduated from Harvard in 1891 in chemistry and natural history. He went to Johns Hopkins to study for a PhD in chemistry, but when his father died in 1892 he decided to cut short his studies to marry, and spent some time in Germany before returning to the United States in 1896.

His first post was as an instructor of physics at the University of Wisconsin, where his love of practical jokes and hoaxes made him an entertaining lecturer. He created 'mirages' in the lab with cut-out palm trees and sand, using bunsen burners instead of the sun, and then would create a tornado with the sand. While he was there, he was asked to undertake a graduate course on physical optics. He knew very little on the subject, but read up on it, keeping one step ahead of the class at first. After a while, he realised that the textbook he was using was well behind the times, and he decided to specialise in optics and write his own. It took five years but it became one of the world's standard texts on the subject.

Meanwhile, he was experimenting with prisms and the spectrum. Prisms that used various materials broke the spectrum up in different ways. Instead of obtaining colours of the rainbow, in order, it was possible to reverse the pattern using aniline dyes contained in hollow prisms. After innumerable experiments, he came across the green flakes of nitrodimethylaniline. He found that these, in solution, absorbed violet rays but transmitted ultra-violet; and by combining nitrodimethylaniline with dense cobalt blue glass, he discovered a ray filter that was opaque to visible light, but which was transparent to ultra-violet. It was a sensation in the world of physics, and the new light it produced was often called 'Wood's light' after its discoverer.

Wood also experimented with colour photography and took the first ever infra-red photographs, in 1908. Infra-red and ultra-violet light have proved invaluable for criminalistics over the years, and are routinely used in document examination.

With all this expertise to hand, it was not surprising that Wood was called in to help police from time to time. His most noted case was a baffling crime in Maryland in 1929.

Seat Pleasant lies just east of Washington, DC, and at Christmas 1929 was still a rural, if not isolated spot. Mrs Anna Buckley was delighted to see what looked like a two-pound box of candy on the porch when she opened her door on 26 December. The parcel was wrapped in brown paper and tied with ordinary white string. Her pleasure was short-lived. Printed in bluish-black ink was the name Naomi Hall. The box had been delivered in error. Mrs Buckley knew no one of that name in the neighbourhood and put the box on a shelf, telling her children that if no one came for the parcel by the end of the Christmas holidays, they could have it.

Her 7-year old, Harold, yearning for the candy, at first didn't tell his mother that he knew a boy named Leslie Hall with a sister Naomi. But on New Year's Day he met Leslie, and his mother's training overcame his greed. He told his friend that there was a Christmas present for Naomi at his house which someone had left by mistake. Leslie collected the package and ran home with it, accompanied by another friend, Steuart Carneal. Leslie took the package indoors while Steuart stayed outside, peering in the window, hoping for a piece of the candy.

Inside, Leslie put the parcel on the kitchen table in front of his mother, Nora Hall, and Naomi, a pretty 18-year-old. Nora's younger daughter Dorothy and the toddler, Samuel, ran in to watch Naomi open her present.

As she lifted the lid, there was a massive explosion. Naomi, Dorothy and Samuel were killed instantly. Nora was flung through the door on to the back porch. She lost an eye and all her teeth, but she was alive. Leslie was flung against a wall, breaking his ribs, and even Steuart, outside the window, was hurt enough to be hospitalised. The kitchen was a mass of wreckage and blood. The table had a hole 18 inches across where the box had been, and there was a 3-foot hole in the earth floor.

There were no clues to the sender in the debris. The only lead was that Naomi was pregnant and, as a matter of routine, her lover was interviewed immediately by police. He was Herman Brady, a big lad and not very bright, who worked on his mother's farm near by. He came forward immediately he heard of the tragedy.

He told police that in fact he and Naomi had been married for nearly a year – since before she was pregnant. They hadn't wanted to tell Naomi's mother, fearing disapproval, but thought that when the baby was born it would soften Nora's attitude. Herman, said to be a good son and a willing worker, wasn't bright enough to have constructed the bomb.

Herman, however, had a clever brother called Leroy. He was a mechanic in Washington's biggest Chevrolet garage, and in his small country community was considered something of a mechanical wizard. But even if Leroy was clever enough to make the bomb, why would he? And why leave it on the Buckleys' porch?

The Maryland authorities asked the US Bureau of Standards, which had a laboratory, to analyse the sweepings from the kitchen floor. Their analysts found some fragments resembling links from a small chain. Some of these were inside what had been a thin steel tube, now completely flattened. The device, they thought, had been set off like a giant cigarette lighter. The lid was attached to the chain, so that when the lid was raised, friction from the chain, passing through the tube, ignited some explosive. The analysts considered that this might be acetylene, from a faint odour given off when the debris was moistened.

Baltimore police called in Wood, and gave him the forensic evidence collected from the Hall residence. The professor called at the house to look at the damage for himself. From his experience, acetylene couldn't have caused such extensive damage. In his view, about half a stick of dynamite had been used.

Under his microscope at Johns Hopkins, he discovered that the broken chain links were in fact scraps of continuous steel wire coiled into a spring, which had been shattered in the explosion. The steel tube was $^3/_8$ inch in diameter with spiral grooves inside, grazed into the metal. There were also some fragments of what appeared to be two steel cylinders, the same diameter as the inside of the tubing, and on the end of one of these appeared to be soldered, or welded, a small disc of copper. Wood thought it likely that this was the remainder of a percussion cap that had become welded to the steel by the force of the explosion. This was consistent with the explosive being dynamite.

Wood could now see how the device worked. He sketched out the mechanism for the detectives and the district attorney. As he described it himself:

> I took a piece of paper and drew a diagram of a short steel tube containing a spiral spring compressed by the cylinder carrying the percussion cap, which was held back by a nail through the two holes in the tube and through the hole in the steel cylinder. At the other end of the tube was another short steel cylinder, also held in place by a nail. A string was tied to the nail, which held the cylinder carrying the percussion cap against the compressed spring; the other end of the string was attached to the lid of the candy box, so that when the box was opened, the nail was withdrawn, the released spring drove the cylinder with its percussion cap against the other cylinder, exploding the detonator that fired the dynamite.

One of the detectives, a countryman, realised instantly that Wood had sketched the mechanism of a rabbit gun. This was usually a .22 rifle fastened to a log with bait dangling in front of the muzzle. When the rabbit took the bait, the trigger fired the weapon in just the same way that Wood had described.

Police knew that Leroy Brady, Herman's brother, was taking such a gun apart only two weeks before the murder. He had told police that the reason was to replace the steel trigger with a brass one as he was afraid that, left in the woods, the steel trigger would rust. Wood told detectives this was nonsense. If the trigger were made of soft brass, it would soon wear away. Brady had obviously taken it apart to see how it worked.

Wood decided to do some detective work himself and try to trace the steel tubing, even though detectives thought it was a wild goose chase. The fragments had been gas-welded in a mass production process and it was just possible that this might link Leroy with the scene of the crime.

No Baltimore hardware store recognised the tubing and thought that, as it was not a standard gauge, it could have come from abroad. Wood wrote to the editor of the trade journal *Iron Age* with his problem. They replied that in fact seven or eight American companies could make such tubing. Wood worked through the list the journal sent him. At the fourth try he struck lucky. Republic Steel recognised the tube from its unusual sizing and said it was made only for General Motors. It was used for the torque rod, part of the choke control on Chevrolet cars. Further enquiries with Republic Steel revealed that the wire spring used in the bomb was part of the Chevrolet door handle.

Wood's microscope had shown that on each of the fragments were two tiny parallel scratches on the seams, probably made by a nick on the polishing machine. He visited Chevrolet headquarters in Baltimore and examined all the torque rods in stock. None showed such scratches. But when police sent someone to buy a couple of torque rods from the garage where Leroy Brady worked, Wood found identical markings to the bomb fragments, indicating that they could be from the same batch.

The percussion cap also yielded some information. It was made of pure copper and was of the type used in the old muzzle-loading guns, not primarily the sort used to explode dynamite. The only firm that still used pure copper, rather than the more common copper plate, was Remington. The police searched the Brady farm, at Wood's request, and reported that there was both a muzzle-loading gun there and a box of Remington percussion caps. When police returned to the farm to take possession of the box as evidence, it had disappeared.

Wood reconstructed the bomb, as he surmised it should have been, and exploded it in a deep hole in the ground. It left the same fragments as in the Halls' kitchen.

The motive for the crime was never fully established, but it seemed that the two brothers were in it together. Herman, who was a bit dense, must have told Leroy how to find the Halls' home but had got it wrong, and Leroy had gone to the wrong house in the dark, fearing to ask directions or put on his headlights.

At the trial the judge would not admit the Republic Steel report on the tubing because it could not be proved without doubt that the fragments the company examined were the ones from the Halls' kitchen. The tracing of the torque rods to the Chevrolet garage was excluded on the same grounds. The continuity of evidence was lacking, perhaps because it had been assembled by an enthusiastic amateur, or perhaps because protocols for the handling of evidence were not sufficiently well developed at that time.

The first jury disagreed on their verdict. A second jury convicted Leroy of second-degree murder but disagreed about Herman. Leroy was sentenced to ten years in prison and the case against Herman was dropped. The publicity given to the case led to an enormous boost for the burgeoning use of science in police work. The fact that such an eminent physicist had solved the mystery of a brutal killing helped those pioneers who wanted to staff and equip crime labs, and the case was one of the many factors which led to the setting up of the FBI laboratory eighteen months later, in November 1932.

Its first home was in a single room in the Department of Justice building in Washington with Charles A. Appel, Junior, as its only member of staff. He had a few microscopes, test tubes and some chemical supplies, and some ultra-violet light equipment. Official examinations began in August 1933 and in the first eleven months of operation 963 examinations were made. Until then, the situation had been more or less as it was in Britain, with a few universities and other laboratories doing *ad hoc* work for the police on an individual request basis. The FBI lab soon grew to fulfil a ready demand, and by its second year of operation was processing examinations at 200 cases per month, ten times the initial rate. An important element in the laboratories was the amassing of reference files for, for example, typewriter face specimens, animal hairs, rubber heels and tyre prints, vehicle paints and watermarks in paper.

A major influence on the growth of the FBI was the bureau's fight against Italian anarchists, and the case against scapegoats Sacco and Vanzetti, which dragged on from 1920 to 1927.

CHAPTER FOURTEEN

SACCO AND VANZETTI
The payroll job

U ntil it was displaced by the O. J. Simpson affair, the 'case of the century' in the United States was that of Sacco and Vanzetti, which ran from 1920 until their execution in 1927. Despite the widespread belief that the men were innocent, there is no doubt that they were anarchists; and it has been 'proved' on four occasions that the gun which fired the fatal bullet was taken from Sacco at the time of his arrest. In 1977, the US government declared that they had not received a fair trial, and side-stepped the question of their guilt or innocence.

To understand what made Sacco and Vanzetti tick, we have to look at their background and the events that led up to the robbery of the shoe factory payroll on 15 April 1920 in South Braintree, Massachusetts.

Nicola Sacco and Bartolomeo Vanzetti were Italian immigrants to the United States. They had come independently from their home country in 1908, just two of a great wave of early twentieth-century immigration, and had both settled in Italian communities near Boston. The two men were followers of the Italian anarchist leader Luigi Galleani, who promoted his ideas through the subversive newspaper *Cronaca Sovversiva,* which he edited. Galleani preached self-determination and direct action, i.e. revolution, to overthrow the capitalist government by violent means. His followers, of which there were thousands, were nearly all manual labourers, in silk factories or the construction industry, working as machinists, or – like Nicola Sacco – shoe factory hands. They rejected the state as well as the private ownership of property, and the most militant of them were prepared to use dynamite and assassination to achieve their ends.

The United States entered the First World War on 6 April 1917, and on 18 May the Military Conscription Act required every male, whether a US citizen or not, to register with the Draft Board. Aliens were not liable for military service unless they had begun the process of naturalisation. Vanzetti had, but Sacco had not. The penalty for failure to register was up to one year in prison. Galleani preached against registration in *Cronaca Sovversiva*: today military service was not required from aliens, but what about tomorrow? The authorities would have everyone on their rolls.

Sacco, Vanzetti and a group of fellow anarchists, including Mario Buda (who was suspected of having planted bombs in 1914 and 1916) and Carlo Valdinoci (publisher of *Cronaca Sovversiva*), headed for Mexico. They

133

were all tradesmen and lived communally in Mexico, doing whatever jobs came to hand, but work was scarce and they each slipped back into the USA one by one over the next few months. Sacco, under an assumed name, got a job in a shoe factory. Vanzetti bought a fish cart from a peddler returning to Italy and plied the streets of Plymouth. For a while things were quiet.

Then, in February 1918, the Bureau of Investigation* raided the offices of *Cronaca Sovversiva* in Lynn. Among the items seized were 5000 address labels for the current issue, including those of Sacco and Vanzetti. The two were active subscribers and contributors to the paper. Indeed, the list gave the authorities much valuable information. Galleani himself was arrested in May 1918, not for the first time, but was freed again. He was, however, a marked man, considered by the authorities to be the leading anarchist in the US, and his deportation order was eventually signed in January 1919. In February that year, his followers circulated a flyer throughout New England threatening to dynamite the government. Mario Buda was thought to be one of its authors.

The flyer was followed by thirty parcel bombs which were sent to prominent politicians and public figures at the end of April. Then, in June, a second wave of bombs was planted at houses in Boston, New York, Philadelphia, Pittsburgh, Cleveland and Washington. The June bombs all went off together, and at every site was found a leaflet on pink paper headed 'Plain Words', and signed 'The Anarchist Fighters'. The labouring masses were going to destroy the tyrannical institutions. Long live the revolution, and so forth.

The one fatality was a night watchman. There were lucky escapes for judges, state representatives, an official of the Bureau of Investigation and, most sensational of all, the attorney general, A. Mitchell Palmer. A bomb demolished the front of his house in Washington. Scattered around the site were about fifty copies of 'Plain Words'. The man who delivered the bomb was blown to pieces by it, having stumbled, it was thought, on the step. His torso was found hanging on the cornice of a house a block away. He was identified from his clothing and his scalp, most of which was retrieved, as Carlo Valdinoci, one of the Mexican exiles. The other suspects, among many, included Buda, Sacco and Vanzetti.

Palmer acted immediately. He set up a sweeping reorganisation of the Justice Department's anti-radical operations. With extra funds from Congress, he was able to expand the Bureau of Investigation, which conducted the department's criminal probes. The bureau had been established in 1908 with twenty-three agents to investigate interstate commerce and anti-trust cases. (The 'trusts' were the big industrial combines like Standard Oil.) The war and the US government's concern about espionage and subversion stimulated the bureau into greater activity, and by the time of

* It became the Federal Bureau of Investigation in 1935.

the armistice there were 580 agents throughout the country. Under Palmer, this trend continued with greater force.

At the time of the bombings, there was a keen young clerk in the Justice Department's Alien Registration Section named J. Edgar Hoover. Palmer promoted the 24-year-old to be his special assistant, assigned to the dynamite investigation. He was put in charge of the General Intelligence Division newly created by Palmer in his post bombings shake up. Hoover, who stayed in the job until appointed head of the bureau in 1924, zealously created an index file of more than 200,000 radicals – communists as well as anarchists – and left no stone unturned to discover the bomb conspirators.

Starting in November 1919, the Department of Justice launched a round-up of radicals from Hoover's list with a view to deporting them. While all this heat was on, there was an attempted robbery, on Christmas Eve, in Bridgewater, Massachusetts. The pay truck of the L. Q. White Shoe Company, carrying the Christmas wages, was held up on its approach to the factory. The gunmen opened fire and this was met with counter-fire from security guards in the back of the truck as it careered out of control and hit a telegraph pole. After a furious exchange, in which, miraculously, no one was hit, the robbers fled in their large touring car, a Buick or a Hudson. They were described as 'dark', not American. The authorities believed that the anarchists were responsible, using the hold-up to finance their operations. The Department of Justice reacted speedily, and on 2 and 6 January 1920 there were up to about 10,000 arrests made in a series of raids, including some 500 in the Boston area.

Arrests continued, and on 8 March, Andrea Salsedo, a typesetter, was taken into custody. Agents were looking for the source of the pink paper on which 'Plain Words' had been printed. Salsedo and Roberto Elia, another printer, were taken to the bureau's headquarters in New York where they were held incommunicado for two months. Then, on 15 April, a paymaster and a security guard were shot while carrying the payroll for Slater and Morrill's shoe factory in South Braintree. (This was not, incidentally, the factory where Sacco worked.) The money arrived at the factory at 9.15 that morning and was checked by Shelley Neal, the American Express agent. It came to $15,776.51. Neal noticed a large black seven-seater sedan near by, with the engine running, and a slightly built man hanging around. The money was packed into wage envelopes and at 3 o'clock in the afternoon it was ready to be taken the short distance down Pearl Street to the factory workers. The paymaster was Frederick A. Parmenter. He set out on foot from the office with a box tucked underneath his arm. He was accompanied by a guard, Alessandro Berardelli, apparently armed with a .38 revolver. Berardelli carried a second box.

The two men walked down Pearl Street and across the level crossing, where they stopped for a chat. Then they strode down the hill towards the factory, Berardelli leading the way. There were plenty of people about. About half-way down, they passed a group of some fifteen Italian labourers digging out the foundations for a new restaurant. Opposite them, leaning on a fence, were two smallish men in dark clothes and caps. They also looked Italian.

The sound of shots made passers-by and workmen look up. A bandit was holding a man roughly by the shoulder. More shots were fired and the man – it was Berardelli – sank to the ground. One of the bandits stood over him and fired again, possibly twice or more. Witness James Bostock thought the gunman fired twice, but at him (i.e. the witness). The two robbers grabbed the payroll boxes and ran towards a Buick seven-seater, together with another bandit, who had been hiding behind a pile of bricks. The three men dived into the car. As it gathered speed towards the level crossing, the crossing keeper began to lower the gates for an oncoming train. One of the bandits yelled at him, gun waving, and he let them through. The gunmen escaped, firing wildly through the back window of the car, and disappeared into thickly wooded countryside.

Next day, a seven-seater Buick with the back window out was found abandoned in the woods, with the tracks of another car leading away from it. Mario Buda, who described himself as in 'food distribution' (he was a bootlegger), had been seen driving a big Buick, and had been suspected of the earlier attempted robbery in Bridgewater. Police visited Buda and discovered that on the day *after* the South Braintree hold-up he had taken his own car, an Overland, to Johnson's garage in Cochesett for repairs. Next time police visited Buda, he had vanished. Now police thought, not unreasonably, that Buda's car could be the second car in the woods. They visited the Johnsons and asked them to phone in if anyone called to collect it.

Vanzetti was active towards the end of April trying to find out what had become of Salsedo, and travelled to New York. He returned to Plymouth on the 29th reporting that Salsedo and Elia were in grave peril inside the bureau. Salsedo had talked. Not only had he confessed to printing 'Plain Words' but, according to the *Boston Herald*, 'Salsedo Gave Names Of All Terrorist Plotters'. Stricken with shame, he had then committed suicide by jumping out of his fourteenth-floor cell window early in the morning of 3 May. The extent of Sacco's and Vanzetti's involvement in the bombings has never been determined, but whatever their activities, they considered it prudent, at least, to dispose of their anarchist literature. Sacco, Vanzetti and fellow anarchist Riccardo Orciani, who had a motorcycle, arranged to meet Buda so that they could use his big car to gather up and conceal the material. On 5 May they arrived at Johnson's garage, Buda and Orciani on the bike and sidecar, Sacco and Vanzetti on foot. Johnson stalled them, saying they couldn't collect the car because the licence plates were out of date, while Mrs Johnson slipped over to a neighbour to phone the police.

Frustrated, the four men went off as they had come, Sacco and Vanzetti to catch the trolley to nearby Brockton, Buda and Orciani on wheels.

Alerted by Mrs Johnson, the police boarded the trolley, and arrested Sacco and Vanzetti for being 'suspicious characters'. Vanzetti was carrying a .38 Harrington and Richardson revolver and some loose shotgun shells. Sacco had a fully-loaded .32 Colt automatic tucked down his trousers and a pocket full of ammunition. They claimed they had been visiting a friend at Cochesett, claimed they had seen no motorcycle, denied they had visited the Johnson's garage or knew anyone called Buda. Police were now convinced that the heavily armed anarchists were the hold-up men.

Buda had disappeared from sight. Orciani was proved to have been at work on 24 December and 15 April. Sacco was at work on 24 December but had been absent on 15 April. Vanzetti, the fish peddler, had no alibi for either date and had the advantage, for the police, of already being in custody. He was charged with the attempted robbery in Bridgewater on 24 December and both he and Sacco were charged with the South Braintree robbery on 15 April.

The DA, Frederick G. Katzmann, decided that Vanzetti would stand trial for the lesser crime first, then the pair would be tried for the South Braintree killings. This was a ploy used by the prosecution in the Marie Lafarge case. It has the effect of damning the accused in the mind of the jury before the real business begins. To be fair, however, Katzmann later stated that the Bridgewater affair was tried first because that was the way the courts happened to be sitting; Plymouth (for Bridgewater) came up before Dedham (for South Braintree).

The first trial began at Plymouth on 22 June 1920 before Judge Webster Thayer, a well-known hard-liner. Vanzetti was defended by J. P. Vahey, a prominent local lawyer, who advised his client not to testify lest his radical views prejudice the jury. His sole defence was that sixteen Italians saw him peddling fish on the day of the hold-up. Christmas Eve was a day that Italians traditionally ate eels and Vanzetti's landlady testified that he had been up till midnight the previous night preparing them. Several customers independently remembered buying the eels on Christmas Eve. His 13-year-old assistant for the day, Beltrando Brini, recalled the day's activities in court, and Katzmann complimented the boy on learning his part so well. Brini was still smarting at the DA's sarcasm when Francis Russell interviewed him thirty years later for his book *Tragedy at Dedham*. Unfortunately, none of the alibi witnesses were Americans whose ancestors had come over on the *Mayflower*. On the other hand, the prosecution was able to produce five witnesses who identified the moustachioed Vanzetti – some from distant glimpses – as one of the hold-up men.

The jury took five and a half hours to find Vanzetti guilty, and Judge Thayer sentenced him to fifteen years in prison. The punishment for armed hold-up was usually eight to ten years in prison. In this bungled hold-up no money had been stolen and no one had been injured.

Vanzetti duly started his sentence, and both men were indicted on 11 September 1920 for the South Braintree hold-up. This prompted Buda, still in hiding, to retaliate. According to Paul Avrich's well researched book, *Sacco and Vanzetti: The Anarchist Background*, Buda went to New York, where he bought a horse and wagon. He loaded the wagon with a large dynamite bomb and a quantity of cast iron slugs. On 16 September, he drove the wagon to Wall Street and parked it on the north side of the street by the United States Assay Office and opposite the J. P. Morgan building. He left the wagon and walked quietly away. A few minutes later, at 12.01 precisely, a tremendous explosion wrecked the street and several of the buildings. The horse and the wagon were blown to bits. Awnings twelve storeys high burst into flames. There were bodies everywhere as people fled the flying glass and rubble. In the Morgan offices, Thomas Joyce, of the securities department, fell dead at his desk in a pile of debris. The toll was thirty-three dead and over two hundred injured. Property damage exceeded $2 million.

One of the Morgan partners was a man named Tom Lamont. He was a summer neighbour of the physicist Robert Williams Wood and had seen his laboratory in a barn at his home at East Hampton. He visited Wood and asked him to help. This was the first time that Wood had been called in on a criminal case, and he was rather dubious, but Captain James Gegan, of the Bomb Squad, welcomed his help. The bomb debris had been swept up into a huge pile, and Wood rummaged among it. The major projectiles – the iron slugs – in fact were cast iron sash-window weights and were all stamped with numbers. Wood suggested that police follow up the serial numbers to trace their origin, but he never learned the outcome. The actual bomb was contained in a thin-walled iron or steel cylinder, about 8 inches in diameter, bound with heavy steel hoops and fastened with rivets. It was probably part of some other machinery, pressed into service for the occasion.

No one was ever convicted for the crime. Whether Buda was the culprit or not, he left the States after the bombing, and headed back to Italy, where he met up again with Galleani and continued his anarchist activities.

It was not until 31 May 1921 that Vanzetti and Sacco were put on trial together, for the South Braintree robbery. Again they were before Judge Thayer, who had asked to be assigned the case. None of the jury were Italian. Four people said they had seen Vanzetti in the neighbourhood of the crime on the day of the payroll robbery and seven identified Sacco. Only one of these people had witnessed the actual shooting. John Faulkner claimed to have seen a nervous foreigner on the train on 15 April who asked him if this was East Braintree. He saw Vanzetti's picture in the paper and then went to the police station where he identified him from five photographs shown him. Only one of the men in the photos was Italian. Ticket agents' records showed that no relevant ticket had been purchased that day.

Another witness recognised Vanzetti among a carload of Italians but could not describe any of the others. The remaining witnesses were of the same calibre. Sacco's photo was also in the paper before the trial. As in Cornelius Howard's case, the witnesses who recognised Sacco became more sure of their identification in court than they had been in the police station. In this case, though, no line-up was used, and Sacco was made to crouch down holding a gun. Twenty-six other witnesses, including the Italian construction team, failed to identify Sacco and Vanzetti.

Sacco claimed that he had been in Boston getting a passport on 15 April 1920. The prosecution did not deny that this incident had occurred, but the trial was over a year later. Katzmann suggested that the event had happened on a different day. Had this been so, and Sacco was guilty, then his time card would have missed a punch on two separate days, which should have been easy to prove. But Katzmann did not produce the punch cards. Sacco had lunch with people in Boston who came forward with plausible tales as to why it could have been only on 15 April that they met him. One friend had a provable doctor's appointment in Boston on that day. But it was difficult for the witnesses to withstand Katzmann's 'go for the jugular' style of examination.

The witness from the Italian Consulate remembered Sacco coming on the 15th because of the large size of photograph he had brought. Unfortunately the official could remember no other applicant on that day or that week. Vanzetti's alibi that he was peddling fish was also difficult to prove so long afterwards. It had been an ordinary day.

A cap had been found near the scene. Katzmann claimed that this belonged to Sacco. The cap had been picked up by a factory worker several hours after the shooting, when hundreds of people had been milling around the spot. The defence argued that it had probably been lost by one of the bystanders. George Kelley, Sacco's employer, was asked to identify the cap as Sacco's. He would say only that it was similar. Even when pressed by the judge, he would only go so far as to say that it was in general appearance the same.

The prosecution stated in court that a tear in the lining was the mark of the nail on which Sacco regularly hung the cap. But it came out after the trial that the cap had been handed to the Braintree police chief, Gallivan, who made the hole in the lining looking for marks of identification. He had then put the cap under his car seat for ten days before it was submitted as evidence. No one called the police chief to the stand. Katzmann brought two more caps into evidence. One was taken from Sacco's home, the other had no connection with the case. Sacco identified his own cap hesitantly, and was asked to put it on. It fitted. When he was requested to try on the cap found at the scene, it perched on the top of his head. The prosecution claimed that he was not really trying and that both caps fitted well.

A more difficult matter to get around was the guilty behaviour of the pair after the crime. The four men at Johnson's garage had quickly dispersed when Johnson said the car was not licensed for 1920. The prosecution claimed that they had seen Mrs Johnson go to the neighbour's house, spotted the telephone wires and realised what she was up to. Secondly, Sacco and Vanzetti were heavily armed on the streetcar. This implied that they had something to fear. They attempted to resist arrest, and after their arrest they gave false accounts about whom they were visiting, and lied about the source of their weapons. But the men had been arrested for being 'suspicious characters'. They were anarchists. They might have been involved in the earlier bombings. Their guilt might have been for different crimes as principals or as aiders and abettors.

Katzmann launched into a character assassination of Sacco. Did he love America? The judge forced him to say yes or no. He naturally said yes. Katzmann then launched into a sarcastic interchange with the hapless anarchist. He had left his wife and child and gone to Mexico to avoid being a soldier and had changed his name until the armistice was signed. Did that show love of his country? He had come back only because he couldn't find well paid work in Mexico. So was his love for America measured in dollars and cents? Jerry McAnarney, for Sacco, did his best to object to this line of questioning but got nowhere with a judge who allowed a seemingly irrelevant line of questioning about patriotism to go ahead. It was just a question of getting Sacco to talk, giving him enough anarchist rope.

The only physical evidence produced by the prosecution was with regard to the guns and bullets. Piecing together of the autopsy and eye-witness accounts indicated that Parmenter had been shot twice. The fatal bullet, probably the first one, entered his body through the back. He must have turned around to his right to look back when he was hit, as the second shot caught him a transverse blow against the right side of the chest. The bullet then exited and caught in his clothes. Berardelli had been hit four times. The first two shots caught him in the back, then he also turned, but to his left, and the third shot caught his left upper arm as he swung round. It travelled across his body and came to rest in the right abdomen. The fourth, and fatal, shot entered his body in his back at the right shoulder and travelled downwards through the body, doing immense damage, severing the main artery and coming to rest on his hipbone, which flattened the bullet. This shot appeared to have been a deliberate and unnecessary shot to kill, fired at short range by someone standing over him as he crouched injured in the street. It was this bullet, bullet III, which caused all the subsequent controversy.

The bullets from Parmenter were numbered 'x' and '5' by the surgeon who found them. This was Dr Frederick Ellis Jones, the medical examiner who conducted the autopsy. He took bullet 'x' from the body and marked it. A nurse found the other bullet on the floor of the operating theatre during a search for it next morning, and Jones admitted in court that he had scratched a '5' on it only the day before he was called to give evidence. The bullets from Berardelli were found by Dr George Burgess Magrath. Magrath, the first endowed professor of forensic medicine at Harvard medical school, was Suffolk County medical examiner from 1907 to his retirement in 1935. His record was unblemished. He was an engaging and impressive witness with an imposing manner, helped by pince-nez and a shock of sandy-red hair turning to glowing white. He had a reputation among prosecutors and defenders for scrupulous fairness and adherence to the truth within the limits of science. Magrath took each bullet as he extracted it from Berardelli's body and immediately scratched it with a pin on the base in roman numerals, I, II, III and IIII, in the order of finding. (This is why the fatal bullet, probably the fourth to be fired, was known as bullet III.)

Witness James Bostock, who held the dying Berardelli in his arms, picked up 'three or four' empty .32 shells and took them to Thomas Fraher, the superintendent at the factory. He said in his evidence that he placed them in a drawer. At some point they were given to police chief Captain William H. Proctor, who had custody of all the exhibits until the trial. No identification marks were put on them. Bostock said that other people also picked up shells, but nothing has ever been heard of them. Officer Shay had also picked up some shells and had given them to detective Sherlock. These were not offered in evidence, presumably lost. Their possible existence came to light only in 1977 in a memorandum unearthed by a researcher which had been written in 1921 by Assistant DA Howard Williams.

Ballistics evidence for the prosecution was first given by Captain Proctor. He identified four empty shells – the 'Fraher' shells, which he described as two Peters, one Remington and one Winchester. They could all have been fired by a .32 Colt automatic such as the one that Sacco was carrying on the tramcar. Proctor also identified the cartridges found on Sacco. They were approximately the same mix – sixteen Peters, three Remington, seven US Cartridge Co and six Winchester. This was not significant as they were all in common use. The Winchesters, however, proved to be an obsolete type, and bullet III was also of this type. None of these potential exhibits were marked at the time of their confiscation, though the stock of Sacco's gun had been marked 'MS' by Officer Merle Spear. He identified it at the trial as the one he had taken off Sacco at the time of his arrest.

If a bullet were to travel straight down the barrel of a gun, it would tumble over in all directions as it headed for its target. In order to make bullets fire straight, the inside of the barrel is rifled: that is, a spiral of grooves and 'lands' (the raised distance between the grooves) is cut into the barrel. There can be perhaps five to seven grooves within a revolver barrel which can twist to the right or to the left. The rifling leaves marks on the bullet, visible to the naked eye, which can help identify which *type* of gun a bullet comes from by the distance between the marks and by their slant, indicating a right or left twisting barrel. These marks are no use, however, in identifying which *individual* gun has fired the shot.

Five of the bullets in the case had a slant to the right, when stood on end, with rifling marks .035 inch apart. These, Proctor stated, were from a Savage .32, as matched by the distance between the marks. One (bullet III) had a slant to the left with marks .06 inch apart. The only American gun which would produce bullets with this slant and with grooves .06 inch apart was a Colt automatic. Proctor said in his testimony that the bullet was consistent with having been fired from Sacco's .32. He was backed up by the other prosecution firearms witness, Captain Charles Van Amburgh (a military title). Van Amburgh was an assistant in the ballistics department of Remington UMC Co. and had also worked for Colt for some years. He tested ammunition on a daily basis for commercial purposes, but this was his first criminal case. He confirmed Proctor's view, saying that he was 'inclined to believe' that the bullet was fired from Sacco's gun.

In saying this, he clearly went further than the evidence suggested, or could suggest, given the state of ballistic knowledge at the time. Proctor seemed on safer ground in using the phrase 'consistent with'. But this answer was the result of a pre-testimony conversation with the DA. Proctor was not prepared to state that the bullet was from Sacco's gun for sure and the DA arranged to put a question to him worded in such a way that he could answer with this useful, but possibly misleading, courtroom phrase.

The bullet, clearly marked with a 'W', was a Winchester. One of the shells picked up at the scene was also a Winchester. A test firing had been done before the trial on behalf of the defence. At this firing, Proctor, together with Van Amburgh and James Burns, for the defence, had fired Sacco's gun and some Winchester and Peters cartridges into a quantity of oiled sawdust (to avoid damage to the bullets). They were produced in court and the jury was asked to compare the Winchester shells with the Winchester shell handed in by Fraher. They were asked to note the similarity in markings of the case shell and the test shells. Burns had been unable to find any of the obsolete Winchesters for the test firing. This fact was said to have impressed itself upon the jury. A juryman, writing many years after the case, said that it was the firearms evidence which was the clincher for them.

What was obsolete about the Winchesters was the knurled cannelure, namely the milling around the waistline of the bullet. This feature had been dropped from the bullet, but the fact that it was obsolete didn't mean it was unobtainable. Burns and the prosecution failed to look hard enough. Investigators of the case were able to get hold of this kind of

Winchester cartridge as late as 1983. It follows, therefore, that it was also available in 1921.

Katzmann's case against Vanzetti was that the revolver found in his pocket, a .38 Harrington and Richardson, had been lifted from Berardelli's body by Sacco and then given to Vanzetti. Berardelli was shown to have owned a .38 Harrington and Richardson. He had taken it to have a new hammer fitted a few weeks before his death, and it was missing after the crime. Vanzetti said he bought his gun from Luigi Falzini. Falzini had bought it from Orciani, an early suspect for the crime. Orciani had bought it from another workman. No one had recorded the serial number nor could identify this revolver for certain. It was a cheap and common make. The men at the repair shop, similarly, could not identify it as Berardelli's gun. It was a busy shop; no one had noted the numbers. The defence argued that if a gunman had picked up a revolver from the dying guard, he would be unlikely to give it to an accomplice and would be mad to be riding around with it three weeks later. In any case, no one had seen anyone rob the dying guard. Berardelli's gun was missing after the shooting. That was all.

Actually, no one had seen the guard with a gun that day. The likelihood is that he was not armed. Maybe he had not yet collected the gun from the repair shop. However, it has been suggested that it was part of the insurance terms that the guard should be armed. To claim the insurance money for the payroll, it was important to prove that Berardelli was carrying a gun, and this became the official line. All the bullets from the scene were .32s, not .38s, and Vanzetti was not charged with having murdered the guards. The part that the .38 Harrington and Richardson had to play in the drama was to link Vanzetti to the scene. The evidence was poor.

The two men were found guilty after an afternoon's deliberation by the jury on 14 July 1921. They faced the death penalty but were not executed for another six years. In the meantime, a defence committee was formed which raised thousands of dollars from the Italian community, trade unions and the New England intelligentsia.

The defence lawyer changed twice and several motions of one kind or another were put before the court in order to get a retrial. In 1923 the fifth supplementary motion concerned the self-styled 'Dr' Albert Hamilton, expert witness for hire in a variety of fields from chemistry to handwriting. He had begun his career as a manufacturer of patent medicines in Auburn, New York, and, needless to say, had no qualifications to warrant his prefix. Hamilton examined both shells and guns through a high-powered microscope and photographed the result. He concluded that there was no connection between the bullets found at the shooting and Sacco's revolver. He claimed that Vanzetti's revolver still had its original hammer, and so could not have been Berardelli's. The prosecution countered by producing experts who said just the opposite.

The defence even found some other likely suspects for the hold-up, the Morelli gang. They were out on bail for another crime at the time of the South Braintree robbery and needed funds for their defence. They drove a Buick which was reportedly never seen again after the payroll robbery. But Joe Morelli, currently hoping for parole from Leavenworth penitentiary, denied everything. The prosecution lawyers would not co-operate with defence on an investigation into the Morellis, and Judge Thayer yet again rejected the motion.

Finally, Governor Alvan Fuller took a personal interest in the case. Not only did he set up a three-man advisory committee under Harvard President A. Lawrence Lowell to review the case, but he made his own investigations. It was at this point, in June 1927, that Colonel Calvin H. Goddard arrived in Dedham with his comparison microscope, attended by the gentlemen of the press.

Neither prosecution nor defence at the Sacco and Vanzetti trial were aware of the pioneering work being done in the new field of forensic ballistics by Charles E. Waite and his team. Waite's interest in this field had started with his involvement in a case in Orleans County, New York, in 1915, when Charles E. Stielow, a simple-minded farm labourer, had been tried for shooting dead his employer and his housekeeper at their farm. The ballistics expert for the prosecution in this case was our old friend Albert Hamilton.

Armed with a microscope and a camera, Hamilton showed the jury at Stielow's trial various marks which demonstrated, he claimed, that the fatal bullet came from the farmhand's ancient and rusty .22. Fortunately, before Stielow was executed, the Governor of New York ordered an independent investigation of the case. On the team was Charles E. Waite, then a lawyer in the state prosecutor's office. This time test firings were made from the gun, which fired rust-covered bullets with regular land and groove markings. The murder bullets were clean and had been fired from a gun with an irregular rifling pattern, a manufacturer's flaw. Stielow was reprieved, and Waite then spent much time over the next ten years in developing the field of forensic ballistics. His first step was to build up a reference library – we would now say database – of all the different guns and bullets and their characteristics, which he did single-handed.

In 1926 Judge Waite, as he became, formed the New York Bureau of Forensic Ballistics with his colleagues Colonel Calvin H. Goddard (an army MD with an interest in firearms), Philip O. Gravelle (a master in photography) and John H. Fisher (an expert in micrometrics). Gravelle had developed a comparison microscope. This microscope had twin eye pieces, focusing on two different bullets on the mount to give one superimposed image. It was able to compare accurately not just the rifling marks but the tooling marks, or striations, that were left on each bullet as it passed

144

through each barrel. The advantage of this was that whereas the rifling marks could only indicate which type of gun a bullet came from, and even that was only to a limited extent, these microscopic marks were in the nature of a fingerprint, which each gun impressed on the bullet as it passed. Shells, as well as bullets, could also be identified surely by the comparison microscope, as the firing pin also left its unique fingerprint.

The difficulty was to demonstrate this to a jury. The fused image seen with the naked eye could not be produced in evidence unless the equipment was brought into court. What had to suffice were photomicrographs taken down each eye-piece of the microscope. These were then cut and pasted together, the left-hand side of one with the right-hand side of the other, to show the striations running into one another in one image.

On the afternoon of 3 June 1927, Goddard demonstrated his microscope in the clerk of the court's office at Dedham to the defence experts for the case (minus Hamilton), a representative of the DA, and the press. He concluded that bullet III had been fired from Sacco's gun and that the Winchester shell had also been fired from the same gun.

Sacco and Vanzetti were electrocuted on 23 August 1927.

There was a further test firing in 1961 after Francis Russell, in researching his book, had tracked down the Colt, the bullets and shells to the house of Van Amburgh's son, himself a ballistics expert. The 1961 experiment confirmed Goddard's findings: the shell and bullet III matched Sacco's gun.

Fifty years after the execution, on 23 August 1977, Governor Michael Dukakis issued a Proclamation stating that whether or not Sacco and Vanzetti were innocent or guilty, there was little doubt that by the standards of the 1970s they had not received a fair trial. The Proclamation was publicly accepted by Spencer Sacco, Nicola's grandson. It stated that 23 August 1977 was a 'Nicola Sacco and Bartolomeo Vanzetti Memorial Day' and that any stigma and disgrace should be forever removed from their names and the names of their families and descendants. The Proclamation was not a 'pardon' because to some minds that carried the connotation that they were, in fact, guilty.

Supporting the Proclamation was a report by the Governor's chief legal counsel, Daniel A. Taylor. He made several major points:

The judge's actions would have been considered improper if they had occurred in 1977. He had asked to be assigned to the second trial, indicating a personal interest in the outcome, i.e. he was prejudiced. He was also reported to have made indiscreet remarks to others, referring to 'those anarchist bastards' and that he would 'get those guys hanged'. It seems hardly necessary to state that he should have been disqualified from hearing the case. Yet not only had he heard the case, he had also made the decisions on the motions for a retrial. This gave one man too much power.

In November 1927 the Judicial Council of the Commonwealth recommended the enactment of new review provisions in capital cases. In the years following this case, the Supreme Judicial Court, rather than just one man, has been given the task of reviewing cases. It is now required to consider both the law and the evidence and it can order a retrial or direct the entry of a verdict for a lesser degree of guilt. The court is also empowered to review the trial judge's decision on a motion for a new trial for 'abuse of discretion' and it can investigate a whole case to see if there has been a miscarriage of justice.

During the trial, Katzmann dwelt on Sacco's trip to Mexico to avoid registering for the draft, although this was irrelevant to the case, in order to rouse the jury's animosity against draft dodgers. The judge further fuelled this animosity in his opening and closing remarks. At the end of the trial, his charge to the jury asked them to respond to the call like true soldiers 'in the spirit of supreme American loyalty'. Even as early as 1926 there was a court ruling that language ought not to be permitted which appealed to prejudice, 'to sweep jurors beyond a fair and calm consideration of the evidence.' In the 1970s such behaviour was considered unprofessional and went against the American Bar Association Standards and Code of Conduct.

Another of Taylor's points was basically that the eye-witnesses cancelled one another out. Furthermore, there was no line-up at the police station. Suspects were shown singly to the potential witnesses and the prisoners' lawyer was not present. The methods of identification used in the case were prejudicial and have been widely condemned.

Above all, the crime remained unsolved. Even if Sacco and Vanzetti were guilty, who were the other participants in the raid? None of the money was traced to the defendants. Even if one of the bullets was traceable to the gun in Sacco's possession at the time of his arrest, who fired the others? The Morelli gang was never adequately investigated. The ABA Code of Conduct 1974 regarded it as unprofessional conduct to avoid pursuit of evidence because the prosecutor believed it would damage the prosecution's case or aid the accused. In Taylor's words:

In short, this was not a trial where the evidence adduced served to explain the entire event in such a comprehensive fashion that each detail gained persuasiveness from being a composite part of a complete whole. Rather, the jury was asked to find that, even though it could not on the evidence know all that had happened, or even most of it, the jurors still could know beyond a reasonable doubt that the two defendants were guilty.

The controversy still rages. In 1983, a self-styled select committee of firearms experts re-examined the surviving evidence. They were all full-time employees of police agencies: Henry C. Lee, director of the Connecticut State Police Crime Laboratory; Marshall K. Robinson, senior firearms examiner with the Connecticut State Police; George R. Wilson, senior firearms examiner with the District of Columbia's Metropolitan Police Department; and Anthony L. Paul, senior firearms examiner with the Philadelphia Police Department. Their report was evaluated by James E. Starrs, professor of law and forensic sciences, George Washington University, DC, in the *Journal of the Forensic Sciences* in 1986. The committee had Sacco's gun, bullet III, now considerably corroded, the 'Fraher' Winchester shells, and the test rounds. They had little to say about the case against Vanzetti, which was always very weak. A new finding was that the gun which fired the other bullets, including the one which killed Parmenter, came from a .32 Harrington and Richardson. (Vanzetti's was a *.38* Harrington and Richardson.)

With regard to the case against Sacco, firstly, the committee found that bullet III was too oxidised to be any use to them; but comparing photomicrographs taken by Hamilton, they came to the conclusion that, given the authenticity of the firearm and of these old photographs, bullet III came from Sacco's gun. Secondly, the Committee confirmed Goddard's view that the 'Fraher' shell was fired by Sacco's gun, based on their own test firings. Thirdly, they also discovered microscopically that six unfired Peters cartridges found on Sacco on the tram matched the Peters shells in Fraher's possession. They were all from the same die-cutting tool. This has no significance in determining probable guilt without knowing how many cartridges came from this tool, or what their geographical distribution in 1920 was. They may have been very common. So, although it is interesting, this last piece of information has no probative value.

The evidence of the bullet and the shell, on the other hand, looks pretty bad for Sacco; but it is not good enough to convict him, given the gaps in the chain of custody from 1920 to 1983. There have been too many opportunities for ineptitude and corruption, and the exhibits have passed unmarked, or poorly marked, through several hands.

Judge Waite died at the end of 1926, leaving Calvin Goddard as the supreme US ballistics expert. His reputation, and that of the New York Bureau of Forensic Ballistics, spread far and wide after publicity gained at the expense of Sacco and Vanzetti. In 1929, he was called in as an expert witness at the special Grand Jury called by a Chicago coroner to investigate the famous St Valentine's Day massacre.

Naples-born Alphonse (Scarface) Capone decided to kill rival gang leader Bugs Moran on 14 February 1929. He arranged for Moran to be tipped off anonymously that a large shipment of recently hijacked spirits was available for purchase. Moran was told that the load would be dropped off at his headquarters, a garage at 2122 North Clark Street, Chicago. Moran said he would be there at 10.30 a.m., but he was late. Seeing a police car enter the garage, he and some confederates ducked into a nearby coffee shop. The police car contained Capone's gang in uniform. They lined up Moran's men against the wall. Thinking they were about to be frisked, the men made no protest. The 'police' then splattered them with sub-machine guns. All were killed. Capone was in the DA's office in Miami at the time of the attack. No one was ever convicted for the crime, but two of the suspects were found murdered some time later, probably by Moran's gang in retaliation.

In his investigation of the incident, Goddard discovered that the job had been done with two .45 Thompson sub-machine guns – tommy guns. Later that year a policeman in St Joseph, Michigan, was shot by a car driver he had stopped for a traffic offence. He was Fred Burke, a known hireling of Capone's, traced by his number plate. An arsenal of weapons discovered at his address was sent to Goddard, who found the two Thompsons responsible for the St Valentine's Day Massacre among them. Burke got life.

After this triumph of detection, Goddard was persuaded to give up his private laboratory in New York and found the public Scientific Crime Detection Laboratory in Chicago. It was established in 1930 as part of the Northwestern University Law School at Evanston, Illinois, with Goddard as its head, and was funded by two of the prominent townspeople who had sat on the coroner's Grand Jury. For this pioneering laboratory, Goddard gathered a staff of specialists covering chemistry, toxicology, serology, document examination, microscopy and photography. At the time, it was the most comprehensive laboratory in the United States. Goddard resigned at the end of 1934, when the laboratory lost financial support in the Depression, to pursue his own researches in Washington, where J. Edgar Hoover was on the point of setting up a special department of forensic ballistics in the FBI.

At the same time that Philip Gravelle was working on the comparison microscope in the States, the New Zealand-born forensic expert Sydney Smith was experimenting on something similar in Cairo.

CHAPTER FIFTEEN

BROWNE AND KENNEDY
The murder of PC Gutteridge

Sydney Smith qualified as a pharmacist in Otago, New Zealand, before sailing to the UK in 1908, aged 25, to study medicine at Edinburgh. He qualified in 1912 and became an assistant in Professor Harvey Littlejohn's department. Littlejohn, like his father before him, was professor of medical jurisprudence and medical police and chief surgeon to the city police. They were the academic descendants of Professor Christison, who had pioneered experimental forensic medicine nearly a hundred years previously for the Burke and Hare case.

In 1917, Smith was invited to head the medico-legal section at the Egyptian Ministry of Justice in Cairo. There were many shootings in the city, and all major crimes were referred to him. It was here that he probably learned of Waite's and Gravelle's work in the United States and started to experiment with putting two microscopes together to compare bullets. Smith was having some difficulty getting both eye-pieces to focus properly and the business was laborious and painstaking, although he was able to make some comparisons from photomicrograph images.

His first significant case, using his own prototype, was the assassination of Sir Lee Stack, commander-in-chief of the Egyptian Army and governor general of the Sudan. Stack was shot by terrorists on 19 November 1924 while driving through the streets of Cairo. From the bullets Smith was able to identify one of the guns as a .32 Colt automatic with a fault at the muzzle end, producing a scratched groove, but this was no use without a matching gun. From an informer, the Egyptian police discovered the whereabouts of some suspects, two brothers called Enayat, and arranged to have them warned that they were about to be arrested. They fled to Tripoli, followed by the police, who arrested them on the train. Their weapons fell out of a basket of fruit during a search. Smith matched the bullets to one of the guns and, confronted with the evidence, the two prisoners confessed and gave the authorities the names of other members of the gang, who had been responsible for other murders in Cairo, using the same gun.

Smith wrote an article on the case for the *British Medical Journal* in January 1926 which brought him many enquiries from police authorities all over the world. So, although Gravelle's work in the States may have been technically further advanced than Smith's, Smith received all the publicity at this early stage.

Smith's autobiography, *Mostly Murder*, points to the shooting of PC Gutteridge in 1927 as the first case in England which used the comparison microscope. Smith himself, however, was not involved in this case. In England, the leading ballistics expert in court at this time was Robert Churchill, a London gunsmith. He had inherited his gunshop in 1910 from an uncle, Edwin Churchill, who had also appeared in court as a ballistics witness, probably due to the convenience of the shop's location, near Charing Cross Hospital.

Robert Churchill had made his reputation with the police after the Sydney Street Siege in 1911. In this famous incident, two anarchists wanted for a shooting incident in Houndsditch, east London, had run for cover to an upstairs room in a house in Sydney Street. Armed police and guardsmen exchanged fire with the two men from early in the morning until the building caught fire at lunchtime. The police were singularly inept and possessed inadequate weaponry. After the siege, Robert Churchill was called in by the Home Office to advise on firearms for the Metropolitan Police. Broadly built, Churchill was often taken to be a relative of Sir Winston Churchill, though a family link was never proved. The famous name, however, did nothing to hurt his reputation, and Macdonald Hastings' biography of his friend is entitled *The Other Mr Churchill*.

The body of PC Gutteridge, of the Essex Constabulary, was found at about 6 o'clock, on the morning of Tuesday 27 September 1927, lying in the road from Ongar to Romford. The constable's notebook was on the ground near by and his pencil was gripped in his hand. His torch was still in his pocket. There were recent car tracks in the road. It seemed likely that just before he was shot, Gutteridge was about to write something down in his notebook by the light of the car's headlamps. The constable's whistle was out and hanging loose, but there were no signs of a struggle. He had been shot twice in the head at close range, and then the murderer had deliberately shot out both his eyes. Two bullets were found. One had passed through his eye and skull and was embedded in the ground. The other rolled out of his clothing when the body was moved.

Scotland Yard was called in immediately and Chief Inspector Berrett was assigned to the case. The scene of crime investigation showed that a motor car had hit the grassy bank at the roadside, but otherwise there were no clues. Dr Lovell, a practitioner in Billericay, about twelve miles away, reported to the police that morning that his car had been stolen. Berrett sent the description to London and it was circulated around the metropolis. It seemed likely that Gutteridge had challenged the car thieves and had got out his whistle to raise the alarm as they tried to make off.

By the evening after the crime, the Brixton police had found Dr Lovell's car abandoned in the street. There was an empty cartridge case under one of the seats and some dark splotches on the running board which might have been blood. Earth scraped off the near-side wheels matched the earth on the grassy bank at the scene of the shooting. Dr Lovell's medical bag was missing from the car. The empty cartridge case was examined by Sir Wyndham Childs, assistant commissioner of the Metropolitan Police. He discovered that the case had held an obsolete type of bullet which was issued to the army until 1914.

Berrett felt that Gutteridge had been shot because the villain was afraid of capture, probably because he already had a criminal record and would get a stiffer sentence this time round. The fact that he shot out the constable's eyes also indicated that he might be a career criminal, rather than an opportunist. There was a superstition among certain types of criminal that the eyes of dead men hold in them a permanent picture of the last thing they saw in life.

Berrett trawled through the criminal records looking for Essex car thieves, and eventually came across the name of Frederick Guy Browne. Browne knew well the part of Essex where the crime had been committed, and had at one time been in the motor trade. His record showed that he carried a loaded revolver with him, though he had not been known to use it. He had been in and out of prison since 1909 for cycle theft, house-breaking and motor theft. A violent prisoner, he was released from Dartmoor just a few months before Gutteridge's murder. Berrett felt sure he had his man, but he could not be found.

Police eventually traced him, from information given by an informer, to a garage he was running in Battersea, but Browne was absent. He had driven down to Princetown, where Dartmoor Prison is situated, to pick up a friend who had just finished a spell inside. Police were waiting for him when he returned, on 20 January 1928. Browne had a small armoury at his home, and a further search revealed a number of surgical instruments hidden in the garage, which were later identified by Dr Lovell. They found a Webley revolver in the car.

Browne denied everything. The informer also identified an associate of Browne's, Irishman William Kennedy, from the albums at New Scotland Yard. Kennedy had met Browne in Dartmoor and the two men began to work together when they were both released. Kennedy had fled his lodgings and was making for Liverpool, where ships could be had for Ireland and the States. He was traced to a lodging house in Liverpool and, as he left the house, Sergeant Mattinson stepped up to him and spoke to him. Immediately, Kennedy drew a revolver, jammed it against the sergeant's ribs and pulled the trigger. Fortunately, Kennedy had failed to release the safety-catch and he was safely arrested.

Once in police custody, Kennedy threw all the blame on Browne. They had gone by train to Billericay to steal a car. They found the doctor's car full of petrol and decided to make for London along side roads, when they had been stopped by Gutteridge.

> When we got some distance up on this road we saw someone who stood on a bank and flashed his lamp as a signal to stop. We drove on, and I then heard a police whistle and told Browne to stop. He did so quite willingly, and when the person came up we saw it was a policeman. Browne was driving and I was sitting on his left in the front. The policeman came up close to the car and stood near Browne, and asked him where he was going and where he came from. Browne told him we came from Lea Bridge Road Garage, and had been out to do some repairs. The policeman then asked him if he had a card. Browne said: 'No.'... The policeman then again asked him where he came from, and Browne stammered in his answer, and the policeman then said: 'Is the car yours?' I then said: 'No, the car is mine.' The policeman flashed his light in both our faces, and was at this time standing close to the running-board on the off side. He then asked me if I knew the number of the car, and Browne said: 'You'll see it on the front of the car.' The policeman said: 'I know the number, but do you?' I said: 'Yes, I can give you the number,' and said 'TW 6120.' He said: 'Very well, I'll take particulars,' put his torch back in his pocket, and pulled out his notebook, and was in the act of writing when I heard a report, quickly followed by another one. I saw the policeman stagger back and fall over by the bank at the hedge. I said to Browne: 'What have you done?' and then saw he had a large Webley revolver in his hand. He said: 'Get out quick.' I immediately got out and went round to the policeman, who was lying on his back, and Browne came over and said: 'I'll finish the bugger,' and I said: 'For God's sake don't shoot any more, the man's dying,' as he was groaning. The policeman's eyes were open, and Browne, addressing him, said: 'What are you looking at me like that for?' and, stooping down, shot him at close range through both eyes. There were only four shots fired. Browne then said, 'Let's get back into the car... He gave me the revolver, and told me to load it while we drove on. I loaded it, and in my excitement I dropped an empty shell in the car.

The cartridge case picked up in the stolen car had a deformation on the base which, when viewed through the comparison microscope, corresponded to a defective striker on Browne's gun. Churchill was also able to prove, with the new microscope, that the bullets which killed Gutteridge came from this gun. Both men were hanged on 31 May 1928. Kennedy had not shot the constable, but what damned him in the prosecution's eyes was that he admitted to having reloaded Browne's gun in the car and handed it back to him, placing a weapon in the hand of a murderer. Because of the confession, the scientific evidence may have had no impact on the jury.

CHAPTER SIXTEEN

JEANNIE DONALD

The Aberdeen tenement murder

In 1928 Henry Harvey Littlejohn died and Smith gave up his extremely lucrative post in Cairo to take over from him as professor in Edinburgh. The unsuccessful applicant for the Edinburgh post, John Glaister Junior, of Glasgow University, playing musical chairs, obtained Smith's post in Cairo.

It was also in 1928 that the Rockefeller Foundation published a survey of forensic medicine departments. There were twenty-four of these, existing and planned, in the Western world – in Austria, Canada, Cuba, Czechoslovakia, Denmark, Egypt, France, Germany, Italy, Poland, Portugal, Romania, Scotland, Sweden, Switzerland and the USA. The glaring omission was, of course, England, which was at this time well behind Scotland and the Continent. Edinburgh had founded its chair of medical jurisprudence and medical police (public health) in 1807, but Glasgow's chair was much later, in 1839, when forensic medicine became a compulsory subject for the university's medical degree. It was similarly styled 'medical jurisprudence and medical police', copying Edinburgh, and had as its first professor Robert Cowan, who was prominent in the public health movement in Glasgow and who also had an interest in forensic medicine. His successor was Harry Rainy, from 1841 to 1872.

Although Rainy had more of an interest in forensic medicine than in public health, he was not used much as a medical witness, being a rather unapproachable man, with a difficult temperament. His legacy to Victorian forensic medicine was 'Rainy's curve'. He made a series of experiments to determine the time of death from the cooling of the body. He and Joseph Coats, lecturer in pathology, took the rectal temperature of patients in the Royal Infirmary just after death and then at hourly intervals until the bodies cooled to room temperature. The theory until then was one of steady heat loss. If a body lost 5 per cent of its heat between 11 a.m. and noon, it would lose 5 per cent of its noon temperature by 1 p.m., and so on. Rainy expected to be able to calculate backwards, in unknown cases, to find the time of death, but he found the pattern to be more complex than he had thought. In eleven of the forty-six bodies tested, the rate of cooling was faster shortly after death, but in another twenty-three cases the rate of cooling was faster towards the end of the cooling period. Rainy could not explain this, but using logarithms he was able to calculate, within a wide margin of error, a maximum and minimum time of death – Rainy's curve. This achieved wide currency as a rule of thumb measure, and modern experts can still get no closer than a margin of error of about four hours, using temperature as the sole determinant.

The Glasgow professor did not become a prominent figure in Scottish medico-legal trials until the time of John Glaister Senior, at the turn of the century. Glaister, who was also police surgeon to the city, took over the chair in 1898. He created two laboratories, one for public health and one for forensic medicine, to accompany the separate teaching sessions. Anne Crowther and Brenda White's history of the Glasgow department, *On Soul and Conscience*, notes that women medical students were taught alongside the men from 1907. 'The classes in forensic medicine, considered particularly indelicate for a female audience, were regarded by both staff and male students as a test of feminine nerves.' These classes were held in the new purpose-built building overlooking the River Kelvin. There was a centrally heated toxicological laboratory with gas, electricity and water laid on, lit by eight double windows to catch the best of the light. There was also a large lecture theatre, chemistry and bacteriological laboratories, a darkroom, museum and a library.

Glaister, 'Old John', was a medical witness for thirty-three years and had a keen sense of theatre. He had a spare, wiry frame, and cultivated a style that developed into eccentricity as he aged. He always retained, for instance, his Victorian frock coat and stand-up collar. His hawk-like features became more prominent after he became bald, and his white moustache added to his idiosyncratic appearance.

His son, 'Young John', was thin-lipped in horn-rimmed glasses and looked the dry, dour Scot. If Old John was a Victorian, Young John was very much at the forefront of forensic medicine. His four-year stint in Cairo had kept him up to date with the latest techniques in forensic medicine, and he came back to take over his father's chair in 1932 brimming with ideas for reform, which didn't go down too well with the old guard.

Until the Glaisters to some extent remedied the balance, Edinburgh had been the top place for forensic medicine in Scotland. In the two great Glaswegian poisoning trials of the mid-century, Madeleine Smith (1857) and Dr Pritchard (1865), Edinburgh had been looked to for its heavyweight medico-legal expertise. Not only was the veteran Dr Christison called in on all the notorious cases, but also Douglas MacLagen, a successor of Christison as professor of forensic medicine, and Henry Duncan Littlejohn, chief surgeon to the Edinburgh police and medical officer of health to the city.

Littlejohn became professor of medical jurisprudence from 1898 to 1905. His son, Henry Harvey Littlejohn, reigned from 1905 to 1927, and Smith, as noted, took over in 1928. Smith had built up the Cairo laboratory based on what he had learned from Littlejohn in Edinburgh, so it was fitting that he should return there to inherit his teacher's post.

The Edinburgh department, in 1928, occupied two floors in the university buildings. It had a large lecture theatre, specimen museum and library, and a photographic as well as a chemical laboratory. Its grandeur stemmed from the fact that when it was inaugurated in 1880, its focus was as a public health laboratory. The two disciplines had been divorced in 1897 when separate chairs were created.

All the facilities of modern forensic medicine in Scotland were used in 1934 when a child was murdered in Aberdeen.

On Friday, 20 April 1934, Mrs Agnes Priestly sent her 8-year-old daughter, Helen, to the Co-operative Store to buy a loaf of bread. It was lunchtime, and the shop was only a hundred yards away across the road, but Helen didn't return. She was due back at school at 2 o'clock and her mother soon became worried. She went along to the shop and discovered that Helen had bought the bread and left the shop with both bread and the receipt. Mrs Priestly continued to the school and arrived just as afternoon school was about to start. She saw one of Helen's friends in the playground, Jeannie Donald, who lived in the apartment below the Priestlys in their tenement. At her neighbour's request, Jeannie went into the school to look for her friend, but she wasn't there.

Now thoroughly worried, Mrs Priestly went back home and called the police. John Priestly, a painter and decorator, left work early and started to look for his daughter. Enquiries were made at the local hospital, but Helen couldn't be found.

A school friend of Helen's, Richard Sutton, came forward at about 6 o'clock that evening and said he had seen her being dragged up the street by a middle-aged man wearing a dark coat with a tear in the back. He had seen them getting on a tram going towards the post office. Helen was still carrying a loaf. A child had been abducted just like this in Aberdeen some months before, so police took the boy's tale seriously. They broadcast descriptions of the man and the girl on the radio, and messages were flashed on the cinema screens. When she left home Helen had been wearing a blue frock, blue woollen jersey with half-sleeves, black stockings and shoes and a tammy, or beret, which had been given to her by her godmother only that lunchtime. The whole city was searched in what proved to be a wild goose chase. When police interviewed Richard again for a better description of the man, he confessed that he had made the whole story up.

In fact, Helen's body was found by a neighbour at 5 the next morning in the tenement in Urquhart Road where the family lived. The building was four storeys high, with two family dwellings on each floor, linked by a communal staircase. On the ground floor was a water closet, near the back door, which was shared by the two ground-floor families, the Topps and the

Donalds. Helen's body had been stuffed in a sack and pushed into the recess under the stairs, near the closet door.

The previous evening and night had been wet and blustery, but both Helen and the sack were quite dry. Moreover, the search had been going on since the afternoon of the previous day and no one had stumbled across the body. William Topp had used the water closet at 1.30 in the morning and had left the house to resume the search at around 4.30. It seemed likely, therefore, that the sack had been only recently brought to the recess, and from somewhere else in the building.

The police called in Dr Robert Richards, the Aberdeen police surgeon and lecturer in forensic medicine at Aberdeen University. Helen was fully clothed except for her knickers and the tammy. The number of the Co-op receipt was visible on her right palm, where she had been clutching the carbon-backed paper. The sack contained some cinders, one of which was between Helen's lips. More cinders were in her hair, and there were signs of vomiting around her mouth and on her dress. Although she was found lying on her right side, the post-mortem lividity on her skin, caused by blood draining down to the lowest point of the body, showed that she had lain for some hours on her left side after her death. Rigor mortis had set in, and there were serious injuries to her vagina.

Dr Richards and Professor Theodore Shennan, professor of pathology at Aberdeen University, performed the post-mortem. They found strangulation marks on Helen's neck and, when her body was opened, there were remains of vomit in her windpipe with bruises to the windpipe and muscles of the voice-box. They gave the cause of death as asphyxia due to compression of the neck.

The time of death was assessed from her stomach contents. Helen had eaten meat and potatoes at 12.30 on the day she disappeared. These were only partially digested and showed that she must have died between one and two hours of the meal. There were two slaters working in Urquhart Road during this time. One of them, George Munro, was standing in the yard of number 59 looking towards the house at about 1.50 when he heard a child's scream coming from his left-hand side (that is, towards number 61, the Donalds' tenement). When he went back into the house he learned that a child was missing, so he returned to the yard and looked in the wash-houses of 59, which adjoined the wash-houses of 61, in case a child had fallen into the water.

Examination of Helen's vagina showed that the injuries had been inflicted before death, but it did not appear to be rape. It had been discovered in 1927 that semen fluoresced under ultra-violet light, and this simple test proved negative. It looked as if the 'rape' was an act committed to make the police believe that a man had been responsible and that an implement of some kind had been introduced, such as a wooden spoon or a porridge stick. Professor Shennan said in his evidence that a hard object about an inch in diameter had penetrated the vagina and torn through into the rectum. It had also been inserted into the anus, pushing faecal matter upwards. These injuries had been inflicted before death because Helen had bled copiously, but only just before, because there was no sign of an inflammatory reaction in the tissues.

There were other tests which could have been done for semen. Victorian tests in rape cases relied on finding sperm under the microscope, but there were two problems with this. One was that any spermatozoa found on a suspect fabric could easily be damaged as they were lifted from the material and transferred to a microscope slide. The tails tended to break away from the heads and could easily be mistaken for textile fibres. The other problem was that, unlike blood, semen was colourless. By the 1870s, French practitioners of forensic medicine had started to use eosin, a red dye, to highlight the sperm on the slide, and then in the 1890s Florence, working at Lacassagne's department in Lyons, developed the Florence test. This was the first test for semen which did not depend on finding sperm. It relied on forming brownish crystals of spermine using potassium iodide and iodine in distilled water. It was also possible in theory to use the serum test on semen, as on blood and saliva and so forth, but this may not have been done very often.

Although the whole neighbourhood seemed to have turned out to search for Helen, there was a notable exception. Alexander and Jeannie Donald, the parents of Helen's friend Jeannie, remained indoors during all the commotion. They were a dour and taciturn couple, not on speaking terms with the Priestlys, although their daughters played together. Jeannie Donald, the mother, was an ardent churchgoer and was very proud of her daughter who, she thought, showed promise as a dancer. On the day of Helen's disappearance, Mrs Donald told police that she had spent the afternoon ironing dancing frocks for young Jeannie to take to a dancing rehearsal that evening. The family had returned after 11 p.m. Mrs Donald seemed calm enough, yet her hands drummed incessantly on the table during her interview with the police, an interview which lasted thirteen hours.

She gave a plausible account of her movements for around lunchtime on the 20th. She had been shopping to the weekly market and had bought eggs and oranges, then had gone to Raggy Morrison's shop for dress material, but found none suitable. As she came home, she had seen Mrs Priestly standing on the corner wiping her eyes, and then as she entered the building she saw Mrs Topp come in from the back door after cleaning her windows.

The police asked the Donalds for permission to search the apartment. The only suspicious findings were some stains at the bottom of a cupboard which they thought looked like blood. On the strength of this, both Alexander and Jeannie Donald were taken into custody. In fact, the stains turned out not to be blood at all, but the couple remained in custody. Alexander was released when police were satisfied that his alibi was sound. At the time of the murder, he had been in the hairdressing salon where he worked.

Jeannie's alibi was much shakier. She could have seen Mrs Priestly wiping her eyes from her tenement window rather than from the street, as she had stated. Mrs Topp agreed that she came in the back door that afternoon, after cleaning her windows, and although she remembered exchanging a few words with Mrs Donald, she did not see her come in from the street.

Morrison's shop, unluckily for Mrs Donald, had been shut that Friday afternoon, and investigations at the market showed that the prices Mrs Donald paid for eggs and oranges were not those for 20 April, but for the previous Friday. She had made the shopping trip, it was true, but on the Friday before. This part of her statement made to the police could not be brought in evidence, however, as it was considered to be incriminating. The prosecution had to rely on medical and scientific evidence, which is how Sydney Smith came to be called in.

He tells the story in his autobiography, *Mostly Murder*. Smith went to Aberdeen and met the procurator fiscal with Professor Shennan and Dr Richards, and visited the scene of the crime. The line of enquiry was twofold, to look at the materials with the body in order to find a link between them and the Donalds' apartment, and to look for items in the apartment which could form a link to the child. The best bet was thought to be the sack which had contained cinders. It was an ordinary jute sack with the letters 'BOSS' painted on it in red. There was a hole in one corner of it where it had been hung on a hook. Although it was hardly conclusive evidence, it was noticed that sacks found at the Donalds' contained similar holes.

The cinders in the sack had been washed. The thrifty housewife would sift and wash her cinders in order to reuse them for lighting the fire. Mrs Donald was the only person in the tenement who was in the habit of doing this, and traces of washed cinders were found in her sink-trap. Smith tried to compare the cinders in the sack with cinders from each of the dwellings in the tenement. He sent samples to the Department of Mines to be x-rayed. They were also ashed and examined by spectrograph and by microchemical methods to see if there was anything unique in the Donalds' cinders, but there was no result, apart, of course, from the destruction of the cinders.

Fluff taken from the sack was examined and proved to contain household debris plus some animal and six human hairs. The Scottish expert on hair was Professor Glaister. He was called in from Glasgow on the strength of having written the most comprehensive work so far on hair: *Hairs and Wools Belonging to the Mammalian Group of Animals Including a Special Study of Human Hair Considered from the Medico-legal Aspect.* This was his thesis for his Doctorate of Science (a kind of super-PhD) and was published in Cairo in 1931 with over 2000 microphotographs. It surely reflected the total amount of knowledge available at this time on the subject.

The six hairs displayed certain irregularities caused by imperfect artificial waving. Hairs taken from Jeannie Donald's hairbrush in prison contained the same irregularities. Both Glaister and Smith examined hairs from both sources under the comparison microscope but although the hairs corresponded in every detail, the two experts agreed that the evidence was not good enough for identification in court. All that Glaister would claim was that the hairs from the sack were strikingly similar. The hairs were definitely not Helen's, at least, because they showed signs of artificial waving, but they could have belonged to any number of adults.

Smith examined the fluff from the sack and his forensic team were able to separate out about 200 different types of fibres of wool, cotton, linen, silk, jute, of varying colours, plus cat, rabbit and human hair. They compared these with fluff taken not just from the Donalds' apartment but from several of the other dwellings in the tenement. Twenty-five different fibres were matched from the Donalds'. The circumstantial evidence was mounting up, bit by bit, but it was not conclusive enough to present to a jury. Other items of evidence were suspicious, but not otherwise very strong, such as the remains of some bread found in the Donalds' home which was similar to the loaf Helen had bought but not like the kind which the Donalds normally ate. In the fireplace were the remains of a shop receipt similar to the one issued in the Co-op.

Helen's knickers and tammy were never found, nor was the instrument used to inflict the injuries. The Donalds' wooden cinder box, usually stored under the sink, was also missing, leaving just a rectangular mark where it had stood. In view of the fact that cinders had been found on Helen, the supposition was that Helen's body had been stored in the cinder box while all the neighbourhood was searching for her. It may have been heavily bloodstained. Helen was blood group O, like so many of the population, and stains from this blood group were found not only on the sack where she had lain, but on a floor cloth found at the apartment. Smith's account tells us that Mrs Donald was a different blood group, but he does not say to what groups her husband and daughter belonged. Spots of human blood too small to be grouped were found on various items in the house – on an evening paper dated 19 April 1934, the day before the crime, on a paper bag, on a packet of Lux washing flakes, and on a woman's stocking. Other items of women's clothing contained traces of blood which were probably menstrual in origin.

Smith had begun with the benzidine test. This was a simple test developed by Oskar and Rudolf Adler in 1904. The sample turned blue in the presence of blood, but a further confirmatory test was required. Smith's report does not state which confirmatory test was used but the wording of his report suggests that it was the serum test.

Blood grouping had been discovered by Dr Karl Landsteiner in 1901 during his time as an assistant pathologist in Vienna. It was already known that red blood cells could clump together – agglutinate – because blood transfusions sometimes failed. The medical profession realised by the end of the nineteenth century that there must be different types of blood to cause this. Landsteiner experimented with blood from himself and his colleagues and found three groups, which he labelled A, B and C. A agglutinated blood B but not A; B agglutinated A but not B; C agglutinated both A and B but was not agglutinated by serums of A or B. C was later re-labelled AB. A few years later, a typeless blood was found which contained no agglutinins (the factors in the blood which produced agglutination). This was termed O. Landsteiner later emigrated to America where he eventually received the Nobel Prize in 1930 for this discovery.

Helen's injuries were so severe that her intestinal wall had been ruptured. Smith thought that it was possible that because of this her blood might have become contaminated with intestinal bacteria. He sent the child's bloodstained garments and the bloodstained articles found in the Donalds' home for analysis at the Department of Bacteriology. This proved to be the strongest evidence in the case and could well be the first time that bacteriological evidence was used in a criminal trial.

Thomas Jones Mackie, professor of bacteriology at Edinburgh University and a doctor of medicine, found that Helen's torn combinations contained an unusual strain of bacteria which was also present on the floor cloths found at the apartment. The Lord Advocate, the Rt Hon. W. G. Normand, MP, KC, for the prosecution, had some difficulty in persuading Professor Mackie to tell him unequivocally that the strains of bacteria from the floor cloths and the combinations were identical and from the same source. The cautious professor, inexperienced in court work, would only state that there was a 'close serological similarity':

> Lord Advocate: Will you express in common language what your conclusion is about the probability or otherwise of the bacilli found in the child's combinations and the bacilli found in that washing-cloth No. 26f, having a common origin, a common human source?

Witness: I have given this very careful consideration and it is my considered opinion that the findings I have stated are very suggestive that these cloths had been contaminated from the same source as the blood-stain on the child's combinations, but I cannot say that this offers positive proof of such connection.

Lord Advocate: Is it a high degree of probability or not?

Witness: I would not go further than to say in my opinion that it is very suggestive.

Cross-examined by Mr Blades: Similarity but not identity?

Witness: Not absolute identity.

Now the judge, the Lord Justice-Clerk the Rt Hon. Craigie M. Aitchison, had a try. He managed to coax Mackie into saying what they wanted to hear by relating the criminal trial to problems that Mackie faced in his daily work.

Lord Justice-Clerk: Supposing you had to advise on a problem of how to treat a particular disease and had to advise as regards identity of bacillus in a matter of that kind, would you be prepared to affirm identity?

Witness: I would be prepared to recommend action on it.

Lord Chief Justice-Clerk: With confidence?

Witness: Yes.

The judge also asked how rare this unusual strain of bacillus was.

Witness: During the last year I have examined roughly 150 different strains of these organisms from the human body and among these 150 strains isolated I have not found this type present. That is less than 1 in 150.

Mackie had also tested other bloodstains, from Mrs Donald's clothes, and found only common types of bacteria, so this added weight to his evidence.

The defence's claim at the trial was that the scientific evidence was inconclusive and stressed the fact that Mrs Donald had no motive for the crime. There was bad feeling between the two families, and Helen had, for unknown reasons, given Mrs Donald the nickname 'Coconut'. Neighbourhood gossip also had it that Helen used to ring the Donalds' doorbell or knock on the door every time she passed, which could be several times a day. Helen had complained to her mother that Mrs Donald kept 'looking after' her as she went upstairs to her own home. Mrs Priestly said that her neighbour was just curious to see who was on the stair. But if Helen had mischievously rung Mrs Donald's bell first, it was hardly surprising if Mrs Donald glowered at Helen going up the stairs.

Smith reconstructed what he thought had happened on that Friday. Helen, entering the building with the bread, had possibly said something objectionable to Mrs Donald as she passed her door. Angry, Mrs Donald may have caught the girl by the shoulders and shaken her, upon which Helen suddenly fell unconscious. At post-mortem it was discovered that Helen suffered from *status lymphaticus*, an overgrowth of lymphatic tissue in the thymus gland in the chest, which can cause a child to lose conscious-ness more quickly and more easily than a normal child.

Mrs Donald may have thought that she had killed her, and in her panic, carried Helen into the kitchen and decided to make it look as if Helen had been killed by a rapist. When she faked the rape with a porridge stick, or whatever was used, poor Helen recovered consciousness and was violently sick. In the struggle she inhaled some of the vomit, and either this caused her death (as Smith thought), or the cause of death was Mrs Donald's hands around her throat (as Professor Shennan thought), trying to stop her screaming. Mrs Donald then put Helen in the cinder box under the sink, cleaned up and spent the afternoon ironing frocks and behaving as normally as possible.

Neither Jeannie Donald nor her husband were called into the witness box, though their daughter, young Jeannie, was. They were kept out of the witness box because their evidence would have been incriminating. One of the couple must have crept out during the night to put the sack out in the hallway. Although Mrs Donald did not give evidence, part of her statement to the police was read out by a police witness. Young Jeannie, who slept with her parents in a big bed in a recess to the living kitchen, had stayed asleep all night. Not so her parents. Alex Donald had got up at about 2.30, according to his wife, to make a cup of tea:

> We had tea and he put out the light and came back to bed. We lay quiet but about half an hour later I thought I heard someone in the back and I said to him, 'Oh, here's the men back again.' He replied, 'Oh, lie down and sleep. You are dreaming.'

Probably the truth was that Mrs Donald confessed over the cup of tea that she had killed Helen accidentally and that her body was under the sink in a sack. After a presumably horrified reaction from Alex Donald, one of them – and my money is on the husband – sneaked out to the closet door with Helen's body, before finishing a troubled night.

There was only one witness for the defence, a 19-year-old woman who had responded to the cinema SOS. She reported seeing a child dressed like Helen in the company of a tramp walking up Queen's Road in the centre of town on the evening of the 20 April.

The jury of fifteen took only eighteen minutes to find Jeannie Donald guilty. She collapsed in the dock and had to be carried from the court. The death penalty was commuted to life imprisonment, which she served in Duke Street Prison, Glasgow, refusing all visitors. She was released in 1944 on special licence when it was learned that her husband was on the point of death.

Glaister was involved the following year in a major case in Lancaster, the Buck Ruxton case.

CHAPTER SEVENTEEN

BUCK RUXTON
The bodies in the stream

Gardenholme Linn is a Scottish beauty spot near the town of Moffat, about an hour's drive, if that, from the Scottish border at Gretna. The Linn is a stream at the bottom of a tree-lined ravine which is thick with bracken and fern. About two miles north of Moffat, the stream is crossed by the main Edinburgh to Carlisle road. On Sunday, 29 September 1935, holiday-maker Susan Johnson was walking over this bridge and stopped to look down into the stream. To her horror, she saw what she thought was part of a human body lying in the gully. She immediately went back to the hotel to get her brother Alfred. Alfred clambered down to the water's edge where he found an arm and various body parts wrapped in a newspaper and a sheet. He called the police.

The local police called in Detective Lieutenants William Ewing and Bertie Hammond of Glasgow CID, who brought in Professor Glaister, regius professor of forensic medicine at Glasgow University, and Dr W. Gilbert Millar, lecturer in pathology at Edinburgh University and a pathologist at the Royal Infirmary. The experts, escorted by the police, arrived on the Monday, and had to fight their way through sightseers to get to the ravine.

Sergeant Robert Sloan, of the Dumfriesshire Constabulary, searched the area and found two heads, one wrapped in a child's woollen rompers, one thigh bone, and two forearms, plus four other bundles. The first, wrapped in a blouse, contained two upper arms and four pieces of flesh. The second, a pillow-slip, contained two upper arm bones, two thigh bones, two lower leg bones and nine pieces of flesh. The third bundle contained seventeen separate portions of flesh wrapped in some cotton sheeting. The fourth and last bundle contained the lower halves of two legs and the chest portion of a human trunk, to which some straw and cotton wool adhered. These, like the previous bundle, were covered in a piece of cotton sheet. All the remains had been drained of blood. Around seventy body parts were eventually found by the police along the stream bed. They might have stayed where they were lodged, under the bridge, but for torrential rain over the previous couple of weeks.

Glaister asked the police to gather vegetable debris from the area where the bodies were discovered. They collected two stretcher-loads of maggot-infested material, among which were further small body parts. The decision was made to take all the remains and the other material to Edin-

burgh rather than Glasgow, as being the nearest place with forensic laboratory facilities.

Glaister called in Professor James Couper Brash, professor of
anatomy at Edinburgh. Brash fitted the remains together to form the bodies
of two females, one something under 5 feet and the other just over. The
shorter body was probably aged between 18 and 25, the taller between 30
and 55, more likely between 35 and 45. Glaister thought the bodies had
been dismembered by someone with anatomical knowledge. Both heads had
ears, eyes, nose, lips and skin removed, and teeth had been extracted. From
two of the hands the terminal finger joints had been removed. Sexual
features had been extensively obliterated, all the mutilations had been done
to prevent identification.

In Glaister's opinion, the head of Body 1 (the smaller and younger of
the two) had been mutilated not just to foil identification but to disguise the
cause of death. The missing soft parts of the face might have borne the
signs of asphyxia, if this were the cause of death. The superficial blood
vessels of the brain showed congestion. There were two fractures to the
skull but it was not possible to determine whether these had been made
before or after death. On the other hand, cuts on the scalp might indicate
an unsuccessful attempt to cut out a wound. There were two bruises on the
face. One under the eye could have been inflicted before death. The other,
on the jaw, was more doubtful. The tongue was bruised and still had the
impression of teeth which had been drawn after death. The line of decapi-
tation was 2 $1/2$ inches below the ear.

A pair of arms which might have belonged to this body showed
ante-mortem bruising. There were four vaccination marks on the left
upper arm. From the state of the legs, Glaister concluded that blood had
been drained entirely from the body before there had been time for the
blood to clot after death. This meant that the cutting up of the body – its
'disarticulation' as Glaister so clinically called it – was performed within a
few hours of death.

The head of Body 2, like the first, had no eyes. Signs of possible
asphyxia had also been excised in that the lips, ears and a portion of tongue
had been cut off. The tongue was swollen, more so than in Body 1. Again,
there were impressions on the tongue of teeth and sockets. The hyoid bone
was broken. This is a small, well-protected horseshoe-shaped bone in the
neck. To find a fractured hyoid bone can indicate manual strangulation. The
one dismembered trunk was considered to belong to this body. It had five
stab wounds to the chest. Glaister thought these had been made in the
course of dismemberment.

The police, meanwhile, were examining the other items found along
the river bank. Although the murderer had attempted to disguise the bodies
by mutilation, he had wrapped them in a newspaper and other items which

were more readily identified. The newspaper gave police a date and a place. It was a *Sunday Graphic* dated 15 September containing part of the head-line '- -ambe's Carnival queen crowned.' The police discovered that this referred to a carnival held in Morecambe, a seaside resort about four miles from Lancaster. They believed that the bodies had been taken to Scotland by car from Lancashire some time on or after this date.

Sydney Smith missed the excitement. He was sailing home from a meeting of the British Medical Association in Australia with Sir William Willcox. At one of the ports, British newspapers came aboard and the two forensic experts read of the gruesome discovery. Then, in another paper, they read that two women had disappeared from Lancaster, a doctor's wife and her young nursemaid, Isabella Ruxton and Mary Rogerson. Smith and Willcox put two and two together. So did the police.

Dr Bukhtyar Hakim, who anglicised his name to Buck Ruxton, qual-ified in medicine at Bombay and London universities before settling down to general practice in Dalton Square, in the centre of Lancaster, in 1930. At the time of the murders he was 36 and Isabella was 34. Their relation-ship was passionate and stormy. He was insanely jealous and suspicious of his wife, and police had intervened already because of his violence towards her. Isabella went the short distance to police headquarters on the other side of Dalton Square in April 1934 to complain of her husband's treatment. Ruxton was brought into the room by a detective sergeant, where he shrieked: 'My wife has been unfaithful. I will kill her if it continues.' The police calmed him down and Isabella agreed to stay with him. The second time, a police constable called at the Ruxtons' house in answer to a telephone message. Ruxton was behaving like a man insane and shouting: 'I will commit two murders in Dalton Square tonight.' He quietened down only after a sergeant arrived on the scene. Isabella was in a distressed condition.

On 14 September 1935, a Saturday, she had gone to Blackpool to see the illuminations with two of her sisters. She drove herself back to Lancaster at 11.30 that evening, and although the car was at home the next day, Mrs Ruxton was never seen alive again. The couple, who had not gone through a marriage service, had three small children, aged 6, 4 and 2, who were looked after by Mary Rogerson, 20. Mary had also disappeared.

Early on the Sunday morning, at 6.30, Ruxton called on Mrs Oxley, one of their charwomen, and told her husband there was no need for his wife to call in that day. 'Mrs Ruxton and Mary have gone away on a holiday to Edinburgh and I am taking the children to Morecambe. But come as usual tomorrow.' Ruxton later denied making this statement and many others made by witnesses for the prosecution.

When he opened the door later in the morning for the paperwoman, Miss Roberts, he seemed agitated, and was holding his right hand against his body. Later that day, Ruxton took the three children to Morecambe to the house of his friend Herbert Anderson, a dentist, and his family. He asked to leave the children there, saying that his wife and Mary had gone away for a few days. He explained away a bandaged hand by telling his friend that he had cut it opening a tin of peaches for the children's breakfast. In fact, the cut was rather more serious than that. It was a slice across three fingers, one of them cut to the bone.

Shortly before 4.30 on the same day he called on a patient, Mrs Hampshire. He told her the decorators were coming the following day, that he had cut his hand badly and that he would need some help in the house as his wife and maid were away. Mrs Hampshire came round and found so much to do in the house that she asked if she might bring her husband in to help. Ruxton had taken up the carpets for the decorators, and the landing and stairs were very dirty. Straw was scattered about, and some was sticking out from beneath the doors of Ruxton and his wife's separate bedrooms. These doors were locked. Presumably Isabella and Mary were bagged up in the locked rooms by then, awaiting disposal.

Mrs Hampshire also found the bath stained a dirty yellow colour up to about 6 inches from the top. Some rolled-up carpet and a suit were in the waiting room, and in the yard at the back of the house were two other landing and stair carpets. These were stained with blood, as was a shirt and some large partly burnt towels. Ruxton told her he had tried to burn these in the yard with petrol but they were too wet. There was a partly full petrol can behind the back door.

Crippen, too, had probably drained his victim's body and dismembered it in the bath, but he didn't invite his patients in to help with the clearing up.

Mr and Mrs Hampshire did sterling work scrubbing the bath and washing down the bathroom lino and stairs. In a curious move, given the circumstances, Ruxton gave Mrs Hampshire some bloodstained carpets and the suit, explaining that the stains had come from his cut hand. This was probably true in some measure, but the cut was more likely to have been made by a bloody surgical knife slipping wetly through his closed fingers than by a tin of peaches. Next day, Mrs Hampshire burnt the waistcoat of the suit, as it was too bloodstained to be of any use, and she tried to wash the blood off the stair carpet, but was unsuccessful.

Neighbours, patients and cleaning ladies reported Dr Ruxton looking unshaven and dishevelled over the next few days. No one could recall seeing a tin of peaches. The doctor kept fires going in the yard, with the charwomen's help, for the rest of the week.

By the weekend he was telling various people that Mary had become pregnant and he suspected that his wife had taken her away to have the pregnancy terminated by an illegal operation. His idea was probably to shame Mary's parents into making no further enquiries. This ruse failed.

Ruxton visited the police from time to time to complain that his wife had left him, and to express annoyance at rumours and press reports linking his name with the remains found at Moffat. They were ruining his practice, he said. The truth is that he was ruining his practice himself by his increasingly bizarre behaviour.

On 9 October, Ruxton went to Edinburgh to see Jeanie Nelson, Isabella's sister, to ask if she had seen his wife. The police were not fooled by this charade. When Ruxton stepped off the train from Edinburgh at 3.50 a.m. on the morning of 10 October, he was met at Lancaster station by Inspector Clark. The police didn't keep him in custody at that time, but he must have known the game was up. Later that day he told Mrs Hampshire to burn the suit that he had given her the previous week. He also asked her about the carpets and when she said she could not get one of them clean, he asked her to burn that as well.

There were more questions from the police on the 11th, and on the 12th he was brought in for a lengthy interview at which the Glasgow police were present. Still in custody, he was arrested at 7.20 a.m. on the morning of the 13th for the murder of Mary Rogerson, the other body not yet having been firmly identified. He was charged on 5 November with Isabella's murder.

The case came up at Manchester Assizes in March 1936, the change to a different town being at the request of the defence. There was a lot of racist feeling in Lancaster against Ruxton, an incomer to a small-minded closed community, married, so they thought, to a white woman. Besides, there weren't many doctors in the town and undoubtedly Ruxton took patients from the others. He had built up a substantial practice quite quickly in the town's main square and had become very popular with the factory workers who formed the bulk of his patient base.

Understandably, the identification evidence was given great emphasis in court. On the day after Ruxton's arrest Detective Lieutenant Hammond went down to the house in Lancaster and stayed there for eleven days searching for prints. He found several matches for the left hand of Body 1 (probably Mary). Her right hand was found only in November in an advanced state of decomposition. Hammond was convinced that the underskin, or dermis, of this hand would bear the same fingerprint characteristics as the outer layer. To prove it, he deliberately burnt the tip of his own finger with a cigarette and, after it had blistered, cut off the surface layer, then he fingerprinted the dermal skin exposed beneath. The result matched his original prints. This dermal evidence was not called in court, but the technique was established by his experiments performed for the case.

169

The police put photographs in the newspapers of the georgette blouse and the child's romper suit found with the remains in the newspapers. The blouse had a patch under the left armpit and both this blouse and patch were recognised by Mary Rogerson's stepmother, who also identified the romper suit as belonging to one of the Ruxton children.

The sheet found in the ravine was identified by F. W. Barwick, director of the testing house and laboratory of Manchester Chamber of Commerce, as being from same batch as a sheet in Ruxton's house. Under the microscope, Barwick could see that both sheets had the same fault in the selvedge. This should have had twenty-six threads but three were missing.

Aside from assembling the body parts into those of two women, Brash also played Prince Charming, fitting casts of the left foot of each body into shoes belonging to Mary Rogerson and Isabella Ruxton. Both fitted.

Once the identity of the two women was suspected, the mutilations, aimed at concealing identity, in fact, aided the police to confirm it. Mrs Ruxton had a bunion on her left foot and her toes were deformed in a recognisable way. It was obvious, therefore, that the mutilation of a left foot found at the stream was to obliterate this feature. Skin from Mary's right arm was removed to prevent identification by a birthmark, and the removal of tissues from her right thumb was because the thumb had a scar.

The photographic evidence of the skulls proved to be the most dramatic of the trial. Norman Birkett, for the defence, objected to the photographic evidence on the grounds that it was constructed evidence and liable to error, whereas the purpose of the evidence was to show exactitude. The judge, Mr Justice Singleton, decided to allow the evidence, saying: 'I am sure the jury will bear in mind what Mr Norman Birkett and Professor Brash have said, and that there is always, or may be, a liability to error; you may get a false value from a photograph at any time, and you may get a doubly false value if one photograph is superimposed on another. On the other hand, it may be of use in some way.'

There was a studio portrait of Isabella wearing a tiara and an evening dress. The photographer had kept the negative and, working with Professor Brash, DC Thomas Stobie, of Edinburgh Police Photography Department, was able to produce a life-size portrait of the victim, the measurements being checked by mounting the tiara and dress on a frame. Then, a life-size negative of the skull was superimposed on the portrait. The two superimposed photographs made a striking image in court.

Similar work was done on a snapshot of Mary next to a low wall. The wall was found and its measurements taken. A life-size superimposition of Mary was then attempted though exact determination wasn't possible in her case.

Glaister's opinion was that ten to fourteen days had passed from the time the women met their deaths until his first examination of the remains. This would implicate Ruxton in the crime. To counter any possible cross-examination on the time of death he asked Dr Alexander Mearns, an entomologist, to look at some sample maggots which he had preserved from the vegetable debris. They belonged to the common blue-bottle and their stage of development was compatible with having been deposited in the ravine twelve to fourteen days prior to Glaister's examination. After all this effort, Glaister was forbidden by Crown counsel to put forward the maggot evidence because of the sensibilities of the jury, in case one of them should fall ill, and a retrial should become necessary. Glaister reserved the right to bring up the evidence in cross-examination, but, in the event, the defence counsel didn't challenge him on time of death, and the maggot evidence, possibly a first for entomology in court, never got a hearing.

To prove that the two women had been killed in Ruxton's house Glaister visited the house, and had much of it dismantled and taken to his laboratory in Glasgow. His report on bloodstains from the house and clothing covers twenty-three pages of close print in the book of the trial. If both women had been throttled and dismembered in the bath, why was there so much blood? A lot of it probably came from Ruxton's hand. Dismemberment had to account for the rest. The apparent vast quantities of blood were suggested entirely from Mrs Hampshire's evidence and some exaggeration might be allowed here. Glaister's enumeration in court of even the tiniest blood splashes could also have made it appear that there was more blood than there was.

Norman Birkett's cross-examination of Glaister certainly made far less of the stains than the prosecution. Counsel for the defence also raised a problem with the serum test. This didn't give Glaister too much trouble. The Glasgow professor was the country's leading expert on the procedure at this time. Although the test was being used on the Continent, and had been used in England, it wasn't used in Scotland at all until the 1920s. Glaister had therefore decided to develop the study for his MD degree. He wanted British courts to be satisfied with the test and to accept it readily as evidence. He needed to be sure that it would work regardless of such factors as age, temperature and contamination of other materials at the scene. To this end he performed over 20,000 individual experiments and obtained his MD on the subject in April 1926. The first Scottish case using the serum test was in the same year at the High Court of Justiciary in Edinburgh.

The test depended, as we know, on a cloudy precipitate being formed in a test tube in the presence of the relevant anti-sera. Birkett wanted to know what would happen if the blood under test were contaminated with soap, as applied by Mrs Hampshire. Wouldn't this produce a cloudiness in the test tube, rendering the results valueless?

Glaister pointed out that if the dilute solution of the colourless part of the blood, the serum, were contaminated with soap, the test tube would not clear prior to the test. In fact, three specimens did have to be discarded because the test tube was cloudy. It was only when the liquid in the test tube was clear that the anti-serum was added. Then, it took about twenty minutes for the mixture to precipitate, indicating the presence of human protein.

Despite Mrs Hampshire's scrubbing, some blood remained on the stairs, in particular, in the eyelets that had held the stair-rods in place. Glaister had unscrewed these himself, having taken the stairs to Glasgow with him. In fact, the stairs were exhibited in court, along with the bath, the bathroom lino and some doors.

There was no evidence for the defence. Birkett put Ruxton on the stand, but he failed to convince the jury of his innocence, and they brought in a guilty verdict in little over an hour. When Ruxton's appeal was heard in London in April 1936, appropriately, he occupied Crippen's cell at Pentonville. The appeal was dismissed and he went to the gallows on 12 May.

After the trial, Ruxton's bath was taken to Lancashire police headquarters at Preston and set in the yard against a wall where a plaque commemorates the case. It is still used as a drinking trough for police horses.

It was unfortunate for Ruxton that he chose to conceal the remains in Scotland, where forensic science, as it was just beginning to be called, was so advanced. England was not so well served. Even in the early 1930s, there was no real difference between forensic science and forensic medicine. All was forensic medicine, that is to say, dominated by the medical profession. The élite practitioners in England were the Home Office analysts. In the 1930s these were Drs Gerald Roche Lynch (St Mary's Hospital) and John H. Ryffel (Guy's). Sir William Willcox was nearing retirement and was elevated to a position of honorary medical adviser to the Home Office. The only full-time Home Office pathologist was Sir Bernard Spilsbury, who was knighted in 1923. Although Spilsbury had been used in major cases since 1910 his Home Office status was not formalised until 1922.

The two Home Office analysts were not getting younger, and there was nobody coming up to replace them. So whereas forensic medicine in Scotland was flourishing, in England it threatened to die out altogether. There had been much talk of forming a medico-legal institute in London, but this came to nothing as no funding body could be persuaded that it was their responsibility to shoulder the financial burden.

When the impetus for action finally came, it was from the Home Office. Arthur Dixon, assistant under-secretary of state at the head of the Police Department, alarmed at the rising crime rate, submitted proposals to the home secretary in 1929 for a police college, with two scientific laboratories and a photographic department.

In fact, there were already some small police laboratories around the country, in Cardiff, Bristol and Nottingham, the last founded by the delightfully named Captain Athelstan Popkess, chief constable. But outside these areas scientific support was little used. When help was needed, consultants were called in on an *ad hoc* basis. Sometimes this would be the local public analyst, who had a laboratory at his disposal; otherwise someone with relevant expertise from the local university would be called in.

When the Home Office was considering setting up the Metropolitan Police Scientific Laboratory, they naturally consulted John Glaister and Sydney Smith as to who could run the lab. Both Glaister and Smith turned down the post, while recommending that a medical man be appointed. Glaister's reasoning was that if a non-medical man were giving evidence for the Crown he might be demolished in court, especially if the evidence for the defence were given by someone with medical qualifications. It would never do to be outranked by the defence. Smith recommended a junior colleague of his, Dr James Davidson, a senior pathologist at Edinburgh Royal Infirmary, who was experienced in medico-legal work.

Roche Lynch was the obvious choice for the post, but he was against the idea of scientific laboratories in principle. The idea was that in addition to the Metropolitan Police Laboratory, there should be regional Home Office laboratories set up around the country. Roche Lynch was afraid that the independence of the Home Office expert would be undermined by this system and that the new Home Office-paid laboratory scientist might be constrained to produce evidence favourable to the prosecution. He didn't see his own government role, of course, as biased towards the prosecution.

When the Metropolitan Police Laboratory opened next door to the new police college at Hendon in April 1935, it was with Davidson at the helm with a staff of six, including analytical chemist L. C. Nickolls. Regional laboratories soon followed at Birmingham, Bristol, Cardiff, Nottingham and Preston, although the war put paid to their immediate development as segments of an integrated regional system. The scientist in charge of the Preston laboratory, chemist J. B. Firth, opened for business in 1938. His first case was a theft from an offertory box in St John's Church, Wigan, by one Patrick Mahoney. Mahoney had kicked in the box, using a metal-toed boot. Firth matched the mark left on the offertory box with the mark on Mahoney's toe-plate. Mahoney was sent down for six months. This laboratory would have been poorly equipped to cope with the Ruxton exhibits.

Before the laboratory system was established in England and Wales, the Home Office analysts had taken on new tasks which stretched their expertise somewhat and although Willcox escaped criticism, Roche Lynch was criticised for being persuaded to undertake glass, hair, fibres, dust and blood-grouping work, for which he had no experience. The coming of the new service did not mean that experienced people were suddenly found to perform these new tasks. It meant rather that the new laboratory personnel with suddenly legitimised expertise were now asked opinions on questions outside their competence.

The system still relied on *ad hoc* experts, of course, as it still does, and on the Home Office analysts until the retirement of Roche Lynch in 1954, when the role died out. Davidson, oddly, does not seem to have been called in as an expert pathologist during his years as director of the laboratory, and remained an administrator. There was more need for pathologists in the 1930s, certainly, but Spilsbury's originally solo role as Home Office pathologist was augmented by Keith Simpson, Francis Camps and Donald Teare, the 'three musketeers' as Simpson called them, and not by Davidson.

It was not until after the war, when botanist H. S. Holden was appointed director of the Metropolitan Laboratory in 1946 to replace Davidson, that forensic science began to take on an identity of its own. This was finally established in 1959 with the foundation of both the British Academy of Forensic Sciences, in London, and the Forensic Science Society, in Harrogate.

With the coming of dedicated forensic science laboratories, discoveries and new techniques tended to be more laboratory-driven, rather than case-driven, as in the past. They followed one another in ever more rapid succession. In the 1950s, for example, ultra-violet and infra-red spectrophotometry, x-ray diffraction and paper chromatography were common methods. In the 1970s these techniques were giving way to combined gas chromatography-mass spectrometry (GCMS), thin layer chromatography (TLC) and high pressure liquid chromatography (HPLC), all of which give chemical 'signatures'. Then, in the early 1980s, pyrolysis gas chromatography became very common in forensic laboratories. This technique had first been introduced in 1965 by Paul Leland Kirk, professor of criminalistics at Berkeley, but it took a few years to gain momentum.

In physics, the electron microscope was first put to forensic use in 1966 in the examination of paint chips, which, by this means, can be done layer by layer. Then the Metropolitan Police Scientific Laboratory pioneered the use of the scanning electron microscope in the early 1970s and an explosion of interest worldwide followed.

Research on blood, however, was not done primarily with forensic ends in view. Its application was therapeutic. Blood transfusion could not be carried out on a large scale at first because the blood dried out while it was being transported. During the First World War, fortunately, a medium was found to keep grouped blood fluid, and transfusions then proved their worth on the battlefields. Other factors in blood were later discovered by Landsteiner and others which had relevance for criminalistics; in the mid-1920s the M, N and P factors were named, and a Japanese team discovered that certain individuals – secretors – secreted blood group characteristics in their other body fluids, which made it possible to ascertain blood groups from, say, saliva or semen; and in 1940 Landsteiner's team discovered the rhesus factor.

Without doubt, however, the development which has caught the public imagination more than any other in recent years is the advent of DNA analysis.

CHAPTER EIGHTEEN

COLIN PITCHFORK
DNA convicts a murderer

When Landsteiner discovered blood groups in 1901, he was disappointed. He had really been looking for small, but particular, differences in the blood which he felt might distinguish one human being from another. Grouping was the closest he came. Although Landsteiner recognised almost immediately that group characteristics could be used for forensic purposes, it was *fifteen years* before the first case was reported in the journals.

In 1916, Dr Leoni Lattes, lecturer and research assistant in forensic medicine at the Institute of Forensic Medicine in Turin, was sent a blood-stained coat of a murder suspect named Aldo Petrucci. Petrucci had claimed that the blood was the result of a nose bleed, an old story. Lattes obtained the blood group of the victim and of Petrucci and put them to the test. The victim was group A, whereas Petrucci was O. The bloodstains also proved to be O. The police looked further into the case and Petrucci was exonerated. Like all forensic tests, they have more probative value when used as a negative test, to eliminate a suspect.

Individual differences, at long last, exploded on to the scientific world on 7 March 1985 when *Nature* published a paper by Dr Alec Jeffreys and co-workers at Leicester University describing the first development of multilocus probes capable of simultaneously revealing hypervariability at many loci in the human genome. Fortunately, they called the procedure 'DNA fingerprinting', which struck a more familiar chord.

Deoxyribonucleic acid (DNA) is found in the nucleus of every cell in the body. For human beings, oddly enough, this excludes red blood cells, which are non-nucleated. Red blood cells are made in bone marrow and when they squeeze out to join the bloodstream, they leave their nuclei behind. When DNA is extracted from white blood cells, saliva, semen or hair roots, it is chopped into millions of tiny fragments, using a restriction enzyme, chemical scissors. These fragments each contain variable sections, so the next stage is to sort these out by size. This is done by letting them move along a slab of gel, pulled by an electric field (gel electrophoresis). The pattern is then transferred from the gel to a nylon membrane and treated with a radioactive probe. Consequently, the pattern becomes radioactive and can be visualised by means of x-ray film. The result, as we all know now, appears like the bar code on supermarket goods.

The first case, a UK immigration dispute, was resolved by the new method in April 1985, only one month after the technique was published. DNA evidence in a paternity suit was soon afterwards admitted in evidence in a British civil court. Its first use in a criminal case was in 1987 when it exonerated the prime suspect in a double murder in Leicestershire and was indirectly responsible for the conviction of the true killer.

Narborough is a small village in the shadow of the M1 motorway and close to the county town of Leicester. Lynda Mann, a cheerful 15-year-old, lived in a semi-detached house in Forest Road, not far from Carlton Hayes Psychiatric Hospital and near to the Black Pad footpath.

On the frosty evening of 21 November 1983, at about 7.30, Lynda set off down the Black Pad footpath to see a friend in Enderby, about a mile away. Her mother, Kath, and stepfather, Eddie Eastwood, also went out for the evening and wound up playing darts with the local policeman at the Dog and Gun. When they arrived home after midnight, they found their elder daughter, Susan, waiting up for them, worried that Lynda was still out. Eddie left to look for her, and although he went down the Black Pad, it was too dark for him to see her body, half buried in the undergrowth.

She was found by a hospital porter going to work at Carlton Hayes shortly after 7 o'clock the next morning. She was so white that the porter at first thought she was a partly clothed mannequin. Soon realising his mistake, with horror, he ran up to the road and flagged down a car. It was being driven by a colleague, an ambulance driver from the same hospital. The two men approached the body.

Lynda was lying on her back with her head turned to the right. She was wearing a donkey jacket which had been pulled up under her head, with the sleeves part way up her arms. Her other clothes – jeans, shoes and underwear – were in a heap some little distance away. Her scarf was wrapped around her neck and the tip of her tongue was protruding through her clenched teeth. She had a bruised chin and had bled from the nose. It looked as if she had been strangled. Out of habit, the ambulance driver bent down and took her pulse, but she had been dead for some hours.

At the post-mortem, chest bruises indicated that her assailant had knelt on the girl to provide leverage as he tightened her scarf around her neck. Her fingernails were long and unbroken, so she hadn't put up a fight. There was no damage to the anus and no tears or bruises to her vagina. Seminal stains indicated premature ejaculation, though penetration had also occurred. Lab tests showed the murderer to be an A group secretor with a PGM of 1+, i.e. he was one of the 80 per cent of people who secrete blood group substances in their body fluids. PGM (phosphoglucomutase) is an enzyme found in semen which can be categorised into various types.

Chief Superintendent David Baker was in charge of the investigation. His first task was to eliminate Lynda Mann's stepfather, Eddie Eastwood, from the field. Ten per cent of the population had a blood group that fitted the bill. Eastwood had not. He was in the clear.

Baker set up an incident room at Carlton Hayes Hospital where a busy team imported computers and started to search laboriously through hand-written records of all known offenders in the area from rapists to flashers, setting them up on the computer. The plan was to link all information with names that might appear on the house-to-house survey. The hospital, too, was on the house list. The house-to-house teams were going back five years and this presented a mammoth problem to the detectives, as a vast number of men – outpatients and residents – had passed through the hospital's doors during that time. Many of them were sex offenders. The 150-strong team were looking at some 10,000 patients, who could now be anywhere.

In January 1984, PC Neil Bunney called routinely at the home of Colin and Carole Pitchfork, in Littlethorpe, the next village. He had with him a *pro forma*, upon which all the house-to-house statements were entered and then signed by the householder. The Pitchforks would have been a low-priority classification as the family had moved into Littlethorpe a month after the crime, but Colin, a baker, had a record of indecency. He had been a regular flasher from an early age; but he had an alibi, of sorts. On 21 November, he had driven Carole to her evening class just before 7 o'clock, with the baby in the back of the car, then minded the baby until he picked his wife up at around 9. He didn't seem a very likely suspect. He had no history of violence and would have had to have left the baby while he murdered Lynda.

By the summer the enquiry had dwindled to nothing. The crime was unsolved.

In the autumn of 1985 another unsolved crime took place. A 16-year-old trainee hairdresser said goodnight to her boyfriend late one evening in Wigston, just a few miles from Narborough. Her boyfriend walked away and round the corner out of sight. The girl headed for the footbridge over the railway. As she came off the bridge, a man was standing on the pavement, apparently waiting impatiently for someone. She tried to walk past but his arm shot out and grabbed her by the neck. He put the blade of a screwdriver against her cheek and put his hand over her mouth, whispering, 'Shut up screaming or I'll kill you.'

The man dragged her backwards along the pavement and down towards some garages. He forced her into one of the garages, pressed her up against the brick wall and made her fellate him. She was terrified. He said, 'Let this be a lesson. You never walk the streets at night. You might not be enjoying this but I ain't hurting you. I could've knocked you off dead easy.' He told her not to tell anyone or he would come back and find her.

Then he was gone. She stayed sobbing in the garage for a little while, afraid he was outside waiting for her, then managed to get home.

Her salon manager called the police next day. Difficult though it is to do, the rape victim should go straight to the police herself where her condition can be assessed by a forensic medical examiner and where swabs can be taken. The longer the victim leaves it, the less likely it is that a conviction will take place. Unless the victim turns up in a distressed state immediately after the attack, there is also the danger that her story will not be believed. Bruises heal quickly.

History repeated itself in the summer of 1986 in Enderby, close to both Narborough and the M1. Dawn Ashworth, 15 years old, and her younger brother Andrew lived in a terraced house in Enderby with their parents, Robin and Barbara. Both parents were working. Robin was a gas engineer and Barbara worked for the Next retail chain, whose headquarters were in Enderby. Dawn, too, was working, now that school was finished for the summer, and had a part-time job at the local newsagents.

On Thursday, 31 July, she left the newsagents at 4 o'clock and set off to see two friends in Narborough. She was wearing a white polo neck pullover, covered by a multicoloured loose-fitting blouse, short white skirt and white canvas shoes. She was carrying her denim jacket. The quickest way to Narborough was through Ten Pound Lane, near the M1, although her parents had told her to go via the motorway footbridge. Everyone in the locality was very well aware that Lynda's killer had not been found. But it was broad daylight. Having reached Narborough, she discovered that neither of her friends was home. A motorist later reported seeing her walking towards Ten Pound Lane on her way back.

When Dawn failed to come home, Robin Ashworth, like Eddie Eastwood before him, went searching around the neighbourhood for his daughter. They called the police later that evening.

The police didn't find Dawn's body until the Saturday morning. It was under a clump of blackthorn bushes in a field by the side of Ten Pound Lane. Like Lynda, she was naked from the waist down, except that her knickers were hanging off her right ankle and she was still wearing her white shoes. She was lying on her left side with her knees pulled up towards her chest. Her bra had been pushed up to expose her small breasts and there was a smear of dried blood from her vagina across her left thigh. She was wearing only one of her silver earrings. Her wristwatch showed the correct time.

Like Lynda, Dawn had been strangled. This time, there were severe internal injuries. The assailant had penetrated her vagina and anus and injured the perineum. It looked as if her attacker had come up behind her and put his arm around her neck, pressing his forearm against her larynx in a stranglehold. There were some blows to the side of the face, indicating a right-handed man, and mouth lacerations suggested that he had gripped her mouth to muzzle her. It was a brutal attack. The only comfort the pathologist could offer was to suggest that the sexual attack occurred after the strangulation, at, or after death.

As before, Chief Superintendent David Baker was in charge. The Ashworths were persuaded to give a press conference and a professor of psychiatry from Leicester University was interviewed on television. He said:

> I think it unlikely that the killer is someone ill in the conventional sense, and very unlikely to be someone at the hospital. He may be someone from nearby who no one suspects. He may be regarded by his family as a quiet, even timid man. It's extremely unlikely that his family and friends will believe he could be responsible for these attacks. It's likely that he's vulnerable in ways not apparent. His abnormality is in his mind and bursts out only occasionally. Once an episode of violence occurs it becomes the focus of an inner preoccupation and fantasy, and this increases the likelihood of it happening again.

And the professor was certain that it would happen again.

Many people phoned in with sightings of suspicious characters. The most promising of these concerned a youth on a red motorcycle, which four witnesses reported at or near the scene on the day of the murder, Thursday, 31 July, and the following day. The youth, who had a red crash helmet, was also seen driving past the Ashworths' house on 2 and 3 August.

A police constable on duty at Mill Lane, in Enderby, on the Sunday evening (the 3rd), spoke to a 17-year-old kitchen porter at the hospital, Richard Buckland. Richard was pushing his motorcycle past and volunteered the information that he had seen Dawn walking up Mill Lane on Thursday evening.

A few days later, a friend of the porter, another employee at the hospital, phoned the incident room to say that Buckland had told him on Friday evening that Dawn's body had been found 'in a hedge near a gate by the M1 bridge'. This was twelve hours before the body was discovered. Another witness came forward to say that Buckland, cruising about on his motorbike, had stopped him at 1.45 p.m. on the Saturday to say that Dawn's body had been found. This was after she had been discovered, but before the press had been informed.

The porter was arrested. He couldn't keep his story straight. He knew Dawn by sight, at least, but had he parked under the motorway bridge and spoken to her? Buckland was very suggestible. He was interviewed by Detective Superintendent Tony Painter and Detective Sergeant Dawe at Wigston police station.

Buckland admitted he had spoken to Dawn that afternoon. 'I saw her walk toward Green Lane [a local name for Ten Pound Lane]. I saw her walk toward the top of the lane. And I saw a man carrying a stick.' The superintendent showed Buckland a picture of Dawn and said: 'I think you were responsible.' The sergeant put in: 'I don't think you *intended* to kill her.' Buckland answered: 'I can't remember. I probably went mad, and I don't know it.'

Painter said: 'Describe to me exactly what happened.' Buckland was incoherent. He confessed, then denied, then confessed, and denied and confessed again. He said he had taken her knickers right off her and thrown them away, whereas they were found on her ankle. He denied having anal intercourse with her, whereas she had internal injuries suggesting anal penetration. He said he wanted a blood test.

The boy's parents believed him to be innocent, and a bit simple-minded. His mother said he had been home watching *Heidi* on the television that Thursday afternoon between 4.45 and 5.15 – although he had actually told his mother he had seen Dawn go across the road to Ten Pound Lane.

Buckland, who had been only 14 at the time of the first murder, denied killing Lynda. He was not a PGM 1+ A secretor. It seemed difficult to believe that there were two murderers responsible. Chief Superintendent Baker decided to try the new technology, which had received quite a bit of press and TV publicity by then. He sent all the samples to Alec Jeffreys at Leicester University – the suspect's, and case samples from Lynda and Dawn. The result came back over a week later. The same man had raped both girls, but he was not the suggestible kitchen porter. Buckland was cleared formally at Leicester Crown Court on 21 November 1986 in a short hearing that made forensic history.

With the release of Buckland, the police were back to square one. They reverted to following up old leads and new ones, but again were getting nowhere. In late December Chief Superintendent Baker decided on a new tack, to call in every male in the locality between 17 and 34 to give blood and saliva samples. This idea was not without precedent.

In 1948 a small child, June Devaney, had been kidnapped from a hospital in Blackburn, Lancashire, and was raped and murdered in the grounds of the hospital. Her head was smashed against a wall. On the floor by the child's empty hospital cot was a bottle labelled 'sterile water'. There were also footprints of stockinged feet which led from the bay window of the ward to the cot, and back again. The bottle contained thumb and finger-prints. The Blackburn police visited the dwelling of every male in the town over the age of 16 and took their prints. It was towards the end of this massive undertaking that the house of Peter Griffiths was visited. His fingerprints matched. He was a 22-year-old schizophrenic and there is some doubt about the degree of his mental responsibility for the murder, although he confessed, and was executed for the crime.

The samples in the Leicestershire case were collected at two testing centres and each male was sent a letter of invitation to report at a specified time. The flaw in the system was apparent to everyone – it relied on volunteers, there being no law to force the general population to give intimate samples, and the killer would presumably fail to come forward. In fact, there were initially about 10 per cent who did not respond, and police took great pains to follow up each of these men. Some had moved away from the area, some were pathologically afraid of needles. At least one man refused on principle. The identity of men reporting to the testing centre was checked ideally by passport. If the donor had no photocard, the police took a polaroid shot of him and checked his identity later with a neighbour or employer. His whereabouts at the times of the two murders was also entered on a *pro forma.*

The first step with the samples was to check if they were PCM 1+ A secretors. If so, these samples were sent on to be DNA tested at the Forensic Science Service's laboratory at Aldermaston. The forensic lab at Huntingdon, which was doing the preliminary testing, was swamped with samples and progress was slow.

Colin Pitchfork was sent a letter of invitation in January 1987. He was upset at being called in. He told his wife he was afraid to give blood because of the earlier flashing convictions and failed to report. When a second letter came, two weeks later, Carole told him in no uncertain terms to take the test. He was in a spot.

He wriggled off the hook by persuading a colleague at the bakery, Ian Kelly, to take the test for him. His story was that he had already taken the test for another man. The other man, Colin said, had a previous conviction for flashing and was scared to take the test and had persuaded Colin to help him out. As Pitchfork didn't live in the village at the time of the first murder he thought he wouldn't be called in. Now he had himself received a letter. Would his colleague help him out? It took some pleading. Eventually Kelly gave in. The pair of them took passport photos of the stand-in at the photo booth on Leicester railway station and Colin substituted his friend's picture for his own in his passport, resealing the lamination with transparent glue. It was surprisingly easy. But calamity struck on the 27th, the day of the test. Kelly had a temperature of 103. Pitchfork needed all his persuasive skills to persuade him from his sick-bed and into the testing centre. He drove him there himself to the evening session and waited outside, then drove him home again. When he returned home, Pitchfork pricked his arm with a pin, put a plaster over it and made much of the experience to his wife.

By May that year, getting on for 4000 samples had been taken, but only 2000 had been checked, due to a backlog at the lab. The response rate was up to 98 per cent, and there were about 1000 more men to do.

In June, a blonde 17-year-old girl accepted a lift from Colin Pitchfork just after midnight. She had had a row with her boyfriend and was walking home alone. When Pitchfork took a wrong turning and headed down a country lane, she grabbed the steering wheel and he had to hang on and slam on the brakes. The girl sobbed hysterically that she wanted to go home, while Pitchfork tried the old line, 'I thought you wanted it'. He obligingly turned the car round and drove her back to the A6. He pulled up and leant over the girl to open the passenger door, but he held on to the handle and said, 'Give me a kiss then.' The girl threw herself against the door and ran off, crying.

The anniversary of Dawn's death came round and still there was no arrest. The Ashworths managed to avoid 31 July altogether by flying to Australia to visit relatives. They left on 30 July and arrived in Sydney on 1 August, crossing the international dateline on the way.

Keeping a secret, especially a big one, is very difficult. Some of the bakery staff were at lunch that 1 August in the Clarendon, a Leicester pub, when Pitchfork's stand-in spilled the beans in a gossip session about his colleague. The manager of one of the bakery shops was in the party and was disturbed by the news. She decided to phone the son of the Clarendon's publican, a police constable, for advice, but he was on holiday. It was September before she got around to it.

The constable immediately phoned the inquiry team. A detective inspector pulled out the old house-to-house *pro forma* on Pitchfork from the Mann investigation and compared the signature with the one taken at the blood testing in January. They didn't match. The manager's story was checked out and the decision was made to arrest Pitchfork. The police called at his house after he came home from work. He put up no resistance. At the police station, he was only too willing to talk.

In 1983 the couple were apparently living a perfectly normal, ordinary married life. Carole knew that he had convictions for exposing himself but forgave him, thinking them youthful misdemeanours. It was more difficult to forgive his infidelities, but she had a baby to consider. They decided to make a fresh start, and to bring up their new child in the countryside. In November 1983 they were on the point of moving to Littlethorpe from Leicester and had found a house in Haybarn Close. The aptness of the street name amused the Pitchforks and they arranged to move in before Christmas.

On 21 November, therefore, they were still living in Leicester, with Carole ignorant of the fact that her husband was still a regular flasher. That evening Colin planned to make tapes from some records so they would have

183

continuous music at their leaving party a few days later. First, he ran Carole to her evening class in his Ford Escort, putting the baby on the back seat in a carry cot. On the way back, he made a detour, looking for a girl to expose himself to. He needed a girl, a lonely spot and a street light: there was no point in flashing in the dark. Lynda, walking home alone, fitted the bill. He parked the car in a drive opposite the psychiatric hospital near where Lynda lived, and waited under the street light for the girl to approach. Then he flashed her. Shocked, she made a bad decision. She ran off the streetlit road towards the dark footpath and then froze, perhaps realising her mistake. Pitchfork, excited, went up to her and grabbed her.

In his interview he blamed Lynda for her own murder. 'One per cent of the time you get someone who goes mad and screams and you have to disappear quick. But all the others walk by you. Just walk *by* you and ignore you. But *she* turned and ran into a dark footpath. She backed *herself* into a corner.'

He confessed everything to the police on tape. Lynda had let him rape her, calm but frightened, hoping he would let her go, but then Pitchfork realised, rather late in the day, that he was coming to live in Narborough in a month's time and she would undoubtedly see him around the village. He had to kill her. Then he collected the car, with the baby in the back, went home and continued taping music for the party before collecting Carole from her evenng class. He didn't feel the need to expose himself to any girls for six or eight months after that.

By the time of Dawn's murder, in 1986, he was the father of two, a toddler and a new baby, born in January. On the afternoon of Dawn's death, Pitchfork was out on his motorbike, a Honda 70, having set out to buy food colouring for a cake. He got off the bike and followed Dawn down the footpath. Again his intention was to flash her. Again he exposed himself, and then blamed the girl for her own murder. He expected her to walk on by, or at least run back the way she had come. Instead she went sideways and jumped into the gateway of the field. He pushed her, and once he had physical contact with her, his excitement took over again. She screamed and he grabbed her, pushing her into the field. Like Lynda, she submitted fearfully to the rape, hoping to be released, but when she sat up, she faced away from him for a moment and he got her from behind in a stranglehold. His account was much more coherent and plausible than that of the kitchen porter. He denied, despite medical evidence, that he had raped her again near the point of death. He showed no remorse. After the murder he hid Dawn's body, rode off to find his food colouring and baked a cake.

He pleaded guilty at Leicester Crown Court on 22 January 1988 not just to the murders, but to two indecent assaults and to perverting the course of justice by letting a stand-in take his blood test. He was given a double life sentence for the murders, a ten-year sentence for each of the rapes and three years each for sexual assaults in 1979 and 1985, plus three years for perverting the course of justice, the sentences to run concurrently.

He had admitted to flashing a thousand girls, but why kill two of them, and why let other girls go? Wambaugh suggests in *The Blooding* that Pitchfork was into control. The two murdered girls let him control them, but the girl who grabbed at the steering wheel was dangerous. He couldn't control her. She would fight for her life. She would mark him, and he lived with his wife, who was always checking up on him because of his infidelities.

Rapists have been categorised into four types and each may respond in a different way to resistance. The victim can hardly be expected to decide on the spur of the moment about the category to which her attacker belongs. The classic sexual rapist usually lacks social skills and appears passive and submissive. He has a poor self-image and possesses unusually strong sexual urges which he feels he can satisfy only through attack. He may have a history of petty sex offences. He is likely to jump out at his victim, saying nothing or simply threatening her. This type is the most likely to back off if offered verbal or physical resistance.

The anger rapist is usually a man with a dominant woman in his life, be it mother, girlfriend or wife. He may be attractive with social graces but will become enraged if his masculinity is threatened. His aim is to dominate, degrade and control. His attacks are often related to a breakdown in an existing relationship and attacks may occur near his home. He is likely to display abusive language and violence. Physical resistance will probably make this type worse. It is best to talk to him and do whatever seems best to stay alive. Urinating, fainting and faking an epileptic fit may be effective, non-provoking forms of resistance.

The sadistic rapist is rare and the most dangerous. He may use an implement in his sexual attack and take his victims to a safe area where he can keep them for several hours. He is turned on by his victims' fear and pain. Keep calm and constantly look for moments to make an escape. Don't attempt physical resistance.

The sociopathic rapist is primarily a criminal who begins to rape while committing other crimes. Most crimes, therefore, occur in the victims' homes. This type doesn't usually resort to violence, although it may be threatened. Other rapists in this category may use social skills to engage their victims in what looks like the promise of a relationship. Beware of the salesman who asks you for a date, or the man who asks you out for a drink after work. With this type of rapist, the victim can end up feeling guilty for having 'asked for it', for not having seen it coming. Try assertiveness, and talking one-to-one before trying any physical tactics.

This advice is from Ray Wyre, author of *Women, Men and Rape*, and is quoted in Diana Lamplugh's book, *Beating Aggression: A Practical Guide for Working Women*. Diana is the mother of estate agent Suzy Lamplugh, who was abducted on 28 July 1986 and has never been seen since. Diana runs the Suzy Lamplugh Trust, 14 East Sheen Avenue, London SW14 8AS, and, having lost her daughter, devotes her life now to protecting the rest of us.

She has this advice, if physical resistance seems appropriate:

(1)   Try to make the knee your first target – it is the weakest joint and when struck or kicked properly it is totally disabled. Remember that when your kick lands, your knee must still be bent. Aim to kick through, not at, the knee.

(2)   The solar plexus is a vital striking area. It is the centre of a web of nerves and a forceful blow with an elbow, umbrella or walking stick has a paralysing effect. The attacker will feel a deep sense of nausea so intense that even a drunkard or a person high on drugs can be stopped.

(3)   The elbow joint is also very weak. Strike the elbow joint with the palm of your hand when the attacker's arm is straight. At the same time, jerk his wrist against the pressure. It is very painful and disabling.

(4)   Under the armpit, slightly to the front, is a very vulnerable spot. It is an area rich in nerves and arteries and a walking stick, umbrella point, key or ballpoint pen jabbed here causes intense pain.

(5)   The large area running down the side of the rib cage. Any blow here can be painful. A palm or heel, a bunch of keys, a pencil or pen, stick or umbrella, even a hardback book, especially if the strike is hard, will cause great pain.

(6)   The shin bone is another prime target. A vicious kick with the inside of your shoe will cause intense pain, even more if you can scrape the edge of your shoe down the shin and stamp on one leg and be sure you can get away.

(7)   The face. Dig in deep under the cheekbone with your thumbs, pencil or key and at the same time push upwards. Try twisting the ears off or shout down them; slap both sides of the head. A sharp quick strike between the eyes can knock your attacker unconscious. If your life is in danger, strike hard.

(8)   The fingers. Bend any finger right back (not just a little way). Stamp on them, bite them, pull them apart. A broken finger is completely disabling.

Do not try aiming at his eyes with your fingers. Most of us find that psychologically impossible and you may draw back at the vital moment and find yourself in an even more vulnerable position. Also avoid trying to knee your attacker in the groin or testicles. This area is usually far too high to be able to reach easily and men are naturally very protective of this part of their body. If you miss you will be left in a highly vulnerable position in which you can easily be pushed over flat on your back.

All you need to do is to disable your attacker and then leave the scene. If you do manage to free yourself, run away immediately. Don't stop to have one more go at him or to see what you have done. The idea is to 'bash' and 'dash'.

CHAPTER NINETEEN

TIMOTHY SPENCER
The first DNA execution

Carolyn Hamm was a 32-year-old lawyer practising in Arlington, Virginia, specialising in architectural preservation. In January 1984, when she failed to arrive at her office two days in a row, her secretary phoned her boss's squash partner, Darla Henry,* and asked her to call at Carolyn's house to see if she was all right. Darla drove past the house, in middle-class South Arlington, in her lunch hour and, seeing Carolyn's car outside, at first thought that everything was fine. But then she noticed that the front door was slightly ajar and that an inch or two of snow had drifted into the doorway.

Becoming alarmed now, Darla got out of the car and peered through the open door. There was mail on the floor of the hallway, and silence. At the far end of the street she could see a neighbour, Larry Ranser, pulling out of his driveway. She called him over and together they cautiously stepped into the house. It was in its usual state of untidiness. Even so, Darla was shocked to see her friend's leather handbag open in the hallway with the contents scattered around it – wallet, cheque book, coins, aspirin, driving licence, business cards, but no notes. In the bathroom, Carolyn's glasses were on the edge of the basin and her squash clothes were in a heap on the floor. Darla and Ranser looked in all the rooms upstairs, but there was no sign of Carolyn. Moving downstairs, they found her dark blue towelling bathrobe crumpled on the living-room rug. Everything else looked in place, except for a length of stereo speaker wire hanging over a chair and a pile of Venetian blind cord lying on the floor.

They found the lawyer's naked body in the basement, lying in the doorway between the utility area and the garage. Her wrists were tied behind her back with Venetian blind cord, and a section of rope, cut from a rolled up carpet nearby, was noosed around her neck. It was looped up over a water pipe and then down into the garage, where it was tied to the bumper of Carolyn's second car, a blue Fiat. There were no visible signs of injury or a struggle, no blood or bruises, just her chestnut shoulder-length hair caught up in the rope that had hanged her.

The medical examiner found petroleum jelly in the pubic hair and around the mouth. Lab tests established the presence of spermatozoa in her

---

*My main source for this chapter is Paul Mones' *Stalking Justice* (Pocket Books, New York, 1995). Mones changes some witness names to protect their privacy.

vagina as well as on the labia and thighs, plus semen stains on the bathrobe in the living room. The time of death was sometime after 10 p.m. on 23 January 1984. The fact that her bag was in the hallway suggested that the killer had broken in some time earlier and had awaited her return.

The case was assigned to Bob Carrig and Chuck Shelton of the Arlington Police Department robbery–homicide unit, to the chagrin of Detective Joe Horgas, a sixteen-year veteran of the department. He had been visiting his in-laws in Pennsylvania when the call had come in. There were only four or five homicides in Arlington per year, so the team worked mostly on robberies. It was Joe's turn, he reasoned, to investigate the next murder. Instead, he had to work through the papers that had landed on his desk in his absence – the 'hot sheets'.

He learned that there had been two break-ins while he had been away, just a few blocks away from the Hamm murder address in South Arlington. Wilma Thoreau had come home from work on 20 January to find that a burglar had broken in through a basement window and had stolen $40 and two gold chains. The curious thing was that the intruder had left certain items behind. These included a paper bag containing three pornographic magazines, a carrot and a length of Venetian blind cord, which were left on the bed. At the foot of the bed was a bucket containing some bags of marijuana, other items relating to drug use, which Wilma had not seen before, and a vial of white powder which turned out to be procaine, sometimes used as a sexual stimulant. It was later discovered that the unfamiliar items belonged to her neighbour. He had also been burgled but, due to embarrassment, had not reported the loss. The *modus operandi* had features in common with the Hamm murder. If Wilma Thoreau had not been late home she might have suffered the same fate.

The second break-in was in the same neighbourhood on the day that Carolyn Hamm's body was discovered. Marcie Sanders came home to find a black male, in his early 20s, in the house wearing a home-made mask and carrying a serrated knife. He took a few dollars from her bag and dumped it on the floor of the upstairs landing. Then he forced her downstairs into the kitchen, made her take off her clothes and gave her a dildo which he had stolen from one of her neighbours. When she refused his demands to use the dildo on herself, he punched her four or five times across the face and cut her across her right calf. Then he grabbed her by the hair and held the knife to her eyes, forcing her to fellate him. After a few minutes he said, 'We're going for a ride now, bitch.' She screamed and kicked her way to the car, afraid – with some justification – for her life. He punched her a few more times and suddenly he was gone, over the back yard fence and away.

It seemed too much of a coincidence that a murderer and a masked rapist were both working the same district, but when someone was arrested for Carolyn's murder, it turned out to be a white man. As a matter of routine, Larry Ranser, the neighbour who had discovered Carolyn's body, was called into the police department about a week later for questioning and fingerprinting. After this interview, Ranser's protective sister Muriel called in to say that at around 8.15 p.m. on the evening of the murder she had seen a man called David Vasquez in the street.

Vasquez, of Latin descent, was a janitor from Muriel's high school some fifteen years previously. He was rumoured at that time to have stolen certain items of clothing from the girls' locker room. She said that Vasquez stared at her in the street and this gave her a creepy feeling. In the past she had always gone inside the house when she saw Vasquez around.

An independent sighting of Vasquez in the road came into the police the same day from a retired military officer, Michael Ansari, who recognised a man called Dave, possibly a school maintenance man. He was white, around 5 feet 10 inches, of Latin descent, medium build. The police report read:

> On the day of the homicide investigation, Dave came to the corner of 23rd and S. Culpepper Streets, looked a while [at the police activity], then left. It was strange to Mr Ansari who stated the whole world was interested in what happened, except Dave.

Vasquez had lodged with Arnold and Debra Harrison, just round the corner from the Hamm residence, until moving recently to Manassas (25 miles away) to live with his mother. He worked as a janitor at McDonalds in Manassas, but sometimes visited the Harrisons, who were genuinely surprised to learn from the police that he had been on the block the previous week. They had not seen him since November 1983. Police found soft porn magazines in his room and some 'peeper' photos. These were shots of scantily dressed women and high-school girls in sports wear taken from a distance, and without the subjects' knowledge.

Detectives Carrig and Shelton visited the FBI's Behavioral Science Unit at Quantico, Virginia, where they met John Douglas and Roy Hazelwood. They discussed the evidence, and showed the FBI men the ropes, the photos from the scene and the autopsy report. Hazelwood and Douglas suggested that the perpetrator might be a white male in his thirties either with a partner or having both a mature and immature side to his nature: mature because of ornate bindings to the wrists and because there was no sign of a struggle or bruising, immature because the handbag had been turned out in the hallway.

They pulled in Vasquez. He said he had been bowling in Manassas on the day of the murder. He had not been to Arlington since November.

Shelton said there had been a burglary in Arlington and asked: 'Is there any reason why your fingerprints should be inside that house?' It was standard procedure. After some intensive questioning about the Hamm murder, Vasquez confessed. In all, he made three confessions, the third being in the form of a dream, 'a horrible dream'. He had broken into the house and cut his hand on the window. The tale sounded like a fantasy from a porn magazine. He had gone upstairs to get help for his cut hand and had startled Carolyn who screamed at the intruder and then demanded sex with bondage, asking him to hang her first by throwing a rope over the basement beam and tying it to the car.

The sensation of choking, or creating mild asphyxiation in some way, heightens sexual satisfaction and the police are sometimes called to auto-erotic accidental deaths. The victim, usually male, is sometimes found strangled by a rope tied, perhaps, to the bedpost after a private session has gone wrong. These deaths at first sight can look like murder. Was Vasquez trying to wriggle out of culpability by suggesting that Carolyn was into achieving sexual satisfaction this way?

The mild-mannered janitor was arrested on 6 February for Carolyn Hamm's murder. Factors against Vasquez being the killer were that he was physically weak. He had difficulty lifting even 30 lb boxes from McDonald's supply trucks. Carolyn was about 30 lbs heavier than he was himself. He didn't drive, and couldn't have got back to Manassas in time for work at 7 a.m. unless he had a partner. He didn't seem bright enough to think through and carry out the crime by himself. Although his hair had the same characteristics as hair found on Carolyn's body, his semen didn't match the case samples. Vasquez was an O group secretor with a PGM of 2–1. Semen found on Carolyn's bathrobe was also from a type O secretor but it was PGM 1+. The fact that Vasquez was a different semen type did not rule him out. The semen might have been from an earlier lover, or might have been from an accomplice. And, after all, Vasquez had confessed.

Before his trial, Vasquez's lawyers had their client take a lie detector test. He maintained essentially the same story as in the dream 'confession'. The lie detector expert, a physician, informed his lawyer, Rich McCue, that the test showed Vasquez had been in Carolyn's home on the night of her death. It was not a dream. Because of Vasquez's suggestibility, McCue was afraid his client would condemn himself to death under cross-examination. He entered into a bargain with the Commonwealth attorney, Henry Hudson, to permit Vasquez to plead to second degree murder and burglary. This would carry a sentence of thirty-five years, but he would be eligible for parole in seven years.

Vasquez was still in prison, on 1 December 1987, when Detective Joe Horgas was called to a homicide again in polite, lawned South Arlington. Susan Tucker, who lived only a few blocks away from Carolyn Hamm's house, had not been seen for several days, nor had she answered her phone. Eventually, a worried neighbour dialled 911. When patrolmen William Griffith and Dan Borelli shone a torch into the house through the partially open back door they could see a handbag on the floor with its contents scattered on the floor.

The patrolmen found Susan Tucker's body face down across her bed. A sleeping bag was draped over the lower part of her back and legs. A white nylon rope was wrapped around her neck and ran down her back, where it was tied several times round each wrist. Her hands were connected by a foot of rope, and from the centre of that was yet another rope, about 2 feet long.

As the police team went about their business, photographing the scene, ribboning off the area, gathering forensic evidence, the phone rang incessantly. Eventually an officer answered it. It was Reggie Tucker, Susan's Welsh husband. He had left Arlington three months earlier to look for work in Wales, and Susan was soon due to give up her job as a publications editor for the US Forestry Service to join him on the other side of the Atlantic. Tucker was frantic with worry when his calls were not answered. He was devastated by her death.

When the forensic team had finished, Horgas and the police team moved into the house. A small window in the laundry area, above the washer-dryer, had been punched out and fragments of broken glass lay up to several feet away. The top of the washer-dryer had been wiped clean. Burglary did not seem to be the main motive; a collection of commemorative and foreign coins remained in the bedroom, although they had been disturbed and lay around the shoe box which had contained them. The killer knew better than to take coins that could easily be traced back to him.

The forensic team had found no useful fingerprints. He had obviously worn gloves. There were a few dark hairs picked off the victim's breast, but no one yet to match them to. The broken window was removed and extensively tested for prints, blood and fibres. The only item of interest was a facecloth found by a neighbour hanging from a tree. Reggie Tucker later identified it as Susan's.

Cause of death was strangulation. Everything about the case shouted to the police that it was Carolyn's Hamm's killer at work again, yet David Vasquez was in prison for that crime.

Routine investigation covered more than interviewing the neighbours. All the recent 911 calls were evaluated, as were all crime reports and FORs, or Field Observation Reports – questionings of suspicious-looking individuals stopped by the police. There had been a nearby break-in on 6 November by a masked prowler who fled when he was spotted by one of the occupants. On the 8th, a man in an army fatigue jacket had been seen hiding in the bushes around the corner from the Tucker home. Screams were heard in the middle of the night on Sunday to Monday (29–30 November).

It appeared that Susan had been killed sometime during the weekend, the first after Thanksgiving. Her husband had spoken to her on Friday 27 November at 6.30. No one had seen her or spoken to her since then.

Tucker, a slightly built man with a dark beard, was in Wales at the time of Susan's death. He told police that his wife had regular habits. She left for work at 6.30 a.m. on a number 6 bus and arrived home the same way at about 6.30 in the evening. Nothing had been taken from the scene that might later connect the murderer with the crime, such as credit cards. The only possible lead was Vasquez. Horgas visited him in prison, where he presented a sorry spectacle, and couldn't, or wouldn't, reveal the name of any confederate. His known associates from 1983 were traced and were each eliminated.

A week after the discovery of Tucker's body, Joe Horgas got around to dealing with the backlog of paperwork on his desk and found a regional request from Detective Glenn Williams at Richmond. Richmond wanted details of any similar cases to two homicides they were currently investigating.

The first dated back to 19 September 1987. As at Arlington, the two Richmond murders had been committed in the respectable leafy suburbs on the south side. Debbie Davis was a 35-year-old divorcee, an accounts clerk at a newspaper who had a second job selling books at a store in Cloverleaf Mall. She was found raped and murdered in her apartment with her hands tied behind her back. Entry was by an open rear window. As in Hamm and Tucker, there was no sign of a struggle in either the assault or the murder. Davis, a medium- to well-built woman, was found lying face down across her bed. She had wavy auburn hair and was wearing only a pair of denim cut-offs and her jewellery – gold earrings and a bracelet. There were slight abrasions around the nose and lower lip. Wound around her neck was a blue wool knee sock. A vacuum cleaner extension pipe had been thrust through the sock and used as a tourniquet. It was twisted so tightly that it had to be cut off at the autopsy. Her wrists were tied with shoe laces. Entry to the apartment was by a 12-inch wide window. Outside, under the window, stood a rocking chair which had been stolen from a neighbour.

Davis had petechial haemorrhages below the eyelids. These are ruptures of the capillaries that look like fine pinpoints. They are caused by extreme pressure and showed that the killer had tortured his victim over some time, perhaps as much as an hour, tightening and loosening the tourniquet. She had been vaginally and anally raped and her shorts put back on. Pure semen samples were found, that is, not mingled with the victim's body fluids. This could indicate that the killer had masturbated over his victim. There were no prints at the scene.

The second murder, on 3 October, was a similar story. Dr Susan Hellams, a neurosurgery resident, was found by her husband in the bedroom closet. He was a law student and came home only at weekends. She had been bound, raped and strangled. Entry was by a window. Hellams was described as 'Rubenesque' with light reddish-brown hair curling to her shoulders. She was tied round the neck with a red leather belt. Other belts and an electrical flex bound her ankles and feet. She was wearing a black jersey skirt and a white silk slip. On her feet were red socks and red leather sneakers. Although there were no obvious bruises, there was a partial shoe print on her right calf. The killer had held her down while he strangled her.

Again, there were no real signs of violence or a struggle. Susan Hellams' eyelids, like those of Debbie Davis, showed petechial haemorrhages, and, as with Davis, there was semen in the vagina and anus. Semen samples from the murders were of the same type. He was an O secretor with a PGM of 1. Samples were sent to Lifecodes in New York for DNA analysis. Lifecodes was founded in 1982 and originally did cancer testing, paternity testing, prenatal screenings and sometimes aided in missing person cases or identifying human remains. DNA testing in criminal cases was their most recent venture.

There was a third murder with certain similarities just over the county boundary in Chesterfield which was being handled by the neighbouring police department. A 15-year-old Korean girl, Diane Cho, living at home with her family, had been raped and strangled in her bedroom. White rope had been wound round her neck and wrapped several times round her wrists. Although Diane was only 15, she was 5 foot 3 inches and 140 pounds. Her physique was, therefore, similar to that of the Richmond victims.

A slender link between the three women was Cloverleaf Mall. Receipts showed that Susan Hellams bought books from the shop where Debbie Davis worked, and Diane Cho had been at the mall on the day she was killed. Perhaps the killer had selected his victims there and stalked them home.

Detective Williams considered it unlikely that the same man would travel a hundred miles to Arlington to kill another victim. Horgas, on the other hand, thought it was significant that, as with the Hamm murder, there had been a rape committed locally by a black man in a mask. He had broken into Ellen Talbot's apartment in Richmond at about 3 a.m., threatened her with a knife and tied her hands. After making her drink half a bottle of Southern Comfort, which he had brought with him, he subjected her to three hours of sexual torture, repeated rapes, oral sex and brutal penetration with a vibrator. The vibrator had been stolen earlier from a neighbour. He was disturbed when her upstairs neighbours came home. They heard her cries and came down to investigate. He fled out of the window by which he had entered. Although there seemed striking similarities with the other two cases, there were also significant differences. Talbot was of a more slender build than Davis, Hellams and Cho. The rape occurred on a Sunday morning and not a Friday or Saturday, as with the other Richmond cases. The rapist did not masturbate over her, nor tie her neck. A different knife was used to cut the ropes. And, in any case, the Richmond police, following advice from the FBI, were targeting white males.

Horgas and the task force at Arlington started all over again. They now looked at all the rapes and burglaries for 1983. From late June to January 1984, nine Arlington women had reported being raped by a young black man in a mask armed with a knife who stole cash from them. The first was 28-year-old Roberta Schwartz. She had been approaching her car in a supermarket car park at 1 a.m. when a young black man came up and put a long-bladed knife to her face. He was skinny, in his 20s. He made her drive around for about fifteen minutes. They stopped in a wooded area where he forced her out of the car at knife point and made her fellate him. Then he forced her to take off her clothes and lie on them. He raped her face to face, then made her go further into the woods where he raped her again, each time without ejaculating. Afterwards he told her to lie on the ground while he went back to the car to fetch something. After a few minutes Roberta realised that he had fled.

The next three victims were attacked in their homes, each attack being accompanied by a continuous rambling soliloquy of death threats and demands to enjoy the sex.

By the fourth victim the rapist had added variations to his MO, taping the victim's mouth and attempting to tie her up with Venetian blind cord. This victim ran from the apartment as he turned to cut the cord off the blind.

Number five, an 18-year-old, was forced to drive, like Roberta, to a remote area. Her eyes were taped with silver duct tape and her arms were tied. She was forced to fellate him, then was brutally raped vaginally and anally. He pushed her into the boot of the car and set light to it. Fortunately, the girl's kicking released the catch and she was able to escape.

The attacks continued through the autumn of 1983 in more or less copy-cat fashion, ending with Marcie Sanders, who lived just six blocks from Carolyn Hamm's home.

From each case there should have been a PERK kit. These were Physical Evidence Recovery Kits – a brown square envelope containing several plastic envelopes, labels, sterile swabs, a fine-tooth comb, nail clippers and rubber gloves. These survived in only three of the cases. Vital hair and semen samples from the other cases had been either destroyed or lost, as was such critical evidence as the victims' clothing. Storage space was limited.

Horgas took what there was to Lifecodes personally, together with samples from Tucker and Hamm. Richmond and Chesterfield had also sent in their samples. Unfortunately, it took ten days just to determine whether DNA typing was possible from a particular sample, then the actual testing took ten weeks.

He also went to see Deanne Dabbs, supervisor of the serology section at the Virginia Bureau of Forensic Science in Fairfax County, and explained the situation fully. Dabbs was the serologist who had found that Vasquez's samples didn't match the Hamm case samples in 1984. She gave the Tucker murder first priority. Negroid hairs were found on the facecloth and on the bed, five in all. She also found pure semen on a blue sleeping bag that had been draped over the victim. The perpetrator was an O secretor with a PGM of 1 (sub-type 1+) and was PEP A1. This was identical to the samples from Davis, Hellams and Hamm.

Horgas also visited the BSU at Quantico and saw special agents Stephen Mardigian and Judson Ray. Ray had surmised that the perpetrator was a white male in his 20s to 30s, living in the Richmond area, as only one black serial killer (Wayne Williams) was known at that time, and female rape and homicides were much more frequently committed by men of the same racial type. The BSU worked on statistical probabilities, having interviewed hundreds of known offenders in prison.

Vasquez looked an unlikely candidate. The eye-witnesses who placed him at the scene around the time of the murder didn't convince the FBI men. Muriel Ranser might have been protecting her brother; Michael Ansari could have been the kind of person who frequently contacts police with information. When he was asked to identify Vasquez from a photograph, he had a hard time recognising him. Furthermore, this type of crime is typically a one-man job and the FBI didn't think that Vasquez had an accomplice who actually performed the rape. As a one-man job, the Hamm murder was too sophisticated for Vasquez's level of intellectual functioning.

The agents explained the 'signature aspect' of the murders, which could all have been committed by the same man. The elaborate construction of the noose and bindings was one such signature. A simple knot would have done the job as easily. The bindings were so rigged that he could choke and release his victims. Other signature aspects were the efforts made to cover the bodies, Tucker with the sleeping bag, Hellams in a closet, Davis in her shorts, and the masturbation over the victims.

The killer was intelligent. The women were stalked, the murders were well planned. He minimised risk of detection by choosing women he knew would be alone. The MO suggested that he had had practice at other offences first (wiping clean the washer-dryer at Tucker's home).

His dominant motive was control. He was an escalating rapist. With each new attack he was learning what worked and what didn't, climbing the ladder of criminality, committing side-by-side burglaries, bringing his own rope.

The big question was where to find him. The FBI advised Horgas to look in the area where the first rape occurred. This was likely to be the rapist's home territory, where he would know the entire area and so reduce the risk of apprehension. The second question was why the four-year gap. It seemed likely that he had been in custody from not long after Hamm's murder until the summer of 1987. He could have been arrested for burglary.

Roberta Schwartz had been the first victim. The area the rapist took her to was a mile from Hamm's and Tucker's homes. He had run off on foot. Horgas drove out to the spot. There were two choices: he could have run to a wooded area, or to Green Valley. This was the predominantly black area of Arlington. Joe had worked the Valley over the years and thought he might have come across the perpetrator in the past, from what the FBI had said.

Joe Horgas and his partner, Mike Hill, started to plough through the probation and parole records for the dates in question. Unfortunately, these did not indicate the crime or the date of incarceration. They were release records. Of 300 files they found only ten possibilities. The criminal records of these ten then had to be called up individually on the computer, which was in a different room. It was slow, painstaking work.

Then Joe remembered a case from ten years earlier: a neighbourhood tearaway had broken into a house. There was no arrest, but the boy, he recalled, had set fire either to his mother's car or house. He remembered the rape victim who had escaped from her blazing car. His memory could only come up with the name Timmy. It was a few days into January 1988, nearly six weeks after the Tucker murder, that he recalled the surname Spencer.

He fed the name into the computer and came up with a long criminal history for burglary. The last conviction was on 29 January 1984. This fitted, but there were no release details. Eventually, Hill found the file and discovered that Spencer had been released from the penitentiary to a half-way house in Richmond on 4 September 1987. The house was less than a mile from the Davis and Hellams homes. The man was technically still in custody, so he would not have figured in Horgas' and Hill's parole search. His home address was in Green Valley, Arlington, some 200 yards away from the first rape and less than a mile from Tucker's and Hamm's homes. Moreover, he had been released from an earlier spell in jail only days before Roberta Schwartz's rape.

Investigations at the half-way house showed that Spencer was signed out most of the evenings when the attacks took place. At other times – well, there was a fire escape near his room. He had gone home to Arlington for Thanksgiving on the weekend that Susan Tucker was killed.

The Richmond police were not as convinced as Horgas that Spencer was the villain. The only way to be sure was to send his blood to Lifecodes. The problem was that the police could require a citizen to submit a blood specimen only if they had probable cause to believe that he had committed a crime. If Spencer's blood were taken illegally, he could get off on a technicality. They had to be very careful.

The Richmond police mounted a surveillance on the suspect. Apart from a shoplifting spree with some friends in Cloverleaf Mall, Spencer was behaving himself. Money for the surveillance was becoming difficult to justify.

Horgas and Helen Fahey, who had taken over from Hudson as Commonwealth attorney, discussed taking the case to a Grand Jury. If a Grand Jury decided that there was a case to answer and indicted Spencer, then that covered the police. They would have 'probable cause' to believe that he had committed a crime and they had the right to take his blood.

The Grand Jury returned a True Bill on murder, rape and burglary relating to the Tucker case and Spencer was arrested. The preliminary blood test done locally showed that Spencer's blood type and enzyme profile matched the Tucker samples. He hadn't objected to having his blood taken, but Joe Horgas thought that was because he didn't understand the implications of DNA analysis. When Horgas told him he was sending his blood to New York for a test that would give 100 per cent certainty, Spencer was disbelieving.

His camouflage jacket was sent to Joseph Beckerman, a forensic scientist who specialised in trace evidence. He scraped all the debris off the coat and the insides of the pockets. Particles of glass were compared with glass known to be from the crime scene at the intruder's point of entry. The procedure involved mounting the known glass on a slide in an oil whose optical properties were standardised. Paul Mones described how it was done in his book *Stalking Justice*:

> Basically the procedure looked at the optical properties of the glass and compared them to the optical properties of the oil, which were well known. A phase contrast microscope with a Mettler Hot Stage could raise and lower the sample temperature to a tenth of a degree centigrade. A monochromator changed the light bathing the oiled sample from pure white to the blue end of the spectrum and then gradually all the way to the end of the reds. Beckerman dialled in several different temperatures and allowed the sample to equilibrate and become stable at each temperature, then went gradually through the light spectrum until he found the precise setting that brought the glass particle to a complete match with the

properties of the oil. At this point the glass particle seemed to disappear under the microscope. Each time this happened he would record the refraction number.

The glass on Spencer's coat matched the glass taken from the window.

The DNA tests finally came back and linked Spencer to the Tucker case and one of the 1983 rapes. Unfortunately there was no usable DNA from Carolyn Hamm. This meant that he could not be charged with her murder and there was no concrete evidence to prove Vasquez's innocence.

The case was the first use of DNA profiling in a criminal case in Virginia and the first time in a rape-murder in the United States. Helen Fahey needed to present her scientific evidence in a convincing way. She herself had no scientific background, but was fortunate in her assistant, Arthur Karp. Karp had studied physics and maths at MIT and had spent twenty years as a systems analyst in the navy. Another bonus was that, with his flowing white hair and bushy beard, he looked like everyone's idea of a scientist.

The trial commenced on 11 July 1988. Arthur Karp called Dr Michael Baird, of Lifecodes, to the stand. Baird gave a clear lecture to the court on DNA, using charts and a pointer. He spoke as if he were conducting a high school science lesson, and showed that the likelihood of an unrelated black American having the same DNA pattern was 1 in 135 million, though such large figures have since been questioned. Baird was followed by colleague after colleague into the witness box. One of these was biologist Dr Richard Roberts of Cold Spring Harbor Laboratory, New York, who certified the reliability of DNA profiling. He assured the jury that it was a generally accepted scientific principle and attested to the reliability of Lifecodes' findings about Spencer.

Spencer was convicted of Tucker's murder and sentenced to death. He was later convicted of the murders of Debbie Davis, Susan Hellams and Diane Cho.

The FBI wrote a report for Helen Fahey explaining why they felt Spencer had killed Hamm as well as the other women. It was signed by Mardigian and John Douglas, founder and director of the Behavioral Science Unit of the FBI National Center for the Analysis of Violent Crime. The letter was instrumental in having David Vasquez freed from prison.

Spencer appealed against his conviction, contending that Lifecodes might have engaged in some of the same deceptive or faulty practices with respect to the testing and computing in his case that the court identified in *People v. Castro*. After Spencer's conviction, a New York janitor, Joseph Castro, was arrested for killing a woman and her two-year-old daughter. A bloodstain on Castro's watch was analysed by Lifecodes and found to match the blood of the young woman. Castro's defence attorneys argued in court that the DNA evidence could not be admitted because Lifecodes had not followed its own protocols for extracting and analysing the DNA. The DNA evidence was disallowed and Castro was acquitted. He later confessed to the crime.

In Spencer's case, his own attorneys, Carl Womack and Thomas Kelley, in view of their client's claim to innocence, had commissioned Cellmark Diagnostics Inc., of Germantown, Maryland, a major US DNA testing laboratory, to analyse and compare Spencer's blood to the semen samples taken from the crime scene. Cellmark confirmed the match. But his attorneys did not leave it there. They also sent a sample to Dr James Geyer, Director of Disputed Paternity Testing at Genetics Design Inc. in North Carolina. Geyer sent it to Lifecodes for DNA testing under a false name as a fictitious paternity suit. The blind testing initiated by the defence confirmed Lifecode's previous result. Spencer was guilty.

He was executed on 27 April 1994.

Chapter Twenty

THE PROBLEMS OF DNA
AND SCIENTIFIC EVIDENCE

The case of *People v. Castro* was the end of a honeymoon period for DNA evidence. The attention in the medico-legal press since then has focused on its problems. Although it is not disputed that DNA finger-printing is the biggest forensic breakthrough of all time, each aspect of the process, nevertheless, is weighed down with difficulties. The sample, the tests, the interpretation of the tests, and the presentation of the evidence in court, have all come under fire.

When a sample of blood is drawn for, say, a paternity test, the inves-tigator can take as much as is needed to produce an unequivocal result. In a criminal case, a sample taken from the victim or the scene of crime may contain elements of DNA from both the victim and the perpetrator, or it may be contaminated by other biological matter at the scene. The sample may also be very small, or have deteriorated over time or by heat. Once in the laboratory, there is always the possibility of contamination, despite precautions, by mishandling of reagents, samples or equipment. DNA labs, and their scientists, have to be scrupulously clean.

Contamination is also possible not just in the environment of the laboratory, but during the actual testing, especially if the case sample and the suspect sample are run side by side. It is safer to run a control sample between the two, as is now done. Another problem is that however carefully samples are handled, there is always a possibility that they can get mixed up, and at least one such case has already been reported.

Since DNA was first used, different methods have evolved; so it isn't always possible to compare samples across time, or from different labs using a different technique. (Prosecution and defence invariably use different laboratories.) There are other difficulties with comparison. What criteria do you use to decide that two profiles are identical? In physical fingerprinting, a rule gradually evolved in the UK that there had to be sixteen points of resemblance for the fingerprint to count as identical. How many bands have to match for a DNA profile to count as identical? If one DNA band is very faint compared with another at the same position, is that a match? Sometimes the DNA material rises up the gel more slowly in one place than another, so that the pattern may be identical but one profile has shifted to be slightly out of alignment. Is this identical? What if one band is slightly thicker than another? The operator needs a great deal of unbiased skill and judgement to make these decisions. Retesting is not always possible if the case sample is very small.

A lot of debate has focused on statistical probabilities. What are the chances that another person, and not the suspect, has generated the sample that was the basis of the test? The normal way that the very high probability figures quoted in DNA cases are worked out is by calculation on the basis of the product rule. According to this, the probability that a number of matches will occur simultaneously is determined by multiplying the probability that each case will occur. To give an example: in 1985 Alec Jeffreys (now Sir Alec) tested twenty Caucasians and estimated the probability of a match as 3×10^{-11} or 1 in 30,000 million. This was how Galton worked out his statistical probability of 1 in 64,000 million for fingerprints. And like fingerprints, DNA bands have the same problem. The maths only works (if it works at all) if the bands, or individual features, are independent of one another. If there are some bands which always occur together, then shorter odds result. It takes a leap of faith to go from twenty Caucasians to 1 in 30,000 million, and more recent calculations have been more plausible.

The Forensic Science Service has statisticians on hand to explain the probabilities to a jury who may be called upon to grapple with the complexities of Bayesian algebra. Roughly speaking, Bayesian algebra relies on the pre-trial, or prior, odds being multiplied by the likelihood ratio (what you get by weighing up the other evidence in court) to get the posterior odds (of whether the defendant is guilty or not). Can a jury understand all this? Should they even be expected to? In 1802, Lord Kenyon ruled out handwriting evidence in a court case because the jury couldn't read, and in 1857 Judge Cockburn refused microscopic evidence of bloodstains because the jury couldn't see for themselves. It is true that today's innovation is tomorrow's everyday knowledge, but it is doubtful that even in twenty years' time an average jury will have Bayesian algebra at their fingertips.

Richard Muir, prosecuting in the Stratton case, had access to Galton's fingerprinting statistics and ignored them. Instead, he put Inspector Collins on the stand to testify that he had looked through 800,000 to 900,000 separate fingerprints on record and had not found a match for Alfred Stratton's thumbprint. Eventually, I hope, lawyers will ditch these complex statistics and go for Muir's simple empirical approach. The UK has already begun moves towards this.

Under the Criminal Justice and Public Order Act 1994, police in England and Wales have been empowered to take without consent a sample of saliva from anyone suspected of involvement in a recordable offence. This Act, therefore, enabled the establishment of a national database of offenders which came into operation on 10 April 1995. Even before this date it had already proved its value. In December 1992 an elderly woman was raped in Shropshire. The rapist wasn't found. However, samples were entered on to the Forensic Science Service's at that time very limited database. Eighteen months later, a young woman working at a Devon hotel was found raped and murdered. Samples from her body were compared with the database and indicated a strong probability that the same individual was involved in both cases. The case was solved in August 1994 when a man's body was found in Cambridgeshire. A suicide note implicated him in the Devon murder and further evidence supported this. DNA profiling showed that he was also the Shropshire rapist.

The challenge of the Castro case was whether DNA, as a novel scientific technique, could be admitted as evidence. DNA is no different from any other type of scientific trace evidence in this respect. At some point the technique has to be tested in court. Many of the controversial toxicological cases of the last century involved the introduction of novel scientific evidence, but although controversy raged, in those days no one thought to ask whether the evidence should have been admitted in the first place. It wasn't until *Frye v. the United States* in 1923 that the problem of novel scientific evidence was articulated in court. The judge said:

> Just when a scientific principle or discovery crosses the line between the experimental and demonstrable stages is difficult to define. Somewhere in this twilight zone the evidential forces of the principle must be recognised, and while courts will go a long way in admitting expert testimony deduced from a well-recognised scientific principle or discovery, the things from which the deduction is made must be sufficiently established to have gained general acceptance in the particular field in which it belongs.

This case led to what are now known in the States as Frye hearings, where the scientific evidence is aired before a panel of scientists to determine whether it can be admitted in court. The Castro decision was made at a Frye hearing. The new evidence in the Frye case itself was a lie detector. This is particularly relevant to today's problems as the lie detector, as mentioned, was the first scientific breakthrough in the States that was the result of research done in a police laboratory. The technique was developed solely for use in court, and this being so, the court was necessarily the testing ground of the science, with the defendant as the guinea pig.

Is this morally justifiable? Suppose the only real evidence against the accused is a single scientific experiment developed for use exclusively for that case? On the other hand, suppose the accused wishes to bring a new technique into court which can clear his or her name. Can this be denied in the name of justice? And if the technique can't be tested in court, then where is it to be tested?

Another problem arises when scientific evidence is unconfirmed. There are only two kinds of evidence, direct (confession and eye-witness accounts) and circumstantial (which includes scientific and medical). Circumstantial evidence plays a part in building up a case against a suspect. It provides pieces of the jigsaw, and to employ forensic evidence as the whole jigsaw is to misuse it. Ideally, scientific evidence should be confirmed by another test of a different nature, or by a different kind of evidence altogether.

There were only two items of circumstantial evidence to link Timothy Spencer to the murder of Susan Tucker, microscopic fragments of glass and DNA. Author Paul Mones' account of the glass analysis, quoted earlier in this context, is very technical and the evidence was uncontroversial. If it was novel scientific evidence, the point was not brought out in court. Yet refraction evidence must have been novel at one time. Moreover, as physical trace evidence, it presents some of the same problems as biological evidence. What criteria were used to decide if the two samples were identical? How sound was the process? What are the chances that the fragments of glass on Spencer's coat were picked up somewhere else? That is to say, how common was the composition of the glass which made up Tucker's window?

If there had been no usable DNA evidence from Tucker, would the case against Spencer have stood up in court? Had there been no glass evidence, would it have been right to bring only DNA evidence against him?

A further problem with scientific evidence is that the samples are getting smaller and smaller. Multi-locus probe testing needed about 50,000 sperm to obtain a good DNA profile, whereas single-locus probe testing needs only 20,000. There is also a replication technique called polymerase chain reaction (PCR), which replicates small amounts of DNA until the sample is large enough to be tested. This needs about 500 sperm. If the sample is contaminated, by the way, the contamination is also replicated.

In July 1997, *The Times* reported that a new advance had allowed DNA to be extracted from a single hair found at the scene of the murder in Chillenden, Kent, in 1996, when Lyn Russell and her 6-year-old daughter Megan were battered to death by a stranger. This was mitochondrial DNA, taken from a strand of hair, rather than its root. If someone is imprisoned for this crime on a match from a single strand of hair, used for the first time in court, and this is the only – unconfirmed – piece of evidence against the accused, will it be a safe conviction?

Forensic evidence in the biological and physical sciences is no longer given by medical practitioners, which may to some extent explain why the techniques have lately come under suspicion. The first experiment for criminal court purposes was done by Professor Christison in 1828. Since then, medical men have given experimental and novel scientific evidence in court time after time, unchallenged. In fact, the science of toxicology could not have progressed at all without convictions that today we would class as 'unsafe'. The evidence was accepted unquestioningly because, and only because, it came from medical men.

Muir was able to manipulate the jury in the Crippen case by his promotion of Spilsbury. He deceived them into believing that Spilsbury was a man of experience and substance, whereas Turnbull, the defence pathologist, was a man of much, much greater experience, yet fluffed his lines in court. Muir knew it was all a game: it was about winning a case, not searching for the truth. Non-medical expert witnesses have never been liked by the prosecution for fear that the defence will outclass them with a witness of better standing. Prosecutors such as Muir knew that the jury would go for someone with a confident manner and a medical degree.

The history of non-medical criminalistics is, consequently, one of failure. When the experts in the sugar bakers' insurance case in 1820 (see Chapter One) tried to get expenses for loss of time, they were unlucky. The matter came up for a Judges' Ruling and their lordships decided, with much pursing of the lips, that 'chymists', who worked with their hands, were mechanics of some description and they could whistle for their money:

> A witness attending the trial of a cause generally is entitled to no remuneration for loss of time, nor has any allowance for such loss been ever made to a mechanic of any description. It is true that evidence of persons of skill is not only admissible, but highly desirable, but are they to acquire knowledge by any experiments they think proper to make, at the costs of the Party? ... I think not.

The medical man has had the edge ever since. Of the seven Home Office analysts in office from 1882 until 1955, only one, John Webster (in office from 1900 to 1927) was not medically qualified. When the Forensic Science Service was founded in the 1930s, it was the advice of the medical profession that was sought, and a medical man who was put, some say disastrously, at the helm.

It is only since the end of the war that the forensic scientist has risen to be level with the forensic pathologist; and now it could be argued that all is forensic science, with forensic pathology and clinical forensic medicine relegated to sub-disciplines.

So what happened in the Spencer case was a reversal of the Spils-bury/Muir trick. Here the prosecutor put her assistant on the stand because he conformed to the jury's notion of the white-haired scientist. She was wise to stay out of the limelight. Studies on the decision-making of juries show that women in general and low status men can create negative reactions. Women sometimes use a less forceful style of presentation and are not taken as seriously. They are more likely to use 'hedge' words and phrases, such as 'It seems like', 'I think', 'Many say'. They use more repetition, hesi-tational murmurs and polite phrases.

The rising professional status of forensic science practitioners has been a conscious progression. One of the most important steps in this context is to ensure that only people with the recognised qualification have the right to practise. In medicine and law this is done by having a professional body to set the exams and then to register or license the successful examinee. There have recently been some moves in this direction in Britain with regard to forensic science. There is as yet no professional body, but the Forensic Science Society is developing along these lines by offering courses and diplomas in various aspects of the subject. The society may well become the professional body for forensic science in Britain, with due registration as an expert witness. Should this happen, forensic science will face certain problems as a result of its tradi-tional use of outside experts such as entomologist Dr Zak Erzinclioglu and Liverpool psychologist Professor David Canter. It will be difficult to register experts from such diverse academic backgrounds, who have not taken, or are averse to taking, the professional body's exams. Furthermore, registration in itself may not be successful in weeding out partisan witnesses and charlatans, like Alfred Taylor in the Palmer case and the bogus Dr Hamilton in the Sacco and Vanzetti case. And again, there may be the problem of what to do if the accused wishes to call the one expert witness capable of clearing his name, and that witness happens not to be registered.

The problems of forensic science and its practitioners are inherent in the system. There will always be partisan witnesses and bad science in court. In theory, the criminal justice system should forestall a poor case from being presented. If it comes to court, the defence should be as able as the prose-cution, with the same resources; the evidence and the judge's summing up should be presented fairly, and even if they are not, the jury should act as a safety net and acquit. If these safeguards fail, there is the Court of Criminal Appeal. When this court upholds an unjust verdict, the only recourse is to use the weight of public opinion to fight for justice, to arouse controversy.

There are three aspects to the history of forensic science. The first is one of case-based developments, where experiments of various kinds performed for particular cases have led to the acceptance of new techniques, such as the Marsh test and the Stas process. The second aspect is one of laboratory-based developments. These came in during the 1880s in France and flourished after the 1930s in the USA and the UK. The third aspect, which runs through the whole period and forms an integral and inseparable part of its history, concerns controversy-led developments. These involve the expression of informed public opinion in order to change the course of events. Public opinion, and the public accountability of people once considered our betters, has never been so powerful as it is today. It is a bitter irony for forensic science that just as its practitioners are achieving equivalent, or even greater, status than medical practitioners in court, we have entered an age of journalistic iconoclasm. No sooner have the forensic scientists risen from the swamp of obscurity, than they are shot down in an open season on experts, as recent cases have shown.

CASES AND CONTROVERSY

In June 1973, lorry driver John Preece was convicted in Edinburgh for the murder of Helen Will and sentenced to life imprisonment. The victim's body was found in Cumberland, near the Scottish border, and the police, assuming that she had been killed in England, consulted Dr Alan Clift, chief biologist at the Chorley forensic science laboratory in northern England.* In fact, she had been killed in Scotland and her body dumped over the border, but Dr Clift was asked to continue on the case. Under Scottish law a witness was required to corroborate his evidence and the biologist next in seniority below Dr Clift was chosen. Clift's evidence formed the bulwark of the prosecution case.

In 1976 Clift took charge of the biology department at the Birmingham laboratory where, the following year, an assistant director was appointed to monitor professional standards. He routinely examined one of Dr Clift's cases and found it unsatisfactory. Clift corrected the errors but when the assistant director examined other cases of Dr Clift, he found them equally unsatisfactory. He reported this to the controller of the Forensic Science Service, Dr Alan Curry, on 1 September 1977. Curry investigated and reported to the Home Office a few days later that there was substantial *prima facie* evidence that Clift had selected results to present in his report, had reported results which were clearly wrong and had been guilty, as he put it, of 'grave technical incompetence'. He was suspended on full pay and the director of public prosecutions appointed a police officer to investigate his Birmingham cases, but not, note, his previous cases at Chorley.

In March 1978, Preece's prison chaplain alerted the authorities to the earlier case that had culminated in the Edinburgh conviction. In September, the director of the Aldermaston laboratory, Margaret Pereira, sent the controller a report on Clift's Birmingham cases with a view to enabling the Home Office to retire Dr Clift prematurely. Although her report did not mention Preece, it contained several references to poor quality casework,

---

* There are six forensic science laboratories in England and Wales: Aldermaston, Birmingham, Chepstow, Chorley, Huntingdon and Wetherby. In 1973 the headquarters was at the Central Research Laboratory at Aldermaston, but has since moved to Birmingham. The Metropolitan Police Laboratory, which also handles City of London cases, was not incorporated into the same set-up until April 1996.

such as conclusions based on flimsy evidence, failure to disclose the full facts, risky decisions, unsound and invalid conclusions, ambiguous reports and 'other indications of incompetence or worse'.

In the summer of 1979, Preece's solicitors contacted the Home Office in an effort to clear their client's name, and it was found that the 1973 case notes were missing. They turned up at the end of July, 'having been wrongly in Dr Clift's personal possession'. It was discovered that after the trial Clift had also retained the slides of the fibres taken from Preece's lorry and clothes, and from the clothing of the deceased.

Preece's appeal was heard in 1981 at the Edinburgh High Court. It transpired that Helen Will, the victim (who had had sex shortly before death), and Preece were both blood group A and that both of them were secretors. Dr Clift had identified neither the victim's blood group nor her secretor status in his evidence at the trial. Her blood group had been mentioned in an earlier report but had been edited out of the final version presented to the court.

Of course, it was vital to know that both victim and the accused were of the same blood group. It destroyed the prosecution's case. Preece's counsel should have been lively enough to have picked up the point and enquired, but did not; and, because of the way evidence was given, Clift could not then volunteer the information. However, Lord Emslie commented at the Appeal that Clift 'did not disclose Helen Will's blood group or her probable secretor status when he knew it was impossible for the defence to discover this for themselves'. So, it seems clear that Lord Emslie felt the onus was on Clift to take the initiative to speak up, whether or not court protocols provided an opening.

Preece's conviction was quashed, causing widespread publicity. The press dubbed Clift 'Dr Blunder' and he resigned. The case was kept before the public eye when it was referred to the Parliamentary Ombudsman in February 1982 to determine why it had taken four years since Clift's inefficiency had come to light for Preece to be freed. Their report, incidentally, was published in January 1984, nearly two years later. Dr Clift's actions were described as 'an unprecedented pollution of justice at its source'. The report went on: 'It is a measure of the excellence of the Forensic Science Service that trust of the forensic scientist has over the years become so profound. But the depth of that trust is a measure also of the extent of the disaster when it is found to have been betrayed.' Clift, unlike Preece, had no right of appeal, and so his side of the story remains unheard.

A major consequence of the case was that a greater tightening of quality control measures was implemented within the Forensic Science Service. These were further improved following the controversies that surrounded the shortcomings of the forensic evidence and police handling of the cases of the Birmingham Six, Guildford Four and Maguire Seven.

The Birmingham Six were convicted in 1975 of bombing two public houses in Birmingham in November 1974 during an IRA mainland campaign which killed twenty-one people.

Scientific evidence revolved around tests for nitroglycerine conducted by Dr Frank Skuse, who was also based, coincidentally, at the Chorley laboratory. Skuse used the Griess test to determine whether any of the suspects had handled nitroglycerine. The test involved swabbing the hands of the suspects with a cotton-wool swab soaked in ether and then squeezing the ether into three separate bowls. Caustic soda and then Griess reagent were added to the first bowl, which should have turned pink if nitroglycerine was present. If a positive result was obtained, then the investigator would add only Griess reagent to the second bowl, as a control. It should remain clear. The third bowl was reserved for confirmatory laboratory tests of a different nature. Skuse found positive results from the right hands of two suspects tested, Billy Power and Paddy Hill.

He used the thin layer chromatography (TLC) test to confirm his results and also had the samples put through the gas chromatography/ mass spectrometry (GCMS) process at the Aldermaston laboratory. The TLC test was considered at least as sensitive as Griess, GCMS much more sensitive. Neither test confirmed the earlier result. However, he had retained a swab from suspect Paddy Hill's left hand, which had previously been negative for nitroglycerine, and subjected this to the GCMS process. The GCMS results came up on the screen in the form of a blip at 4.2 seconds into the test, indicating the presence of a sample of the unique atomic mass of nitroglycerine. No printout of the blip was produced in court. Skuse's opinion was that there was a 99 per cent probability of the presence of nitroglycerine on the two men's hands.

The defence called Dr Hugh Black, former Home Office chief inspector of explosives. Despite a career spent in advising government departments on explosives, he was an inexperienced witness. His opinion was that there were other common substances that would give the same reaction as nitroglycerine. He named the nitro-cellulose found in lacquers, varnishes and paint. In addition, he said that if the Griess test results were not confirmed by further tests, Dr Skuse should have come to the conclusion that nitroglycerine was not present. Furthermore, he should have confirmed his findings by taking three readings from the oscilloscope screen, and not relied on just one.

Under cross-examination Black was forced to admit that he had never swabbed anyone's hands, nor carried out a GCMS test and had never been in a forensic science laboratory. But he was right, nevertheless.

At the end of October 1985, Granada TV's *World in Action* screened a documentary throwing doubt on the specificity of the Griess test for the presence of nitroglycerine and questioning Dr Skuse's conclusions.

The programme commissioned Dr Brian Caddy of Strathclyde University and Mr David Baldock, a former Home Office forensic scientist, to make further experiments. They obtained positive results from a variety of substances tested by means of the Griess test, including some nitro-cellulose products (aerosol, lacquer and chips) and, most significantly, two old packs of playing cards. Caddy had the programme producer, Ian McBride, shuffle a pack of cards for five minutes before testing his hands. The test was repeated. Results for both tests were positive. The Birmingham Six were known to have been playing cards on a train shortly before their arrest.

Three days after the programme Dr Skuse retired, aged 50, from his position at the Chorley laboratory following uncompleted moves by the Home Office to secure his compulsory retirement on grounds of 'limited efficiency'. The Aldermaston lab conducted a detailed study of the Griess test after this. It confirmed Caddy's and Baldock's results, and the test fell into disuse. Experiments were also done by Dr John Lloyd who discovered that there was some, as yet unknown, component of smoke which is deposited on the hands of smokers. This can give an identical response to nitroglycerine when using GCMS. In addition, Lloyd suggested that Skuse could have washed his bowls out with a soap containing nitrite ions and this may have been an accidental source of contamination.

At the first Appeal in 1987, the court learned more about the single oscilloscope reading. According to Chris Mullin's book *Trial and Error*, Skuse gave evidence at the appeal that he had timed the blip with a stop-watch and that this was witnessed by Dr Janet Drayton, a young scientist at Aldermaston. Her notes read, 'Possible ng present. Very small increase.' Although Skuse admitted that Dr Drayton was more experienced with the process than he was, he thought that she was not 'as strong' as she should have been in reporting the result.

Dr Drayton had not been called at the original trial. Now, at the appeal, everything hinged on her evidence. She said that all the printouts were given to Dr Skuse. (These, however, were missing and might have gone missing before the original trial, but they had existed, as Dr Black had seen them.) She did not recall the stopwatch. Some pages were missing from her notebook recording the tests previous to the one on Hill's left hand. She had searched for them and did not remember tearing pages out and giving them to Dr Skuse. It was not normal practice to do so. The surviving pages later surfaced at Chorley, where Skuse had formerly worked.

This evidence was not good enough to overturn the verdict either at this Appeal in 1987 or the next one in 1990. What finally freed the Six a year later was evidence which cast doubt on the validity of police notes of interviews with the suspects at the time of their arrest and interrogation. This was provided by Dr David Baxendale, of the Forensic Science Service, using the technique of electrostatic document analysis (ESDA). ESDA is a simple means of showing up the indentations on a piece of paper which are made by writing on the previous sheets. It was invented at the London College of Printing in the 1970s and was therefore not available at the original trial of the Six, although it is now used by forensic laboratories all over the world. Using ESDA, Baxendale found that four pages had been added to the notes of one interview, and he also discovered discrepancies involving dates, inks, paper, staple holes and spacing among the other documents. The Court of Appeal concluded that four police officers had deceived the court at the original trial. The convictions were quashed in March 1991.

The Guildford Four were convicted in 1975 of bombing pubs in Guildford and Woolwich in October and November 1974 in which seven people were killed. Scientific evidence was not involved in this case. Statements made by the accused, however, led to the conviction of Anne Maguire, her family and friends (the Maguire Seven) in 1976 for illegal possession of explosives – the implication being that her house in London was an IRA bomb factory. This case involved tests for nitroglycerine performed by the Royal Armament Research and Development Establishment at Woolwich (RARDE). This means that they were government forensic scientists but not part of the Home Office Forensic Science Service.

In the Maguire case the TLC test had been used as the primary (if not the only) test. The substance to be tested is dissolved in ether and a drop is applied to one end of a specially coated absorbent plate and allowed to dry. A spot of a known substance (in this case nitroglycerine) is applied alongside it. The plate is then stood end-up in a dish of solvent with the samples at the base. The solvent is drawn up the plate like water up a sheet of blotting paper, carrying with it known and unknown samples. Their final positions are revealed in a coloured spot by spraying a developer on to the plate (Griess's reagent again). The colour and final position on the plates are compared. Using this test, hand swabs had proved positive for nitroglycerine for six of the seven members of the Maguire family. The seventh was incriminated by positive results from several pairs of plastic gloves.

At the trial it became known that an explosive substance called PETN caused a similar reading. If PETN gave the same reading as nitroglycerine, perhaps other substances could as well. The defence produced a strong expert witness in John Yallop, formerly principal scientific officer in charge of explosives at RARDE. Yallop had developed the TLC test in the 1960s as a method of detecting explosives. He stated that a single TLC test wasn't good enough on its own and that confirmatory tests should be carried out. Apparently, all that had been done, according to Robert Kee's book *Trial and Error*, was to take sniffer dogs to the Maguire home. The dogs had found no evidence of explosives. If the sniffer dogs qualified as a confirmatory test, the results should have been reported as negative.

The Maguire Seven and Guildford Four cases went to Appeal in 1977 but their convictions were upheld. The campaign to clear their names continued through the 1980s as the Maguire Seven were gradually released at the end of their sentences. This was with the exception of one family member who had died in prison. Anne Maguire was the last to be set free, in February 1985. Now the campaign intensified. Television programmes and newspaper articles championing the innocence of the Seven and the Four kept the cases before the public.

Under constant pressure, the home secretary ordered a police investigation into the police handling of the Guildford Four case in the summer of 1988. Their convictions were quashed in October 1989 on the grounds that notes of confessions had not been taken contemporaneously even though the police swore they had (ESDA again). Following their acquittal, the home secretary commissioned Sir John May to hold an inquiry into the circumstances surrounding the convictions of both the Guildford Four and Maguire Seven. May commissioned Professor D. Thorburn Burns, professor of analytical chemistry at Queen's University, Belfast, to investigate the scientific aspects.

Thorburn Burns found that PETN and nitroglycerine could not be differentiated in the test result, and that innocent contamination was also possible. A hand which had handled nitroglycerine could contaminate plastic gloves and a person could become innocently contaminated, even under the fingernails, by handling contaminated articles such as a towel. Furthermore, it was discovered that the parameters within which the scientists were prepared to report a TLC test as 'positive' were wider than they alleged at the trial. A final reading within 6 per cent of each other was regarded as the same. This was not made explicit to the jury. The incident echoes problems encountered in matching DNA bands.

Sir John examined notebooks and case files from RARDE which had not previously been disclosed. Walter Elliott, senior scientific officer at RARDE, and Douglas Higgs, his superior, gave evidence at the trial and before Sir John that it had not been possible to test the suspect samples a second time, but the notebooks showed that this had in fact happened before the trial when scientists had been trying to identify the particular brand of explosive present. The results had been negative. The results of two further tests had not been communicated.

Sir John's first report, in July 1990, concluded that the scientists involved 'imperfectly understood their duties as forensic scientists and as witnesses'. The prosecution was criticised for not being open minded with regard to the disclosure of the scientists' notebooks, which might have changed the course of events. He recommended that the case of the Maguire Seven be referred to the Court of Criminal Appeal.

The Seven's convictions were quashed in June 1991 on the grounds of the possibility of innocent contamination. The other matters were dismissed as red herrings. The Court of Appeal considered that a forensic scientist advising the prosecuting authority was under duty to disclose relevant material.

Following the acquittals of the Birmingham Six and Maguire Seven, the case of Judith Ward was also referred to the Court of Appeal. She had been convicted in 1974 of bombing Euston Station, the National Defence College in Buckinghamshire and a coach on the M62. Dr Frank Skuse and the RARDE scientists had also been involved in these cases, using the Griess test and TLC on Judith Ward's hands and in the caravan where she lived. The defence had claimed innocent accidental contamination. Her conviction was quashed in June 1992 on the grounds that new light on the scientific evidence rendered the convictions 'unsafe and unsatisfactory'.

In *Ward*, the appeal judges criticised the RARDE scientists Douglas Higgs, Walter Elliott (now deceased) and George Berryman for taking the law into their own hands. They had acted in concert to conceal from the prosecution, defence and the court matters which could have changed the course of the trial. It had been a lamentable catalogue of omissions and obstructions. They had suppressed evidence to demonstrate that boot polish could produce findings that showed traces of nitroglycerine; and Higgs had not wanted to disclose anything that might encourage investigation by the defence. Dr Skuse's conclusions were described as 'wrong'. The jury had also been unaware of an 'avalanche' of undisclosed material as to Judith Ward's troubled state of mind.

Injustice is inherent in any criminal justice system. This was recognised in 1907 by the establishment of the Court of Criminal Appeal in England following two major controversies of the early years of the century, the cases of Adolf Beck and George Edalji. These stories are too complex to relate here. But what is striking is that, like Sacco and Vanzetti, the two men were both from outgroups. Beck was a foreign-born Jew in an anti-Semitic age, and Edalji was a half-caste Indian. Sir Arthur Conan Doyle ran a newspaper campaign in the summer of 1907 to clear Edalji's name. A vicar's son, and a solicitor in Birmingham, Edalji had been imprisoned for maiming colliery ponies in his home village. The campaign led directly to the Court of Criminal Appeal, which was founded the same summer. Some years later, Doyle became involved in the case of Oscar Slater, a disreputable German Jew who was accused of murdering an old lady in Glasgow in 1908. Slater spent many years in prison. His name was cleared by the Court of Criminal Appeal for Scotland in the late 1920s only after an Act of Parliament had been passed permitting the court to hear cases from the period prior to the court's foundation in 1926.

Members of outgroups crop up again and again in injustice stories. The latest concerns African-American superstar and sports hero Orenthal James Simpson.

On 3 October 1995, a mainly black Los Angeles jury acquitted O. J. Simpson of murdering his ex-wife Nicole Brown Simpson and a friend, Ronald Goldman, just outside her home in Los Angeles on 13 June 1994.

The reason we know so much about this case, and doubtless will know more in future, is that it occurred in the United States, where, in comparison with the UK, there are three fundamental differences in the laws applying to criminal hearings.

In the UK, reporting restrictions first enacted in the Criminal Justice Act 1967 confine pre-trial media publicity within such bounds as will ensure a fair trial. The State of California evidently has no such restrictions. Consequently, the outside world was bombarded with 'facts' about the Simpson case from the media, leaked – according to the newspapers – by the usual 'police sources'. Alan Dershowitz, one of Simpson's defence lawyers, who wrote *Reasonable Doubts* about the case, accused the police and district attorney's office themselves of orchestrating a campaign to shatter O. J. Simpson's popular public image as 'Mr Nice Guy'. The release of a tape to the media of Nicole Brown's 911 call accusing her husband of threatening her was the most damning of these leaks, although some of them were trivial and proved to be no more than rumour. All of them, however, were surely aimed at prejudicing any future jury.

The second area of difference is that the jurors in the trial are entitled to go public following the conclusion of the trial. They have, in fact, made comments to journalists and written books to describe how they felt in the jury room, and what prompted them to cast a not-guilty vote. In the UK such comment would be viewed as contempt of court. In 1980 the left-wing *New Statesman* published an interview with a member of the jury in the trial of Jeremy Thorpe, the former Liberal Party leader. A year later the Contempt of Court Act 1981 made it an offence for anyone to obtain, disclose or solicit any information about the secrets of the jury room. This also blocks any academic research into how juries arrive at their decisions.

Finally, and most obviously, the trial was televised, whereas in the UK, where both television and still cameras are prohibited, court artists are employed by the media to sketch the proceedings.

Much of the controversy surrounding the Simpson case relates to the police handling of the exhibits. Physical evidence must be sealed and labelled and logged as soon as possible. In the Simpson case, Dershowitz claims in *Reasonable Doubts* that several mistakes were made.[*] The police

* Dershowitz is my sole source here. I have been unable to corroborate his information.

contaminated the scene of the crime by covering the bodies with a blanket from Nicole Brown's home, casting doubt on hair and fibre evidence later retrieved. Approximately 8 cc of Simpson's blood had been taken from him on 13 June. That meant, according to the nurse who took the blood, between 7.9 and 8.1 cc. Detective Philip Vannatter, in charge of the investigation, carried around this vial of blood in an unsealed envelope for three hours and went for a cup of coffee before booking it. The defence later argued that 1.5 cc of blood was missing. Documented booking of samples didn't start until two days after the crime and the blood samples weren't counted. A juror later told the press that the jury found Vannatter's decision to carry around the blood for three hours suspicious because it gave him the opportunity to plant evidence at Simpson's home.

A bloodstained glove which was alleged to match one at the crime scene was found at Simpson's Rockingham estate. The blood was a DNA match with Goldman, Brown and Simpson. Blood of all three was allegedly found in various places in Simpson's Ford Bronco. Three weeks after Simpson gave the blood sample, bloodstained socks were found on his bedroom floor and on the back gate at the crime scene.

Dershowitz suggests that Detective Mark Fuhrman took the glove from the scene of the crime and left it on Simpson's property, and that he could have transferred blood from the crime scene into Simpson's white car by getting in and sitting at the driver's seat. There was no corroboration for Fuhrman's statement that he found the glove on Simpson's property and he was exposed in the trial as being racially prejudiced, especially against blacks married to whites. The glove didn't fit Simpson any more than the cap had fitted Sacco seventy-five years earlier.

The prosecution claimed that DNA from the bloodstained socks matched that of Simpson and Brown, and that samples from the blood on Brown's gate matched Simpson's. The blood from both sources was sent for analysis at the FBI laboratory at Washington. Again, according to Dershowitz, they were both found to contain a preservative called EDTA which is added to blood in test tubes to prevent it from coagulating, but which does not occur naturally in blood. The socks had no other traces to link them with the crime scene, and the pattern of splashes was consistent with the blood being dabbed on a sock later. In *Reasonable Doubts* Dershowitz explains that he experimented with red wine to demonstrate this to his family. If the sock was splashed while on the foot, then only one stain showed, but if it were put on a flat surface and dabbed with wine, then the wine showed up on both sides, as on Simpson's sock.

Further spots of blood were found around Simpson's own home, which was not surprising. (Sydney Smith had found several innocent blood-stains at the home of Jeannie Donald in 1935.) Simpson told police that he had cut his finger retrieving his cellular phone from the Bronco. The defence argued that the officer collecting these spots of blood had left them in a hot car for four hours, which had degraded the DNA. When the blood finally reached the lab, defence claimed that the serologist handled the samples at the same time as a reference tube of Simpson's blood, not following proper procedures of changing gloves and washing down between handling separate samples. These DNA samples can be very tiny indeed, microscopic. Dershowitz's argument was that cross-contamination in the laboratory occurred, creating a false positive match with Simpson. Unlike the other controversial samples, these were never sent to be tested for EDTA, so we'll never know.

It remains to be seen whether any reforms in procedures have been put in hand among the Los Angeles police following this case. If the defence claims are true, then the case marks a backward step in a state which pioneered both police science and academy training for police officers.

In England and Wales, the controversial cases of the 1980s led directly to a massive shake-up of forensic science and of the criminal justice system in the early 1990s. Aside from Sir John May's inquiry, the House of Commons set up a Home Affairs Committee of MPs to look at the state of forensic science. Not to be outdone, the House of Lords convened a Select Committee to do the same. The most prestigious body, however, was the Royal Commission on Criminal Justice of 1991 to 1993, headed by Lord Runciman, 'to examine the effectiveness of the criminal justice system in England and Wales'. It was set up on the same day in March 1991 that the Birmingham Six's convictions were quashed. Despite this obvious link, there was no analysis of the Irish cases which led to its being set up, nor indeed of any other miscarriages of justice. The Royal Commission was not concerned merely with forensic science or injustice, but with safeguarding the criminal justice system as a whole in what has been described as a damage limitation exercise.

The committees, generally, reported that quality control had improved a great deal since the occurrence of the controversial cases in the 1970s. Laboratories now have a rigorous system of quality control whereby fake case samples are submitted randomly. These are subjected to tests where the results are already known and the results are compared. The tests themselves are gradually being accredited under the National Measurement Accreditation Service (NAMAS). This is part of a government department aiming to establish national and international recognition of the competence of accredited testing laboratories. Essentially, each laboratory that carries out a certain test should achieve the same results as any other laboratory carrying out the same test. A drawback is that independent laboratories and individual court experts remain outside this scheme. And so are the police.

Many of the recommendations of the committees were aimed at levelling the playing field between prosecution and defence. Both are normally funded by the government – it's unusual to find a defendant rich enough to pay for his or her own defence – so Legal Aid supplies the cash, including funding for forensic laboratory work. But the prosecution always holds the best cards.

The defendant is at a natural disadvantage with regard to forensic science. The police and prosecution agencies have been first on the scene and have taken away exhibits. They are first to be informed of any results. The defence are in the position of having to respond to the evidence that the prosecution has discovered. To reduce the inequity, the Royal Commission on Criminal Justice recommended that the prosecution should disclose all relevant information before the trial, and that the defence lawyer should have the right to find comparable forensic expertise and be able to pay for it.

The Royal Commission recommended, moreover, that the defence should have access to the original notes of any experiments if they felt it would throw doubt on the validity of the tests done for the prosecution. Pre-trial discussions were also recommended to clarify agreements and disputes between the experts, and at the trial, where the evidence is disputed, the judge should ask expert witnesses before they leave the witness box if there is anything else that they wish to say.

One result of all this debate was the Criminal Procedure and Investigations Act 1996, which came into force on 1 April 1997. It requires the prosecution to disclose to the accused any material in its possession which might undermine its own case. This sounds good, but harbingers of doom worry that the decision on what to disclose remains in the hands of the prosecution, and that defence lawyers will no longer be able to sift routinely through every piece of evidence gathered by the police. Such a system has no effective means of appeal.

To help the defence find suitable forensic expertise, it was recommended that more use be made by the defence of the Home Office forensic science laboratories. Although such assistance had always been available to the defence in the past, it was seldom employed, as the exhibits had to be submitted to the laboratory by the police, who had legal responsibility for them. Furthermore, the results of any tests made for the defence were reported by the laboratory to the senior police officer in charge. The result was that separate laboratories were established, sometimes staffed by former Home Office Forensic Science Service personnel, to serve the needs of the defence. These laboratories tended to have less sophisticated equipment, and the quality control measures imposed on the Home Office labs were not applicable. The situation was especially difficult in DNA cases, and in the early years it was very difficult for the defence to find suitable expertise and to pay for it.

To make the situation more equitable and to convey a semblance of independence, the Forensic Science Service was put at arms' length from the government in 1991 by being reorganised into an executive agency of the government under a chief executive, Dr Janet Thompson, who oversaw the change. The Metropolitan Police Scientific Laboratory has now been placed under Dr Thompson, but the Scottish and Northern Irish labs are not involved. Dr Thompson, by the way, has an Oxford DPhil – a scientific rather than a medical doctorate. The Royal Armament Research and Defence Establishment at Woolwich was similarly transformed into the Defence Research Agency (DRA).

Along with agency status came direct charging, rather than funding from central government. Today anyone can use the former Home Office laboratories and pay in the normal way. The police are the main customers and instead of their lab work being funded centrally, it is now paid for by each individual police authority. This idea of customer payment is, of course, not unique to forensic science, but has rippled through the entire English Civil Service as part of the drive for privatisation which started in the Thatcher years. The much smaller Forensic Pathology Service is included, but has always maintained its independence, since pathologists, in London at least, are paid by their hospitals.

There is always a risk that if the forensic science labs charge on a case by case basis, the police may be less likely to send an item for analysis which may exculpate a suspect and that they may look for the cheapest (and not the most reliable) source of expertise, or increasingly use in-house facilities or independent forensic science laboratories with unknown levels of quality control. A recent case highlights this problem.

In May 1992, 89-year-old Florence Jackson was found floating in the River Brede in East Sussex, a short distance from where her niece, Sheila Bowler, had left her when their car broke down. The prosecution claimed that Mrs Bowler took her aunt from her residential home, tipped her into the river and then faked a car breakdown. When she returned with help, she feigned surprise that her aunt had left the vehicle. Mrs Bowler, a middle-aged music teacher of impeccable background, had no motive for dispatching her aunt, but was given a life sentence for murder at Lewes Crown Court. The only evidence was that Mrs Jackson was unable to walk far without help. Being afraid of the dark, however, she might have got out of the car in a panic and could have fallen into the river without any assistance from her niece.

It was important to establish how far the body, or any walking stick the old lady might have carried, could have floated after death. The police sent a constable to the river bank where he threw in sticks to see how fast they moved. He noted that they showed very little movement and concluded that the tidal flow was slight. A television company took up Mrs Bowler's case and consulted the National Rivers Authority and the Institute of Hydrology in Wallingford, becoming veritable experts in tidal flows. They discovered that the constable's experiment had been conducted at slack tide, which invalidated his conclusions. Mrs Bowler's case was referred to the Court of Appeal, and she was acquitted after a retrial.

Journalist and author David Jessel, discussing the case in a talk to the British Academy of Forensic Sciences, blamed direct charging and the constraints on budgets for the short-cut approach adopted by the police in building their evidence. This problem may be alleviated as the role of forensic support manager becomes more widespread. The manager is normally a civilian, sometimes a forensic scientist, who supervises procedures, quality assurance and training with regard to forensic work done in-house. He or she is the liaison officer between the laboratory and the police force and is in charge of the exhibits.

The distancing of the government, as the prosecuting body, from forensic science began in 1882 when the Home Office analysts were appointed. This degree of sensitivity is peculiar to the Home Office. Other government departments, such as the Department of Social Security and Customs and Excise, prosecute without any such coyness, away from the heat of public debate.

The police were distanced from being a prosecuting body in the Crown Courts in 1987 when this function was taken over by the Crown Prosecution Service. The CPS decides whom to prosecute and this provides an additional buffer. These checks should make the enhancement of cases more difficult in England and Wales, as should the tape-recording of interviews, which was introduced in the UK in the 1980s.

Independence of establishment, however, can only go so far when central government ultimately foots the bill, and when the very same personnel perform a test on the Friday as part of the Home Office Forensic Science Service and on the following Monday as an 'independent' executive agency. It's worth mentioning here that the two police laboratories in Great Britain, in Strathclyde (Glasgow) and London, have never been criticised for partisan personnel.

Another move to independence is the coming into force in April 1997 of the Criminal Cases Review Commission. That such a body should be set up was the least controversial recommendation of the Royal Commission on Criminal Justice. It was established by the Criminal Appeal Act 1995 which replaced the home secretary's power to refer cases to the Court of Criminal Appeal with an independent body. Before the Act came into force, the home secretary received about 800 petitions a year claiming wrongful conviction.

Only a tiny percentage of these reached the Appeal Court. It remains to be seen how many will now be referred. The stumbling block is that the Court of Criminal Appeal itself remains unreformed.

Michael Mansfield QC, in his book *Presumed Guilty*, criticises certain judges for being elderly and some for being out of touch. The recruitment of judges is not based on a legal career structure as it is in France or the USA; it is the self-perpetuation of like choosing like. The result can be intense loyalty to the establishment. Halting the Birmingham Six's civil action against the police for assault in 1980, Lord Denning, master of the rolls, said: 'If the six men win, it will mean that the police were guilty of perjury, that they were guilty of violence and threats and that the convictions were erroneous... This is such an appalling vista that every person in the land would say: "It cannot be right if these actions should go any further."' In 1988, Denning spoke again on the case, in relation to the growing clamour for the release of the Six: 'It is better that some innocent men remain in jail than the integrity of the English judicial system be impugned.'

Mansfield doesn't agree. His view is that the greatest condemnation of any judicial system is that it should imprison innocent people and then place the interest of that system above the interests of those it was designed to protect. Mansfield's is one of the loudest voices to call for changes in the Court of Criminal Appeal.

This court, should it so wish, is in a position to undermine all the reforms of the 1980s and 1990s. The doors are gradually being opened to let justice in, but the last door can still be slammed shut. As one of the few people who sees the workings of the criminal justice system on a daily basis from the outside looking in, David Jessel's view is that the Appeal Court has historically 'displayed little doubt'. He is not alone in detecting, in recent judgements, a determination by the Appeal Court to draw a firm line under the era of miscarriages of justice, the implication being that these unfortunate cases were a feature of the 1970s: remedial action has been taken; they couldn't possibly happen again. But of course, they aren't a feature of recent history.

After the freeing of the Birmingham Six in 1991, Andreas Whittam Smith wrote in *The Independent* newspaper: 'It is a shocking thing that the legal system can no longer be trusted to provide a fair trial.' After an earlier case, *The Times* reported: 'We never read any reports where medical evidence is given without blushing for the state of medical science in England.' *The Lancet*, reporting the same case, called the medical witnesses 'interested advocates'. These last two quotations, however, are from contemporary reports of an insurance case in *1832*, over 160 years ago. The witness in question was Alfred Taylor, who gave evidence on the cause of death of the insured party without even viewing the body.

Forensic science progresses like air disasters. Every time a crash happens, the investigation makes sure that particular fault doesn't happen again. As a result, air travel is safer now than ever before. But there will always be human error, despite all the safeguards. When a criminal case goes down, it doesn't make a splash. We only know about it via the media and the controversy it generates. Moreover, nobody is immune from human error; the Court of Criminal Appeal *will* fail again, and when it does, it is up to us, through the media, to use public opinion to call for justice. We need a free press and media controversy to right wrongs. But controversy irritates the judges. Lord Chief Justice Taylor rebuked the media in one case for showing 'no hesitation in substituting their judgement for that of the court'. Yet the whole idea of justice is to by tried by one's peers – one's equals – not a bigwig in a big wig.

If recent judges of the Court of Criminal Appeal have quashed obviously unsafe convictions, this isn't proof that the criminal justice system works. It is proof that public pressure works. But before we start congratulating ourselves as members of the campaigning public, it might be wise to remind ourselves that a jury made up of people like us has first convicted the innocent. Only rarely does a jury bring in a perverse verdict, one that goes against the presented evidence or against the judge's directions.

We mustn't let ourselves be bamboozled by authoritative figures in court who say that white is black. We are the jury. It's up to us, in the end, to see justice done.

SELECTED SOURCES

Introduction

James, P. D., and Critchley, T. A., *The Maul and the Pear Tree* (The Ratcliffe Highway Murders), London, 1971

Leonard, T. C., *The Power of the Press*, Oxford, 1986

Rhodes, H. T. F., *In the Tracks of Crime*, London, 1952

Sayers, Dorothy L., Introduction, *Great Short Stories of Detection Mystery and Horror, Part I, Detection and Mystery*, London, 1928

Thorwald, J., *The Century of the Detective* (*Dead Men Tell Tales, Proof of Poison* and *The Marks of Cain*), London, 1966

Thorwald, J., *Crime and Science*, London, 1967

Ward, Jenny, *Origins and Development of Forensic Medicine and Forensic Science in England, 1823–1946*, PhD thesis, Open University, 1993

Wilson, C., *Written in Blood: a history of forensic detection*, London, 1990

Times

1. Burke and Hare: Immigrant enterprise

Christison, R., *Life*, edited by his sons, Edinburgh, 1885

Christison, R., 'Murder by suffocation. Injury of the spine after death imitating an injury during life. Experiments on the effects of blows soon after death', *Edinburgh Medical and Surgical Journal*, 1829, p. 236

Clarke, J. F., *Recollections of the Medical Profession*, London, 1874

Cole, H., *Things for the Surgeon*, London, 1964

Edwards, O. Dudley, *Burke and Hare*, Edinburgh, 1993 (second edition)

Fullmer, June, 'Technology, chemistry and the law in nineteenth-century England', *Technology and Culture*, 1980, pp. 24–5

Lock, Joan, *Dreadful Deeds and Awful Murders: Scotland Yard's first detectives, 1829–1878*, Taunton, 1990

Mohr, J. C., *Doctors and the Law: medical jurisprudence in nineteenth-century America*, Oxford, 1993

Peterson, M. Jeanne, *The Medical Profession in Mid-Victorian England*, Berkeley, 1978

Richardson, Ruth, *Death, Dissection and the Destitute*, London, 1987

Roughead, W. (ed.), *Burke and Hare*, Notable British Trials series, Edinburgh, 1948 (third edition)

Sheehan, A. V., *Criminal Procedure in Scotland and France*, Edinburgh, 1975

Williams, L. P., *Michael Faraday*, London, 1965

Contemporary medical journals and newspapers

2. Marie Lafarge: The gateau from the chateau

Browne, D. G., and Tullett, E. V., *Bernard Spilsbury: his life and cases*, London, 1952

Browne, G. L. and Stewart, C. G., *Reports of Trials for Murder by Poisoning*, London, 1883

Glaister, J., *Medical Jurisprudence and Toxicology*, Edinburgh, 1921

Hartman, Mary S., *Victorian Murderesses*, London, 1985

Orfila, M. J. B., 'Memoire sur l'empoisonnement par l'acid arsénieux par M. Orfila (lu à l'Académie royale de médicine, le 29 janvier 1839)', *Annales d'hygîene et de médecine légale*, 1839, pp. 421-65

Saunders, Edith, *The Mystery of Marie Lafarge*, London, 1951

Shearing, J., *The Lady and the Arsenic*, London, 1937

Simpson, C. K., *Forensic Medicine*, London, 1964

Thorwald, J., *Proof of Poison*, London, 1966

'Trial of Madame Lafarge', book review in *Edinburgh Review*, April–July 1842, pp. 359-96

Weiner, Dora B., *Raspail, Scientist and Reformer*, New York, 1968

3. Count and Countess Bocarmé: Deadly nicotine

Orfila, M. J. B., 'Mémoire sur la nicotine et sur la conicine', *Annales d'hygîene publique et de médecine légale*, July 1851, pp. 147-230

Stas, J. S., 'Observations upon a general method for detecting the organic alkaloids in cases of poisoning', *Monthly Medical Journal*, 1852:2, p. 313

Stas, J. S., *Œuvres Complètes*, in 3 vols, Brussels, 1894

Thorwald, J., *Proof of Poison*, London, 1966

4. Professor Webster: Killing the golden goose

Boston Medical and Surgical Journal, vols 41 and 42, 1850

Bradbury, S., *The Evolution of the Microscope*, London, 1967

Cottone, J. A., and Standish, S. M., *Outline of Forensic Dentistry*, Texas, 1982

Dilnot, G., *The Trial of Professor Webster*, Famous Trials series, London, 1928

Taylor, A. S., *Manual of Medical Jurisprudence*, several editions

5. Dr William Palmer: The Rugeley poisoner

Browne, G. L., and Stewart, C. G., *Reports of Trials for Murder by Poisoning*, London, 1883

Graves, R., *They Hanged My Saintly Billy*, London, 1971

Taylor, A. S., 'On poisoning by strychnia', *Guy's Hospital Reports*, 1856, pp. 269-404

Taylor, A. S., *On Poisons*, London, 1859, p. 796

Watson, E. R. (ed.), *Trial of William Palmer*, Notable British Trials series, Edinburgh, 1952

Illustrated Times, Illustrated London News, Lancet

6. Dr George Henry Lamson: The poisoned pill

Adam, H. L., *Trial of George Henry Lamson*, Notable British Trials series, London, 1913

Browne, G. L., and Stewart, C. G., *Reports of Trials for Murder by Poisoning*, London, 1883

Malot, H., *Le Docteur Claude*, huitième édition, Paris, 1882. (As this was after the murder, Lamson must have read the septième edition.)

Malot, H., *Doctor Claude or Love Rendered Desperate*, London, 1882

Parliamentary Debates, House of Commons (Hansard)

Stevenson, T., 'Poisoning by aconitine (case of *Reg. v. Lamson*)', *Guy's Hospital Medical Reports*, 1883

Stevenson, T. (ed.), *Taylor's Principles and Practice of Medical Jurisprudence*, London, 1883

Thompson, C. J. S. (Curator of the Historical Section of the Museum of the Royal College of Surgeons of England), *Poisons and Poisoners*, London, 1931

Analyst, British Medical Journal, Daily News, Graphic, Illustrated London News, Lancet, Medical Directory, Medical Register, New York Times, Times

7. Harris and Buchanan: The pinprick pupils

Flower, R. P., 'In the matter of Carlyle W. Harris: Denial of application for clemency,' 4 May 1893. State of New York, Public Papers of Governor Flower

Gettler, A. O., 'The historical development of toxicology', *Journal of Forensic Sciences*, vol. 1, 1956

Hamilton, A. M., *Recollections of an Alienist*, New York, 1916

Pearson, E., *Murder at Smutty Nose and other Murders*, London, 1927

Smith, E. H., *Famous American Poison Mysteries*, London, 1927

Stevenson, T. (ed.), *Taylor's Principles and Practice of Medical Jurisprudence*, London, 1894

Witthaus, R. A., *Manual of Toxicology*, New York, 1911

New York Times, 1892–3

8. Eyraud and Bompard: An essay in decomposition

Darmon, P., *Médecins et assassins à la Belle Époque: la médicalisation du crime*, Paris, 1989

Gribble, L. R., *Famous Feats of Detection and Deduction*, London, 1933

Lacassagne, J. A. L., 'L'Affaire Gouffé', in *Archives de l'anthropologie criminelle*, 5, 1890, p. 642

Locard, E., *Mémoires d'un criminologiste*, compiled by Robert Coruol, Paris, 1957

Mannheim, H., *Pioneers in Criminology*, London, 1960

Thorwald, J., *Dead Men Tell Tales*, London, 1966

9. The Stratton brothers: The thumbprint on the cash box

Ambage, N., *Origins and Development of the Home Office Forensic Science Service, 1931–1967*, PhD thesis, University of Lancaster, 1987

Carter, Detective Superintendent W. E., 'Photography at New Scotland Yard', *Forensic Photography*, 1974, vol. 3, no. 9

Galton, F., *Finger Prints*, London, 1892

Galton, F., *Memories of my Life*, London, 1908

Harrison, R., *The CID and the FBI*, London, 1956

Henry, E. R., *Classification and Uses of Fingerprints*, London, 1900

Lambourne, G., *The Fingerprint Story*, London, 1984

Metropolitan Police Museum, New Scotland Yard, Standard Note File 96, 'Precis and annotated index of correspondence re anthropometry and fingerprinting', 1894–1907

Parliamentary papers, various

Thorwald, J., *The Marks of Cain*, London, 1964

Ward, Jenny, *Origins and Development of Forensic Medicine and Forensic Science in England, 1823–1946*, PhD thesis, Open University, 1993

Whitehead, D., *The FBI Story*, 1957

Wilton, G. W., *Fingerprints: history, law and romance*, 1938

10. Dr Crippen: The London cellar murder

Browne, D. G., and Tullett, E. V., *Bernard Spilsbury: his life and cases*, London, 1952

Cope, Z., *The History of St Mary's Hospital Medical School*, London, 1954

Dew, W., *I Caught Crippen*, London, 1938

Goodman, J., *The Crippen File*, London, 1985

Oddie, S. I., *Inquest*, London, 1941

Young, F. (ed.), *Trial of H. H. Crippen*, Notable British Trials series, Edinburgh, 1920

11. Cornelius Howard / Mark Wilde: The double acquittal

Duke, Winifred, *Six Trials*, London, 1934

Goodman, J., *The Stabbing of George Harry Storrs*, London, 1983

Thorwald, J., *Crime and Science*, London, 1967

Thorwald, J., *Dead Men Tell Tales*, London, 1966

12. Charles Henry Schwartz: The burnt-out lab

Block, E. B., *The Chemist of Crime*, London, 1959

Gribble, L. R., *Famous Feats of Detection and Deduction*, London, 1933

Vollmer, A, and Schneider, A., 'School for police as planned at Berkeley', *Journal of the American Institute of Criminal Law and Criminology*, March, 1917

13. Leroy Brady: The candy box murders

Loth, D., *Crime Lab: science turns detective*, New York, 1964

Seabrook, W., *Doctor Wood: modern wizard of the laboratory*, New York, 1941

14. Sacco and Vanzetti: The payroll job

Avrich, P., *Sacco and Vanzetti: the anarchist background*, Princeton, 1991

Goddard, C. H., 'Scientific identification of firearms and bullets', *Journal of the American Institute of Criminal Law and Criminology*, XVII, 1926-7, pp. 254-63

Goddard, Col. C. H., Obituary in *Journal of Criminal Law, Criminology and Police Science*, 46, 1955-6, pp. 103-4

Jackson, B., *The Black Flag: a look back at the strange case of Nicola Sacco and Bartolomeo Vanzetti*, London, 1981

Russell, F., *Tragedy at Dedham: the story of the Sacco-Vanzetti case*, London, 1962

Sacco-Vanzetti Case, Transcript..., Henry Holt and Co, New York, 1928

Seabrook, W., *Doctor Wood: modern wizard of the laboratory*, New York, 1941

Starrs, J. E., 'Once more unto the breech: the firearms evidence in the Sacco and Vanzetti case revisited', *Journal of Forensic Sciences*, April 1986, pp. 630-54, July 1986, pp. 1050-78

Thorwald, J., *The Marks of Cain*, London, 1965

Whitehead, D., *The FBI Story*, 1957

Young, W., and Kaiser, D. E., *Postmortem: new evidence in the case of Sacco and Vanzetti*, Amherst, 1985

15. Browne and Kennedy: The murder of PC Gutteridge

Gribble, L. R., *Famous Feats of Detection and Deduction*, London, 1933

Shore, W. T., *Trial of Browne and Kennedy*, Notable British Trials series, London, 1930

Smith, S., *Mostly Murder*, London, 1959

Thorwald, J., *The Marks of Cain*, London, 1965

16. Jeannie Donald: The Aberdeen tenement murder

Crowther, M. Anne, and White, Brenda, *On Soul and Conscience*, Aberdeen, 1988

Glaister, J., 'Forensic Medicine Department, University of Glasgow', in *Methods and Problems of Medical Education*, Rockefeller Foundation, Division of Medical Education, ninth series, New York, 1928

Littlejohn, H. H., 'Department of Forensic Medicine, University of Edinburgh', in *Methods and Problems of Medical Education*, *ibid.*

Smith, S., *Mostly Murder*, London, 1959

Thorwald, J., *Crime and Science*, London, 1967

Wilson, J.G. (ed.), *Trial of Jeannie Donald*, Notable British Trials series, Edinburgh, 1953

17. Buck Ruxton: The bodies in the stream

Ambage, N., *Origins and Development of the Home Office Forensic Science Service, 1931–1967*, PhD thesis, University of Lancaster, 1987.

Blundell, R. H., and Wilson, G. H., *Trial of Buck Ruxton*, Notable British Trials series, London, 1937

Browne, D. G., and Tullet, E. V., *Bernard Spilsbury: his life and cases*, London, 1952

Firth, J. B., *A Scientist Turns to Crime*, London, 1960

Glaister, J., *Final Diagnosis*, London, 1964

Glaister, J., and Brash, J. C., *Medico-legal Aspects of the Ruxton Case*, Edinburgh, 1937

Maehly, A., and Stromberg, L., *Chemical Criminalistics*, Berlin, 1981

Potter, T. F., *The Deadly Dr Ruxton*, Preston, 1986

Simpson, C. K., *Forty Years of Murder*, London, 1980

Smith, S., *Mostly Murder*, London, 1959

Willcox, P. H. A., *The Detective–Physician*, London, 1970

18. Colin Pitchfork: DNA convicts a murderer

Godwin, G., *Trial of Peter Griffiths*, Notable British Trials series, London, 1950

Jeffreys, A., 'Molecular sleuthing: The story of DNA fingerprints', *Science and Public Affairs*, autumn 1993, p. 24

Jeffreys, A. J., Wilson, V., and Thein, S.L., 'Hypervariable "minisatellite" regions in human DNA', *Nature*, 7 March 1985, p. 67

Lamplugh, Diana, *Beating Aggression: a practical guide for working women*, London, 1988

Landsteiner, K., 'Individual differences in human blood', *Science*, 17 April 1931, p. 403

Odell, R., *Landmarks in 20th Century Murder*, London, 1995

Pena, S. D. J., *et al.*, *DNA Fingerprinting: state of the science*, Introduction and A. J. Jeffreys' and S. D. J. Pena's chapter, 'Brief introduction to DNA fingerprinting', Basle, 1993

Wambaugh, J., *The Blooding*, London, 1989

19. Timothy Spencer: The first DNA execution

Discovery Channel, 'The south side strangler', 30 January 1997

Mones, P., *Stalking Justice*, New York, 1995

20. DNA and scientific evidence

Freckelton, I. R., *The Trial of the Expert: a study of expert evidence and forensic experts*, Oxford, 1987

Fullmer, June, 'Technology, chemistry and the law in nineteenth-century England', *Technology and Culture,* 1980, p. 24

Imwinkelried, E. J., 'The evolution of the American test for the admissibility of scientific evidence,' *Medicine Science and the Law,* 1990, vol. 30, no. 1, p. 60

Jeffreys, A. J., Wilson, V., and Thein, S. L., 'Individual-specific "fingerprints" of human DNA', *Nature,* 4 July 1985, p. 76

Werrett, D. J. 'DNA: From bones to body fluids', talk at Science, Crime and Justice Day, Science Museum, 4 November 1995

Conclusion: Cases and controversy

Caplan, J., 'Trial by television for the jury', *Times,* 19 November 1991

Dershowitz, A., *Reasonable Doubts,* New York, 1996

Freckelton, I. R., *The Trial of the Expert: a study of expert evidence and forensic experts,* Oxford, 1987

Heaton-Armstrong, A., 'Disclosure, hearsay and previous misconduct', *Medicine, Science and the Law,* April 1997, p. 93

Home Affairs Committee First Report, The Forensic Science Service, Session 1988-9, HC 26-I; Evidence, HC 26-II, 13 February 1989

House of Lords Select Committee on Science and Technology, Session 1992-3, Paper 24-I

Kee, R., *Trial and Error: the Maguires, the Guildford pub bombings and British justice,* London 1989 (orig. 1986)

Malleson, Kate, 'The Criminal Appeal Act 1995 (2) The Criminal Cases Review Commission: How will it work?', *Criminal Law Review,* December 1995, p. 929

Mansfield, M. *Presumed Guilty,* London, 1993

'May Report', Sir John May's Report into the Circumstances Surrounding the Conviction arising out of the Bomb Attacks in Guildford and Woolwich in 1974, Session 1993-4, HC 449

McKee, G., and Franey, Ros, *Time Bomb,* London, 1988

Mullin, C., *Error of Judgement: The truth about the Birmingham bombings,* London 1990 (orig. 1986)

Parliamentary Commissioner for Administration ('the Ombudsman'), Fourth Report for the Session 1983-4. Investigation of a complaint about the delay in reviewing a conviction for murder. 26 January 1984, HC 191

Parliamentary Debates, House of Commons (Hansard), various

Pereira, Margaret, 'The Forensic Science Service, past, present and future', *Medico-Legal Journal,* vol. 156, p. 74

Redmayne, M., 'The Royal Commission and the forensic science market', in McConville and Bridges, (eds), *Criminal Justice in Crisis,* Oxford, 1994, p. 219

Sprack, J., 'The Criminal Procedure and Investigations Act 1996 (1) Duty of disclosure', *Criminal Law Review*, May 1997, p. 308

Thornton, P., 'Royal Commission on Criminal Justice (5) Miscarriages of Justice: A lost opportunity', *Criminal Law Review*, December 1993, p. 927

Scotsman, Sunday Times, Times.

INDEX